THE DARK INVADER

CLASSICS OF ESPIONAGE

General Editor: Wesley K. Wark

Other titles in the Series

IN THE DOCK

American version

CAPTAIN VON RINTELEN
(Franz Rintelen von Kleist)

THE DARK INVADER

Wartime Reminiscences of a German Naval Intelligence Officer

With an Introduction by
Reinhard R. Doerries

FRANK CASS
LONDON • PORTLAND, OR.

First Published in 1933 by Lovat Dickson Limited.
This edition first published in 1997 in Great Britain by
FRANK CASS PUBLISHERS
Newbury House, 900 Eastern Avenue
London IG2 7HH

and in the United States of America by
FRANK CASS PUBLISHERS
c/o ISBS, 5804 N.E. Hassalo Street
Portland, Oregon 97213-3644

Website http://www.frankcass.com

Copyright © 1998 Captain von Rintelen
Introduction Copyright © 1998 Reinhard R. Doerries

British Library Cataloguing in Publication Data
Kleist, Franz Rintelen von
    The dark invader : wartime reminiscences of a German naval
    intelligence officer. – 2nd ed. – (Classics of espionage)
    1. Kleist, Franz Rintelen von 2. World War, 1914–1918 –
    Secret service – Germany 3. World War, 1914–1918 – Personal
    narratives, German
    I. Title
    940.4'8743'092

ISBN 0-7146-4792-6 (cloth)
ISBN 0-7146-4347-5 (paper)
ISSN 1363-0164

Library of Congress Cataloging-in-Publication Data
Rintelen, Franz von, 1878–1949.
    The dark invader : wartime reminiscences of a German naval
    intelligence officer / Captain von Rintelen (Franz Rintelen von
    Kleist) ; with an introd. by Richard Doerries.
        p.   cm.
    Originally published: London : L. Dickson Ltd., 1933.
    ISBN 0-7146-4792-6. — ISBN 0-7146-4347-5 (pbk.)
    1. World War, 1914–1918—Secret service—Germany. 2. Espionage,
    German—United States—History—20th century. 3. Intelligence
    service—Germany. I. Title.
D639.S8R6 1997
940.54'8743'092—dc21   97-21328
                                                            CIP

Printed in Great Britain by
Bookcraft (Bath) Ltd, Midsomer Norton, Somerset

TO MY DAUGHTER
MARIE-LUISE

The original publisher's pagination has been maintained.
Part One therefore begins on page 15.

CONTENTS

ILLUSTRATIONS

INTRODUCTION

T HE MYSTERIOUS 'Captain von Rintelen (Franz Rintelen von Kleist)' named on the title sheet of the 1933 first edition of *The Dark Invader*, in fact, is Franz Dagobert Johannes Rintelen, born in Frankfurt on the Oder on August 19, 1878.[1] The father of Franz Rintelen was a legal official with considerable banking interests.[2] Little is known about Franz Rintelen's youth, his education or upbringing, except that he had a sister and five brothers. He was close to some of his brothers and later visited them, even during the Nazi period, when travelling to Germany became an extremely risky undertaking for the once highly respected German naval officer.[3]

Young Rintelen spent a couple of years with a London banking house, leaving England in 1905 for New York, where he is said to have been with Ladenburg, Thalmann and Co. until 1907.[4] Sources suggest that, while in the US, he was already connected with the Disconto-Gesellschaft, a well-known German bank in Berlin.[5] Apparently, his father at one time served as director of the Disconto-Gesellschaft.[6] During his stay in New York, Franz Rintelen was able to establish a number of valuable contacts in the financial market which would turn out to be very useful during his later stint in the US as an agent of the German military.[7]

The Dark Invader, the first of two volumes of Rintelen's memoirs, initially was offered to the Ullstein publishing house for serial publication in the *Berliner Illustrirte Zeitung* and thereafter as a book with the catchy title *Von Admiralstab bis Zuchthaus* [*From the Admiralty Staff to the Penitentiary*].[8] However, some time in 1930 officials of the German Foreign Office were shown a copy of the manuscript, and after closer scrutiny in January 1931, expressed rather strong reservations concerning its publication.[9] The memo recording the meeting between the publishers and representatives of the Foreign Office was signed by (Karl Alexander) Fuehr, who in World War I worked with the German propaganda office at 1123 Broadway in New York, together with such well-known German propagandists as George Sylvester Viereck and Matthew B. Clausen. In his memo Fuehr emphasizes how he tried to dissuade the publishers. They, in turn, requested a list of alterations desired by the German Government. But Fuehr could hardly be expected to put on paper what the Wilhelmstrasse thought of Rintelen's memoirs.[10] Thus it happened that one of Imperial Germany's most illustrious agents took his memoirs to the former enemy. Lovat Dickson in London was the winner.[11]

While the beginning of Rintelen's involvement in covert operations against the neutral United States remains shrouded in mystery, circumstantial evidence in the records points to late 1914. Since the early days of the war Kapitänleutnant Rintelen had been attached to the Admiralty Staff, and economic questions, as well as financial transfers to other countries in connection with the needs of

INTRODUCTION

German cruiser warfare, were his specific responsibility.[12] Though later almost everyone in Berlin would claim to have had nothing to do with or to have known nothing of the undertakings of the brash naval officer, Rintelen's departure on his mission to the United States in the spring of 1915 was anything but a secret operation. On February 20, 1915, the Ministry of War, upon the suggestion of the General Staff and after consultations with the Foreign Office and the Treasury, requested the temporary transfer of Rintelen, and on February 29 (*sic*), 1915, the Chief of the Admiralty gave his permission. We cannot be certain whether Rintelen received additional instructions from the navy, but the records clearly show that he was sent to the United States by the Ministry of War and that his basic instructions came from that office.[13]

Rintelen's main assignment seems to have been the stoppage of shipments of war material from the United States to Germany's enemies.[14] Whether his efforts were to be limited to giant purchases of the respective material or whether his instructions from the beginning also included the possibility of sabotage, is a difficult question, the answer depending largely on one's interpretation of the less than explicit records. As most of the records in question were produced after the event, that is either in the course of investigations held in Germany after the collapse of the empire or later in the US and in Germany in connection with the work of the Mixed Claims Commission, there is ample reason to assume that most participants were not primarily interested in the truth. Evidently, Franz Rintelen would have wanted to demonstrate that while in

America he acted on instructions from the military leadership in Berlin, and the military and political leaders in Berlin after the war would have wanted their orders to Rintelen to appear as quite normal, namely concerning the purchase of war material in America in order to prevent its shipment to Germany's enemies.

Franz Rintelen had managed to achieve some notoriety, even before his departure to the United States. Admiral Gustav Bachmann, Chief of the Admiralty Staff from February to September 1915, had to defend his officer against charges of improper conduct levelled by the office of the Imperial Chancellor Theobald von Bethman Hollweg. It would appear that Kapitänleutnant Rintelen had used his connections in Berlin to influence the chancellor towards a more aggressive submarine war, regardless of American warnings. When the chancellor's office wanted the young naval officer disciplined, the Chief of the Admiralty Staff demonstrated considerable understanding for Rintelen and described him in most favorable terms: 'He has through his energetic successful activities been of very valuable service to the Admiralty staff and proven to be an officer of fine education and extensive knowledge, possessing an honest, open personality, great energy, quick comprehension, and a lively, impulsive temper.'[15]

In another episode, before his departure for the United States, Rintelen contributed to the transfer of the American Military Attaché in Berlin, Major George T. Langhorne. The bald statement of Colonel Walter Nicolai, German army intelligence chief in World War I, that 'Major Langhorne was recalled due to pressure from the Entente'[16] deserves a brief explanation. The German Admiralty Staff had forwarded to the US what Langhorne thought were his coded cables but which, in fact, appear to have been decoded and altered. The British intercepted some of these messages, and promptly lodged a protest with Lindley M. Garrison, the American Secretary of War. Whether the British had to decode Langhorne's messages, or whether Rintelen sent them uncoded for the American Military Attaché, remains unclear. The effect would have been the same: Langhorne had to leave Berlin. Not surprising, the German General Staff became enraged when it read what the *Daily Telegraph* had to say about the matter: '... the Kaiser's Government has been using Major Langhorne's name to send extremely pro-German reports to the United States by wireless, in an effort to deceive the allied Governments ... In the hope of misleading the enemy, the Germans craftily inserted false information and pro-German sentiments in Major Langhorne's messages ...'[17]

From the records of the German Foreign Office it is quite apparent that Langhorne not only cultivated contacts with the German military in Germany, as was part of his professional activity, but also continued such contacts after his return to America. Why he went to see Franz von Papen, the German Military Attaché in Washington, remains less than clear. Whatever the American's motivations may have been, Papen reported to Berlin that Major Langhorne would prefer to keep the affair under a lid. If the matter could just be ignored long enough ('tot zu schweigen'), Papen thought, one might actually succeed in getting Langhorne sent back to Berlin.[18] Despite such expectations, the

THE DARK INVADER

American Military Attaché was not returned to Berlin. Unshaken in his positive appraisal of the Germans, he wrote to Captain von Papen shortly thereafter: 'I trust that all will come out well between our countries ... I hate to think of having had to leave your country on account of that fearful mistake and I am sure that R[intelen] – and the others were sincere in thinking that those words could not be caught.'[19]

At least one of Rintelen's American assignments had been prepared in advance in Berlin. Arrangements had been made for liaison with Melvin Rice, who claimed close connections with the American chemical industry, particularly Dupont. From the records, it is difficult to determine just how much the Germans knew about Mr. Rice and his business acumen, but there can be little doubt that the latter was to assist Rintelen in buying up war material in the US.[20]

Rintelen boarded the *SS Kristianiafjord* departing for the US from Kristiania on March 22, 1915. He travelled under a false Swiss passport as Emile Victor Gaché, one of a string of aliases used by him on various occasions.[21] He landed in New York on April 3, 1915, checked in at the Crest Northern Hotel on April 7 and, according to the Secret Service, stayed there with some interruptions until July 27, 1915. To comprehend the full impact of his operations in the US during the short stay of four months, it is necessary to recall that Rintelen did not arrive as a stranger, but instead had access to a number of well-connected people, and that much of the groundwork for his activities had been laid earlier.

INTRODUCTION

On the American side, the government by the spring of 1915 already had gained considerable knowledge of German intelligence operations in different parts of the country and had begun to organize a number of surveillance schemes. The small and relatively inexperienced Bureau of Investigation welcomed helpful assistance from a number of British agents operating in the United States. Count Bernstorff, the Imperial German Ambassador in Washington, told his Foreign Office in Berlin: 'We are undoubtedly surrounded by a far-reaching British intelligence service.'[22]

On the German side, it was decided to engage in sabotage in the neutral United States, and the records contain a number of papers clearly documenting that decision. The best known of these papers may well be the telegram initialled in the Berlin Foreign Office by Adolf Count von Montgelas and Richard Meyer on January 23, 1915, and dispatched to the Washington Embassy on January 25, 1915, on order from the General Staff. Its content was brief and to the point: 'Secret. I ask ... to send the following telegram to the Military Attaché in Washington. From the following persons the names of suitable people for sabotage in the United States and Canada can be obtained: 1) Joseph MacGarrity [sic], 5412 Springfield Philadelphia, Pa 2) John T. Keating, Maryland avenue, Chicago 3) Jeremia [sic] O'Leary, Park row, New York. No. 1 and 2 absolutely reliable and not talking; No. 3 reliable, not always discreet. The sabotage in the United States can extend to all kinds of factories for war material deliveries; railways, dams, bridges are not to be touched there. Embassy must under no circumstances be compromised by sabotage plans nor Irish-German

xv

propaganda.' Someone in the Foreign Office added the sentence: 'Persons have been named by Sir Roger Casement.'[23] Some time later the British handed the Americans an 'interlinear decoded copy', and one can only speculate when it was that both governments knew the names of these Irish-American leaders and were aware that Casement discussed topics of this nature with the Germans.[24] In the 1920s and 1930s when the Mixed Claims Commission was occupying itself with the sabotage cases, representatives of the German Government were to go out of their way to state that Rintelen's orders had called for buying up war material which otherwise would have been shipped to Germany's enemies. If Rintelen had become involved in sabotage, the Germans argued, he would have done so entirely on his own volition and without instructions from Berlin.[25] Going through the voluminous papers of the Mixed Claims Commission, it is difficult to avoid the impression that most German operatives in the years after World War I rather unanimously did not care to remember anything at all of Rintelen or his activities.

Rintelen's involvement in sabotage should not be a surprise when seen in the context of other sabotage plans and operations in North America of both the General Staff and the Admiralty even before April 16, 1917. In late autumn 1914, officials in Berlin were concerned about the transport of Japanese troop contingents across Canada.[26] On December 15, 1914, the Wilhelmstrasse therefore notified the German Embassy in Washington: 'General Staff desires energetic action for effective destruction of Canadian Pacific Railroad in several places. Captain [Hans] Boehm whom you know and who will return [to the US] soon is acquainted with matter. Please inform military attaché and give needed funds.'[27] A telegram from the Embassy to the Foreign Office on January 8, 1915, indeed states that the military attaché had initiated plans for sabotaging three Canadian railroad lines but that the actual invasion of Canada by operative units, needed to execute the planned sabotage undertakings, would be held up until just prior to impending Japanese troop movements through Canada.[28] On January 19, 1915, the General Staff agreed to abandon 'larger military action against railroads in Canada for the time being' but at the same time ordered Captain von Papen to be prepared to disrupt Japanese troop transports.[29] Only a couple of weeks later Werner Horn, a German officer taking his orders from the admiralty agent Boehm, who in turn seems to have followed orders from von Papen, was apprehended after attempting to blow up a bridge in Canada.[30] Thus, in February 1915, well before the arrival of Rintelen, press coverage of German activities in the United States had moved from passport forgeries to sabotage.[31] What Americans did not know was that the bridge at Vanceboro was only one of five targets Boehm and von Papen had wanted to destroy simultaneously. The big fireworks had only been cancelled because their agents did not turn up for the final preparatory meeting in Portland, Maine, on February 23.

In late 1914 and early 1915, correspondence between Washington and Berlin, concerned with sabotage and military operations by Germans and Irish from the territory of the United States against Canada, seems to have passed between Rudolf Nadolny of the Abteilung IIIb of the

German General Staff and Captain Franz von Papen, even if many of the Papen messages are over the name of the Ambassador Count Bernstorff. These documents leave no doubt that large-scale sabotage and the deployment of platoons of operatives were a part of German strategy in America long before April 1917. It may well be that Count Bernstorff was not or did not care to be aware of the full extent of all operations, but the records certainly indicate that he was cognizant of most projects.[32] Indeed, Bernstorff more than once attempted to curb the activities of the agents.[33] The records also show that Rintelen had one or more encounters with the ambassador. Whether Rintelen was called in by the ambassador, as Rintelen remembers, or whether Rintelen took the initiative to see Count Bernstorff, in retrospect would appear to be less than important. Yet, during acerbic exchanges between Rintelen and German Government officials in the immediate post-war years, these encounters in America between ambassador and naval agent were to become a matter of considerable controversy.[34]

If Rintelen had contemplated sabotage in the United States, the attachés Franz von Papen and Karl Boy-Ed certainly had laid the groundwork, albeit with little success and much publicity.[35] Although we have no eyewitness accounts, political and legal records on both sides of the Atlantic strongly suggest that Rintelen revived the faltering sabotage campaign and relied on an extremely diverse network of operatives consisting of naval personnel from German ships tied up in New York harbor, a motley group of adventurers, and German agents. They ran a dangerous operation which involved placing incendiary devices on ships leaving the harbor with cargo for the Entente. At the same time Rintelen and some of his men evidently were involved in a scheme of organizing labor and fomenting strikes in American ammunition plants.[36] Beyond that, Rintelen engaged in an undertaking to return the ousted General Victoriano Huerta to power in Mexico.

The futile attempts of Imperial Germany on behalf of Victoriano Huerta continue to be surrounded by some mystery. In his books Rintelen presents a somewhat incomplete picture, and specialists, such as Friedrich Katz or Barbara Tuchman, seem to be short of reliable documentary evidence.[37] Presumably, Rintelen conferred with Huerta in Spain, some time before both headed for the United States, and once both were in New York, contacts between the Mexican leader on one side and Rintelen, Boy-Ed and von Papen on the other were intensified. General Huerta was offered financial support and arms in return for establishing a pro-German government in Mexico. Germany's real hope was a war between the United States and Mexico, conveniently tieing up American resources of manpower and material. Indications are that Germany invested considerable funds in the Mexican undertaking. The money was expended by Rintelen and Boy-Ed, presumably with the knowledge of Heinrich Albert who, among other things, functioned as a financial manager for German propaganda and covert action in America. Rintelen is said to have deposited $800,000 in one of Huerta's accounts,[38] and the records point to other additional expenses related to German plans in Mexico. Liberal spending, however, was unable to stop the ceaseless efforts of Emanuel Victor Voska, a Czech working for

Thomas Masaryk and apparently having close ties to the British Naval Attaché Captain Guy Gaunt. Voska's agents succeeded in placing bugging devices in New York hotel rooms used by General Huerta for his meetings with the Germans.[39] The Americans, therefore, were well informed about the German schemes in Mexico, and Huerta found himself arrested by a military posse and a federal marshall before he could cross the border at El Paso to create further problems for Washington.[40] When the distressed Mexican leader sent off an urgent cry for help to the German Ambassador, Count Bernstorff passed the letter on to the American government, causing the puzzled Woodrow Wilson to comment: 'This is truly extraordinary.'[41]

Rintelen's return to Berlin, or rather his departure from New York on the SS *Noordam* on August 3 and his capture by the British on August 13, 1915, in some ways are as mysterious as most of his activities that summer. As British intelligence and the American Government were tuned in on his negotiations with the Mexican general, it comes as no surprise that they would welcome the opportunity to put a stop to the work of this agent. By contrast, however, one wonders why Berlin would have felt inclined to recall Rintelen after such a brief stay in the United States. True, he and those responsible for sending him out in the first place, may have concluded that buying up American war material would not halt US aid to Germany's enemies. Also, since the American press regularly reported on purported or real German conspiracies in the still neutral United States and since no remarkable achievements had been registered, sabotage, on the whole, may not have appeared very promising. Yet, the continued intelligence activities of other agents, even in Mexico, such as Anton Dilger or Kurt Jahnke would suggest that the General Staff was not recalling Rintelen because of some general change of policy towards America.

Franz Rintelen's own occasionally careless behavior such as his social gallivanting with a young lady who happened to be Anne L. Seward, a niece of the famed secretary of state, may have contributed to the somewhat abrupt end of his stay. As it was, Miss Seward wrote to the President that the 'prominent Berlin banker' whom she had 'met socially' was 'a secret but intimate emissary from the Kaiser'. '[H]is utterances are distinctly offensive and his threats alarming', she reported.[42]

Rintelen himself always assumed that the attachés von Papen and Boy-Ed suggested to Berlin that he be recalled. Rintelen's belief was that by successfully organizing a functioning group of sabotage agents in America he had caused the attachés to perceive him as a meddling competitor. This was certainly not unfounded. Papen later reported that one day Rintelen had told him that he was employing the chemist Dr. Scheele to produce bombs to be placed on outgoing steamers. According to this version, the military attaché thought himself greatly endangered by these activities of Rintelen, because the chemist was also connected to Papen in the relatively harmless illegal shipment of rubber and oil to Germany. To prevent the worst, von Papen dispatched an urgent request to the Ministry of War advocating the recall of Rintelen.[43] Other records indicate that Boy-Ed, von Papen and their unsuccessful associate, the financial and propaganda advisor Heinrich F. Albert, worked together to get Rintelen recalled from the US.[44]

Whoever was behind it, the result was a wire from Berlin to the Naval Attaché Boy-Ed, instructing him to inform Rintelen that he was to return to Germany.[45] Since Captain 'Blinker' Hall's decoders in the famed 'Room 40' of British Naval Intelligence were making good headway in reading German cables, the British were alerted that the German agent was about to cross the Atlantic.[46] When exactly and how he would do it, was an added piece of information easily obtained in New York City.

When the Holland-America liner was off Ramsgate on August 13, 1915, and underwent the usual British naval scrutiny, 'Blinker' Hall netted his catch. Rumors in the press had it that Rintelen was executed, and the Wilhelmstrasse actually requested the American Ambassador in Berlin, James W. Gerard, to query London and to offer German legal defence and coverage of related expenses, in case he were still alive.[47] The War Office was quick to respond that Rintelen was neither imprisoned nor was he about to be shot. He was, the British replied, merely a prisoner-of-war, and 'no criminal proceedings whatever have been taken against him'.[48]

Indeed, Franz Rintelen was being held at Donington Hall just outside of Derby, a building complex used as a camp for captured German officers. When the Zimmermann Telegram and unlimited German submarine warfare brought the United States into the war in April 1917, the German agent's fortunes rapidly changed. Since the summer of 1916, Washington had worked at getting him extradited, and now, with America in the war, the British handed him over. Though London did intercede to have him treated as an officer, the Americans insisted that 'he is in the Tombs in exactly the same status as any other person who has been indicted for violation of the Federal criminal laws ... and ... he is entitled to the same rights which any other federal prisoner has, and no more'. Even Frank L. Polk, in May 1917, personally intervened: 'My only fear is that we will be making trouble for some of our prisoners when the Germans get them and we will probably make trouble for some British prisoners in the very near future.'[49] The Department of Justice, however, was not impressed and had such legal procedures carried out as originated from indictments filed in New York, charging Rintelen with 'perjury ... conspiring in restraint of foreign commerce, conspiring to secrete bombs on vessels, and conspiring to attack vessels'. In November 1918 Rintelen was sentenced to twenty months,[50] probably somewhat generous considering the time and prevailing spirits.

Prior to his being sentenced, the German Government had made several rather half-hearted attempts to bring him back to Germany in return for the release of a British subject, of an American sentenced for espionage in Warsaw, or in connection with a group exchange of prisoners. It is true that negotiations for the Germans were difficult, due largely to the fact that since February 1917 they had no direct diplomatic relations with the United States and that much of the paperwork in this context had to pass through the Swiss diplomatic representatives in Washington who were attending to German interests in the US. The records indicate that the British had already declined an exchange. The Americans, for their part, resented the thinly veiled German threat of possible reprisals against US citizens still living in Germany, and Washington did not forego the opportunity to remind the Germans of the great number of German citizens living in the United States.[51] Germany's military and political collapse in the autumn of 1918, of course, did not alleviate the lot of the imprisoned agent in America. Franz Rintelen had little choice but to await the end of his detention in the penitentiary in Atlanta, Georgia.

On November 21, 1920, Woodrow Wilson commuted his sentence under the condition that he depart from the United States prior to January 1, 1921.[52] Though the Germany he returned to was another country than the one he had left on his mission in early 1915, one might have assumed that he would have been received with the usual military honors and that he would have begun a new life in some civilian or military capacity, whatever his preference. Quite to the contrary, Rintelen's life, following his arrival in Germany in February 1921, took a number of unexpected turns and in the end the daring naval officer and agent of the German Empire became a hunted suspect pursued by the secret police of the new totalitarian Germany. In the early phase following his return, there was, to be sure, some recognition of his dangerous mission to the United States during the war, and he was duly promoted to the rank of *Korvettenkapitän* and awarded the Iron Cross.[53]

INTRODUCTION

The generally receptive climate in Berlin, however, changed immediately once Rintelen took steps to seek reimbursement of personal funds he said he had lost as a consequence of his activities in the United States. Things took a turn for the worse when Rintelen insisted on contradicting the dubious, if not to say false witnessing of his contemporaries in America, namely Count Bernstorff, Boy-Ed, and von Papen. Rintelen was not the kind of man to buckle under and submit without audible protest to rude treatment by those in power. Without exaggeration, it can be said that the enduring battle between Rintelen and the representatives of the Weimar Republic, who in many instances were the same as the representatives of Wilhelminian Germany, created more records than the agent's activities, including the court cases, in the United States. A good part of his conflict with the bureaucratic structures of the Weimar government is told in Rintelen's second book *The Return of the Dark Invader*, but he had no access, of course, to the documents of the German military branches and the German Foreign Office, captured later in World War II by allied forces and largely returned to the Bonn government some years ago. Other than the medals of military recognition and a few letters from the brass who knew of his risky task and the years of incarceration that followed his capture,[54] there was neither recognition nor any visible attempt in Berlin to pacify the angry naval officer who demanded his backpay and what he had lost of his own funds in America. Surely, Rintelen was anything but a very smooth or extremely patient negotiator when it came to his demands from the government. On the other hand, the General Staff and the Ministry of War had not entrusted him with the very difficult mission to the United States because he was such a kindhearted fellow.

From the relatively scarce personal information we have about Rintelen's life after his return to Germany, we know that he travelled a lot, in and outside of Germany. There are several indications that over the years he had acquired a certain liking for Anglo-Saxon ways, and it is not surprising that he began to travel to England. In late 1926, the British admiral who had arrested the German agent in World War I had a lengthy and extremely amicable meeting with his former prisoner. Though Rintelen had no reason particularly to seek out Admiral Hall who, from Rintelen's perspective, had acquiesced when in 1917 he was taken under guard on the SS *Adriatic* to America in order to stand trial, it was he who apparently notified Hall that he was in London. There followed a lengthy luncheon at the Garrick Club that went so well that Hall invited Rintelen to his home for dinner. The family dinner just before Christmas 1926 turned out to be a memorable event, for among the other guests at the table were Alfred E. W. Mason, who had worked against German agents in Spain and Mexico during the war, and Arthur Pollen, the barrister and inventor of a mechanical device to improve the accuracy of shells being fired from ships. As the coming years were to show, Hall and Rintelen had begun to like each other earnestly, a feeling which, however, would not prevent 'Admiral, Sir W. Reginald Hall, K.C.M.G., C.B., D.C.L., L.L.D.' from reporting the event and what was said to the American Consulate General in London.[55]

In later years – and it is difficult in this context to over-look his continued futile negotiations with the German Government over money owed to him – Rintelen decided to publish his memoirs. A further motive, besides financial considerations, may well have been the German denial that Rintelen had been sent on his mission by the Ministry of War, or rather the insistence that he had been sent out to purchase war material, not to sabotage American industrial installations and their ammunition shipments to Germany's enemies. Seen in the context of international relations at the time, the German refusal to give Rintelen any kind of recognition is not at all surprising. The United States and Germany, in the 1930s, were still at loggerheads in the Mixed Claims Commission over large claims originating from sabotage charges. The two largest explosions, at the Black Tom terminal in New York harbor and at an assembly plant of the Canadian Car and Foundry Company in Kingsland, New Jersey, occurred in July 1916 and January 1917 respectively, that is well after Rintelen's departure from the United States in 1915. Yet, the American press kept the activities of Germany's wartime agents in the public light, and the Germans could have no interest in any additional publicity.[56]

It is an open question whether the clamp put on German publishers to prevent the publication of Rintelen's memoirs was an intelligent decision. That an author with Rintelen's international experience might find a foreign publishing house should not have been altogether incon-ceivable, and it might have occurred to the responsible officials in Berlin that while some changes in the text would

have been possible in the case of a German publication, there would be little chance to put pressure on British or American publishers. It is, of course, difficult to be certain, but in retrospect it would appear more than plausible that Rintelen had at some point decided that German officials would neither recognize his intelligence work in the United States, nor allow him to publish his memoirs with the unfriendly references to Franz von Papen, the former military attaché who became chancellor of Germany in 1932. Martin Bormann, in December 1933, wrote that Rudolf Hess, the 'Stellvertreter' of the 'Fuehrer', went so far as to get a German publishing house to buy Rintelen's book with the explicit purpose of preventing it from appearing in German. Otherwise, Bormann wrote, Rintelen probably would have found a Swiss publisher to print a German version to coincide with the English publication.[57]

Understandably, reactions to *The Dark Invader* were different in Berlin than in London or New York. No less a person than the British writer and intelligence *aficionado* A.E.W. Mason wrote the 'Preface' to the book and told the reader (page xli): '... [Rintelen] went abroad in 1915 and only saw his own country again after the lapse of six strenuous and, in part, unhappy years. The history of those years is told in this book. The conversations which he records depend, of course, upon his memory; the main facts we are able to check, and we know them to be exact.' One may wonder what Mason meant by 'main facts', for evidently Rintelen embellished his memoirs with decorative elements and likely inventions.[58] In some ways,

The Dark Invader may be a classic, a revealing report about operations generally denied by governments, but not the whole truth. The whole truth in every case might have been harmful to other persons or to the author himself. Rintelen was neither a traitor who would carelessly harm others nor a man willing to accept the shoddy treatment accorded to him by the government after his return to Germany.

The press in Britain and the United States greeted the publication with favorable comments, and in view of the ongoing negotiations in the Mixed Claims Commission it is no surprise that American officials specially welcomed Rintelen's story as further evidence of German malevolence during World War I. Yet, in the end, Rintelen's memoirs were disappointing because though Rintelen 'has contributed a revealing amount of background and atmosphere to the twelve-year, twenty-million-dollar Mixed Claims Commission Conflict between the United States and Germany over the Kingsland–Black Tom losses ... he always has stopped just short of naming names'.[59] The Germans were painfully aware of the influence the book was likely to have on American public opinion. Certainly, this was Karl Alexander Fuehr's major reason for doing everything in his power to obstruct the publication of the German text: 'The whole depiction of Rintelen's sabotage activities which will warm up long forgotten stories about German [text burned] acts in America, of course, will [not – word burned] be helpful for our image in the United States.'[60]

Rintelen apparently spent less and less time in Germany and, perhaps sensing the danger of being arrested by the political police, began to settle in Britain. The records show that, in 1933, von Papen dictated a letter to Hess, asking that the 'Staatspolizei' find out 'whether Rintelen is in Germany, and, in such case, to have him arrested for high treason [wegen Hoch- und Landesverrat]'.[61] Needless to say, the former German agent had no inclination to allow himself to be incarcerated again, this time in the fatherland. He published his two books in London and New York and travelled to the United States, where he had no problem being admitted on a non-immigrant visa. He lectured across Britain, and, it would appear, closely followed developments at the Mixed Claims Commission. In fact, his interest in the troubled legal procedures between Germany and the United States took him so far as to intervene and offer himself as a witness to the commission.[62] As if he had given up on possible reconciliation with Germany, in 1933 he even went public in the American press and discussed his activities, naming projects and agents. For the American government the articles in the *Washington Herald* contained no revelations, but to the man on the street, shortly after the rise to power in Germany of Adolf Hitler, the articles could only recall a particularly ugly chapter in American–German relations.

In Britain he strengthened his friendship with Admiral Hall and his family. They indeed became so close that Rintelen's daughter Marie Louise was one of the bridesmaids when the admiral's only daughter, Faith Elizabeth, wed Lieutenant Peter William F. Stubbs, Royal Navy, on April 7, 1934. The former German agent himself was among the large number of high-ranking British naval officers in attendance at Lyndhurst.[63] Rintelen eventually began to criticize openly the Nazi regime in Germany and considered himself a refugee.[64] In 1938, the *Washington Star* reported that 'a disagreement with his fellow saboteur, von Papen, made it advisable for him to live in England'.[65] In fact, Rintelen applied for 'British naturalization' and had hopes of eventually becoming a British citizen. When the British summoned him to appear before the so-called Aliens' Tribunal, it was Admiral Hall who vouched for him, and, as a consequence, he was allowed to live free of restrictions as a 'friendly alien'.[66] Several sources suggest that Rintelen volunteered to serve Britain in the war[67] and that before the Aliens' Tribunal he had exclaimed: '… my ambition is to wear the uniform of a British naval officer … I want to serve Britain. I hate Nazidom and all it stands for. I want a chance to fight it.'[68]

On May 24, 1940, only two weeks after Winston Churchill had taken office as Prime Minister, Rintelen was again called before the Aliens' Tribunal in London. This time he lost, and in the company of a policeman he was allowed to return to his home to gather essentials before being packed off to a camp.[69] It must have been a curious crowd that awaited him there. The British did not always separate such different internees as Jewish refugees from Germany, suspected foreign agents, Nazis and fascists, and, well, people such as Franz Rintelen. Some years ago a Jewish refugee from Hamburg told this author that he had been interned together with Franz Rintelen. He remembered going for walks often with Rintelen and talking about politics and current events. He recalled his conversations with Rintelen rather favorably but spoke of the

Heil Hitler salutes of German Nazis interned with them.[70]

Information on Rintelen's life in camp and the final years of his life afterwards is still very scarce. Up to now, no personal papers, comparable to the mass of documents from the years prior to World War II, have surfaced. A rather astonishing message from the American Consul Walter R. McKinney for the American Ambassador in London to the Secretary of State from March 1941 suggests that a 'Captain Francis John Von Rintelen ... now interned at Huyton Camp, near Liverpool, England' had written to the American embassy in London that he intended to apply for an immigration visa to the United States. The letter from Rintelen apparently had also hinted that he might be willing 'to give certain evidence',[71] presumably in connection with the old sabotage cases from World War I dealt with by the Mixed Claims Commission.

Press reports indicate that Rintelen was held in the internment camp until early 1945 shortly before the defeat of Hitler's Germany.[72] Rintelen did not know that the Germans had not forgotten him. Their ignominious *Sonderfahndungsliste G.B.*, an alphabetical list of 2,820 names of persons to be arrested after German troops occupied Britain, on page 173 lists 'Korvettenkapitän a.D. Franz Rintelen', incidentally just a few names before that of his conversation partner in the camp.[73]

On May 30, 1949, Franz Rintelen collapsed at South Kensington Station in London and died shortly thereafter in hospital.[74]

March 1997   REINHARD R. DOERRIES

INTRODUCTION

NOTES

1. Family tree in Paul and Jost Rintelen, *Das Geschlecht der Rintelen* (Freising: Bode, 1977). Regrettably, even important sources for the history of intelligence such as Patrick Beesly, *Room 40* (London: Hamish Hamilton, 1982) continue to use the wrong names and aliases (p. 229).
2. Synopsis Franz von Rintelen, 55, RG 87, National Archive, Washington, D.C. (NA). Memo signed by Herbert Parsons, July–September 1917 (sic.), 9140-646, Military Intelligence Division (MID), RG 165, NA.
3. Information from members of the Rintelen family. Cf. W.R. Hall and A.J. Peaslee, *Three Wars with Germany* (New York: G.P. Putnam's Sons, 1944), p. 163.
4. Henry Landau, *The Enemy Within* (New York: G.P. Putnam's Sons, 1937), p. 43. A memo by H.H. Martin, December 16, 1930, Box 16, Entry 76, RG 76, NA, claims that Rintelen was with Kuhn Loeb & Co.
5. Cf. Memo by Arthur von Gwinner, December 31, 1906, Archive, Deutsche Bank. *Deutsches Bankier-Buch*, 11th edition (Berlin, 1909), pp. 102–3, lists Franz Rintelen as a *Prokurist* of the Disconto-Gesellschaft. The *Handbuch der Deutschen Aktien-Gesellschaften*, edition of 1912–1913, pp. 49–50, names Franz Rintelen as a member of the *Vorstand* (board of directors) of the Nationalbank für Deutschland. Cf. Dresdner Bank to German Foreign Office, October 29, 1935, Rechtswesen 6, Bd. 41, Politisches Archiv, Auswärtiges Amt, Bonn (PA, AA). He continued to be listed as a director of that bank until 1920. Suggestions that Rintelen also had a position with the Deutsche Bank (Landau, *The Enemy Within*, p. 43) could not be substantiated.
6. 9140-646, MID, RG 165, NA.
7. Rintelen had met George Plochmann of the Trans-Atlantic Trust Co. before the war. Cf. Memorandum by H.H. Martin, December 20, 1930, Entry 76, Box 16, RG 76, NA. Later Plochmann apparently introduced Federico Stallforth, a man of varied financial talents and engagements, to Rintelen. 862.2-406, RG 165, NA. Cf. Reinhard R. Doerries, *Imperial Challenge* (Chapel Hill: University of North Carolina Press, 1989), pp. 179, 336.
8. Cf. Captain von Rintelen, *The Return of the Dark Invader* (London: Lovat Dickson & Thompson Ltd., 1935), pp. 198–9.
9. Information from Rintelen family. German Foreign Office to German Embassy Washington, January 28, 1931, Rechtswesen 15, Rintelen, PA, AA.
10. Memo, Fuehr, January 24, 1931, R 80149, PA, AA.
11. For details of his encounters with Ullstein see Rintelen, *The Return of the Dark Invader*, pp. 173, 198–9, 202–3.
12. German naval report from New York, October 25, 1914, 2189, RM 5, Bundesarchiv-Militaerarchiv, Freiburg (BAMA).
13. Vanselow to Admiralty, Charlottenburg, October 1, 1919; Reichswehrminister to Admiralty, October 11, 1919, fol. 1-263, RM 5, BAMA. Memorandum by Hossenfelder, August 5, 1927, Auswaertiges Amt III B, Schriftwechsel Min.Dir. de Haas-Rintelen, PA, AA.
14. There has been much confusion about the instructions Rintelen may or may not have received. Initially, the German naval officer with a letter of introduction from

the German Foreign Office even approached the American ambassador in Berlin, James W. Gerard, for safe conduct on his way to America. Whether his original instructions were actually connected with a Belgian project, or whether this had served merely as an excuse for the safe conduct request, must remain an open question. Rintelen to Heinrich Albert, Paris, January 6, 1928, Rechtswesen 20, Rintelen, PA, AA. Gerard to Secretary of State, December 20, 1915, *Papers Relating to the Foreign Relations of the United States. The Lansing Papers 1914–1920*, vol. I (Washington, D.C.: Government Printing Office, 1939), p. 673. Message from Rintelen to German Investigating Commission, via Swiss Legation to German Foreign Office, November 29, 1919, Weltkrieg adh. 4, no. 3, Bd. 2, PA, AA: 'Upon Minister Helferich [*sic*] expressing me [*sic*] financial objections once more declined delicate mission. Agreement was reached between ministers Helferich [*sic*] and Wandel and latter distinctly accorded me full powers in every respect. After consultation Berlin with Governor General Bissing regarding possibilities improvement conditions Belgian Relief through my personal acquaintance with New York Chairman was given written introduction by Undersecretary Zimmermann to Ambassador Gerard who vainly tried to obtain safe conduct to America.'

15. Memo of Admiral Bachmann, March 31, 1915, sent to Admiral Georg Alexander von Müller, April 2, 1915, 1127, RM 2, BAMA. Concerning the submarine war issue at this stage of the development see Karl E. Birnbaum, *Peace Moves and U-Boat Warfare* (Stockholm: Almqvist & Wiksell, 1958), pp. 23–6. Doerries, *Imperial Challenge*, pp. 80–2.

16. W. Nicolai, *Nachrichtendienst, Presse und Volksstimmung im Weltkrieg* (Berlin: Ernst Siegfried Mittler und Sohn, 1920), p. 64.

17. Clipping, *Daily Telegraph*, March 26, 1915, no page reference; General Staff to Foreign Office, Berlin, March 30, 1915; both Deutschland No. 127, Secret, No. 22, Bd. 4, PA, AA.

18. Von Papen to General Staff, Washington, D.C., March 26, 1915; Count Bernstorff to Foreign Office, April 5, 1915; both ibid.

19. Langhorne to von Papen, Fort Bliss, July 1, 1915, Entry 538, Box 8, RG 59, NA. Rintelen's description of the affair in *The Dark Invader* certainly corresponds with the information in the German records.

20. Synopsis Franz von Rintelen, August 1918, 55, RG 87, NA, where Rice is referred to as a US citizen and President of D.W. McLeod & Co. According to this source, Rice agreed to work with Rintelen in return for certain business concessions in Belgium. Memorandum 'Rintelen–Bernstorff Contacts', March 11, 1939, Box 14, Entry 76, RG 76, NA. Cf. Telegram from Berlin, passed on by German Embassy to the Military Attaché von Papen, Washington, D.C., April 6, 1915. Dr. Albert's Papers, Numbered Series, Box 21, RG 65, NA (where he is called Malvin Rice).

21. Among the aliases found in the records are Emile Victor Gaché, E.V. Gasche, Emile Victor, Fred Hansen, Edward V. Gates, E.V. Gates, E.V. Gibbons & Co., Costa, d'Costa, National Manufacturing Export Co., Meloy, Fred Jones, Fred Haywood, F. Brown, Fred Brown, Fred Gill, Fred Harrison, Miller, Muller, Mueller, Mexico Western Ry.

22. Draft, Count Bernstorff to Foreign Office Berlin, Cedarhurst, August 28, 1915, Dr. Albert's Papers, Subject File, Box 1, RG 65, NA.

INTRODUCTION

23. The unusual telegram has been reproduced in several publications, at times, however, with the wrong date of January 25, 1916. This literal translation of the German text in Doerries, *Imperial Challenge*, pp. 179–80, 337–8.

24. Handwritten note without signature, undated, Box 3, Entry 542, RG 59, NA.

25. Brief on behalf of Germany, Before the Mixed Claims Commission, Botschaft Washington, MCC, Bd. 2, Teil 1, PA, AA.

26. Jagow to Embassy Washington, December 1, 1914, WK 11h, secr., Bd. 1, PA, AA.

27. Zimmermann to Count Bernstorff, December 15, 1914, ibid.

28. German Embassy Washington to Foreign Office for General Staff, January 8, 1915, ibid.

29. Nadolny (Abteilung III b, General Staff) to Foreign Office for Embassy Washington, January 19, 1915, ibid.

30. Werner Horn attempted to set off an explosion at a Canadian Pacific Railroad bridge crossing the St. Croix River near Vanceboro, Maine. Clipping, *New York Times*, February 3, 1915, ibid.

31. Early German infringements of US law were connected to the need to produce false papers for German reserve officers travelling back to Germany through the British naval blockade. The operation was run by Hans Adam von Wedell.

32. Count Bernstorff for instance authorized funds in connection with some of the intelligence operations.

33. Doerries, *Imperial Challenge*, pp. 335–6.

34. Statements of Count Bernstorff and reactions of Rintelen in Parlamentarischer Untersuchungs-Ausschuss 20, PA, AA.

35. Whether Rintelen was sent to the US because the attachés had failed, as is claimed in various records, in the absence of hard evidence must remain an open question. Cf. Richard Levering of MID to A. Bruce Bielaski, Chief of Bureau of Investigation, March 28, 1918, 10546-39, MID, RG 165, NA.

36. Arthur S. Link, *Wilson*, vol. III (Princeton: Princeton University Press, 1960), pp. 561–2. Cf. the personal experience of Samuel Gompers, as recalled in his *Seventy Years of Life and Labor* (New York: E.P. Dutton, 1948), p. 339 ff.

37. Friedrich Katz, *Deutschland, Diaz und die mexikanische Revolution* (Berlin: VEB Deutscher Verlag der Wissenschaften, 1964), pp. 339–40, who refers to Barbara W. Tuchman, *The Zimmermann Telegram* (New York: Viking Press, 1958), pp. 79–83. Tuchman, however, does not name her sources. A revised and translated edition of Katz's book is available: Friedrich Katz, *The Secret War in Mexico: Europe, the United States and the Mexican Revolution* (Chicago: University of Chicago Press, 1981).

38. Katz, *Deutschland, Diaz und die mexikanische Revolution*, pp. 339–40. Michael C. Meyer, *Mexican Rebel* (Lincoln: University of Nebraska Press, 1967), pp. 124–5.

39. Emanuel Victor Voska and Will Irwin, *Spy and Counterspy* (New York: Doubleday, Doran, 1940), pp. 192–5.

40. George J. Rausch, Jr., 'The Exile and Death of Victoriano Huerta', *Hispanic American Historical Review*, 42 (1962), pp. 138–9.

41. Tuchman, *The Zimmermann Telegram*, p. 83, without naming a source.

42. Anne L. Seward to 'My dear President Wilson', Boston, July 2, 1915, Box 209, Records of the Office of Counselor, RG 59, NA. Memorandum by Chandler P.

Anderson, July 8, 1915, ibid.

43. Von Papen before the Parliamentary Investigation Committee on April 16, 1920, Rechtswesen 6 Sabotage Claims, Bd. 12, PA, AA. 'Rintelen–Bernstorff Contacts', Box 14, Entry 76, RG 76, NA. Ministry of the Army to Chief of the Admiralty, Berlin, October 11, 1919, fol. 1-263, RM 5, BAMA.

44. Boy-Ed to Admiralty Staff, Luebeck, September 1, 1919, fol. 1-263, RM 5, BAMA.

45. Cf. Ministry of War to Admiralty Staff, Berlin, July 2, 1915, *Secret*, Rechtswesen 6 Allg., Bd. 3, PA, AA.

46. Sir W. Reginald Hall and Amos J. Peaslee, *Three Wars with Germany* (New York: G.P. Putnam's Sons, 1944), pp. 6–7. Beesly, *Room 40*, pp. 229–30. William James, *The Code Breakers of Room 40* (New York: St. Martin's Press, 1956), pp. 100–1.

47. James W. Gerard to Walter Hines Page, November 4, 1915, Foreign Office (FO) 383, Public Record Office, Kew (PRO).

48. War Office to Foreign Office, December 2, 1915, ibid.

49. See also Franz Rintelen to the British Ambassador, Sir Cecil Spring Rice, May 5, 1917: 'I am not accorded the treatment that I think I am entitled to as a naval officer of Germany ...', reproduced correctly in *The Dark Invader*, pp. 260–1. This and related documents such as Polk to Charles Warren, May 13, 1917; Warren to Polk, May 17, 1917; Polk to Warren, May 21, 1917, are held in Collection 656, Yale University Library.

50. Nolle Prosequi, August 8, 1927, US District Court, Southern District of New York.

51. A number of documents relating to the proposed exchanges can be found in 4597, RM 3, BAMA.

52. Reproduction of document in *The Return of the Dark Invader*, unnumbered pp.

53. Untitled document, dated April 24, 1933, Rechtswesen 6 Sabotage Claims, Bd. 30, PA, AA.

54. Cf. Chief of the Naval Staff, Admiral Behncke to Rintelen, Berlin, February 16, 1921, Rechtswesen 20, PA, AA.

55. Memorandum by Peaslee of statements of Admiral Hall regarding Rintelen's recent visit to London, London, December 27, 1926, with an appended statement under oath signed by Admiral Hall and Russell H. Rhodes, Vice Consul. Collection 'Admiral Sir Reginald Hall (1870–1943)', Churchill College Archives, Cambridge. Cf. description by Rintelen, *The Return of the Dark Invader*, pp. 120–1, which places the dinner in January 1927. See also Rintelen's version of his preparations for the meeting with Hall (p. 116ff.).

56. For instance in *The Saturday Evening Post* in May 1940, clippings, Box 24, Entry 76, RG 76, NA.

57. Martin Bormann to Demann, Muenchen, December 21, 1933, Registered, Rechtsfragen betr. Rintelen, Geheimakte, PA, AA. The documents now in this folder were heavily burned and partially restored. They consist only of left-over pieces of the former papers. Bormann sounds as if the major reason for this action was to protect von Papen from being smeared.

58. Concerning the fictional elements cf., for instance, William James, *The Code Breakers of Room 40* (New York: St. Martin's Press, 1956), pp. 99–100 (on Rintelen's account of meeting Guy Gaunt, the British Naval Attaché in the US) or p. 150 (on a British press attack on the intelligence section of the Admiralty).

59. Leon M. Siler, 'How a Kaiser's Protege Works Abroad', *New York Post*, May 11, 1936, clipping, Box 20, Entry 76, RG 76, NA.

60. 'Aufzeichnung', Fuehr, January 1931, Rechtswesen 15, Geheimakten, Vereinigte Staaten, PA, AA. Fuehr expresses his opinion that it would still be very harmful politically if it were to become known that during the period of US neutrality the German Government had tried to involve America in a war with Mexico.

61. Heavily damaged, partially restored document; of the date only 'ber 1933' remains, signed Fuehr. Ibid.

62. See, for instance, Rintelen to Mixed Claims Commission, Basel, September 15, 1930; Rintelen to 'Chairman of the Mixed Claims Commission', London, November 11, 1932, as enclosure to George Gordon Battle (Rintelen's American lawyer) to Harold H. Martin, Counsel to the American Agent, Mixed Claims Commission, New York, November 20, 1932; Box 16, Entry 76, RG 76, NA.

63. On the wedding see 'War Foe at Wedding of Captor's Daughter', clipping, *New York Times*, Box 16, Entry 76, RG 76, NA. 'Marriages', *The Times*, April 9, 1934, p. 15d.

64. 'Britain Arrests Von Rintelen In Big Spy Suspect Roundup', clipping, *Evening Star*, May 24, 1940, Box 19, Entry 76, RG 76, NA.

65. 'Von Rintelen Repeats Social Success in London', clipping, *Washington Star*, November 10, 1938, Box 17, Entry 76, RG 76, NA.

66. Albert H. Robbins, Attorney, to David Wiener, London, February 9, 1940, Box 19, Entry 76, RG 76, NA.

67. 'Plotted Black Tom, Says Von Rintelen', clipping, *New York Times*, January 3, 1940, Box 17, Entry 76, RG 76, NA.

68. 'Von Rintelen Dies in London', clipping, *New York Herald Tribune*, May 31, 1949, Presse-Archiv, Berlin.

69. 'Rintelen Seized In Fifth Column British Dragnet', clipping, *New York Herald Tribune*, May 25, 1940, Box 19, Entry 76, RG 76, NA.

70. Conversations and correspondence with Eduard Rosenbaum, London, especially Rosenbaum to this author, November 1, 1976.

71. Walter R. McKinney for the Ambassador to US Secretary of State, London, March 24, 1941, MID, RG 165, NA.

72. 'Von Rintelen Dies in London'.

73. *Sonderfahndungsliste G.B.*, Facsimile Reprint as *The Black Book* (London: Imperial War Museum, 1989).

74. 'Von Rintelen Dies in London'.

From Admiral Sir Reginald Hall, the Chief of the Naval
Intelligence Division during the War.

                    Hawk's Lease
                    Lyndhurst
                        August 13th 1932[1]

My dear Rintelen,

I wish to tell you to-day that I, as
you know, have the greatest sympathy
for you. I know well that you have
suffered more than a man should be
called on to suffer, and I am full
of admiration for the manner in which
you have retained your balance of
mind and your courage.

That the fortune of war made it my
job to bring so many disasters on you,
that is my sorrow, and if by anything
I can do I can in some manner assist
to get you peace and happiness, I
shall feel happy myself.

            Sincerely yours,

                W. R. HALL

[1] The anniversary of my capture by the British—off Ramsgate.

PREFACE

MEN engaged in Intelligence Services during a war divide their particular opponents into two classes. One consists of neutrals who go out of their way to help the enemy for the sake of gain ; and for such men we have not much compassion should they fall upon misfortune. They are interfering in great matters with which they are not concerned, in order to make a little money. The other class is made up of men who, abandoning the opportunities of their own careers, go secretly away in the sacred service of their country, play a lone hand, and run the gauntlet of foreign laws. For such we can have nothing but respect while the fight is going on and friendship when it is over.

Captain FRANZ VON RINTELEN belongs to this latter class. A young naval officer with every likelihood of reaching to high rank, he went abroad in 1915 and only saw his own country again after the lapse of six strenuous and, in part, unhappy years. The history of those years is told in this book. The conversations which he records depend, of course, upon his memory ; the main facts we are able to check, and we know them to be exact.

The book is written, as one would expect from his record, without the least rancour, and I think I am not trenching upon the province of criticism when I add— with admirable simplicity. It is a record which is more detailed and concerned with endeavours on a vastly wider scale than is usual in such accounts. One cannot, I think, read it without recognising, apart from the magnitude of the things attempted and done, the terrific strain under which he lived; and this gives a moving and human quality to the narrative which sets it a little apart from any other which I have read. Those who are most saturated in spy stories will find much to surprise them in this volume, and they will not be likely to forget the poignant minutes which he spent on the top of an omnibus in London and the way in which those minutes ended.

The book has other grounds for consideration. It throws a clear light upon the efficiency of the English Intelligence Services, for one thing. For another, it reveals that the jealousies of Departments—which in other countries did so much to hamper the full prosecution of the War—were just as rife in Germany itself, and that the picture of German concentration with which we were all terrifying ourselves in 1914 had no solid foundation in fact. Finally, here is as good an argument against War as a man could find in twenty volumes devoted to that subject alone.

A. E. W. MASON

LATE MAJOR, R.M.L.I.

G.S.O.(2)

PART I

ADMIRALSTAB
The Naval War Staff in Berlin

IT is the afternoon of August the 4th, 1914. We junior officers of the Admiralty Staff sit at our desks and wait and wait. War has been declared, and every now and then the troops, who are being dispatched to the Western and the Eastern Front, march past our windows. The music of a band bursts into our quiet rooms, we tear open the windows for a moment, and wave to the comrades whom the War is sweeping into action.

It is the afternoon of August the 4th, 1914. We sit in our offices at the Admiralty, and our nerves can hardly stand the strain of waiting any longer. From time to time a rumour runs through the building. Our Chiefs are said to have indicated to the Government once more that, according to information received from our Naval Attaché in London and from our secret agents, England will certainly not remain neutral. We, the officers of the Admiralty Staff, are convinced that soon the English warships will turn their bows towards the south. At night, as we sit anxiously in our rooms and talk in hushed voices, we wait for something to happen, for some news that will turn our presentiment into fact. The war with France and Russia is a war to be conducted by the Army, a military war, in which important tasks presumably will not fall to the Navy. But if England . . .! We wait and wait.

It is the afternoon of August the 4th, 1914. The door of my room opens, and an order comes from my Chief telling me to go immediately to the Foreign Office to

receive an important piece of news. The order directs
me to bring this news with the greatest expedition to
the Admiralty in the Königin Augustastrasse.

As my instructions are handed to me I rise from my
chair. A few more officers happen to be in the room,
and they hold their breath as I read out the order.

" Every minute counts "—so the instructions end.

We all have the feeling that something is about to happen that touches us closely. We suppress our agitation
before the orderly, but while I quickly get ready to leave,
one of my comrades takes up the telephone-receiver
to inform Police Headquarters that in a few minutes a
service car of the Admiralty will be racing through
the Bendlerstrasse, the Tiergartenstrasse, and the Voss-
Strasse, and that the road has to be kept clear for it.

The car races away. I am soon standing on the steps
of the Foreign Office. An attendant throws open the
door, and I pass through the hall, to find myself suddenly
in a large room.

On a red plush sofa sit two gentlemen—Sir Edward
Goschen, the Ambassador of His Britannic Majesty, and
Mr. James W. Gerard, the Ambassador of the United
States. Sir Edward looks depressed and, half-turned
towards Gerard, is talking in a low voice.

It is the afternoon of August the 4th, 1914, and as I
stand in the room, with this scene before me, I at once
realise its meaning. I now know the nature of the news
that I have to take back as quickly as possible to the
Admiralty. I know that Sir Edward Goschen has just
handed over England's declaration of war, and that the

American Ambassador, Mr. Gerard, has come to the Foreign Office with him to explain that he will take over the representation of British interests in Germany.

For a moment my knees tremble as the whole significance in world-history of this incident opens up before me. Then I remember that I am a naval officer, and enthusiasm rises high in me. I see the Fleet setting out in a few minutes, with the heavy smoke-streamers of the German torpedo-boat flotillas hanging in the evening sky over the North Sea.

But suddenly I sober down. I notice the look of indifference on the face of Gerard, sitting on the sofa in a brown lounge suit, not, like Goschen, in top-hat and frock-coat. Goschen sits in a correct attitude and is visibly much distressed, but Gerard is leaning over, half-turned towards him, resting against the sofa cushions. He has one leg crossed over the other, and lounges there, nonchalant and comfortable, turning his straw-hat on the handle of his walking-stick with his fingers. With disconcerting coolness, his eyes fixed on the ceiling, he quietly murmurs : " Yes, perhaps the only peaceful country in the world will soon be Mexico."

Mexico ! A country which was then distracted by civil war !

Herr von Jagow, the Secretary of State for Foreign Affairs, enters the room and gives me a sealed envelope. I know what it contains. I bow, first to him, and then to the two Ambassadors, and hardly know how I get down the steps. My car starts, and rushes through the Voss-Strasse, the Tiergartenstrasse, and the Bendlerstrasse to

the Admiralty. At the street corners, at the busy cross-
ing-places, stand policemen, who, the moment our car
comes into view, raise their hands high and stop the
traffic so that we may not be held up.

Before the Admiralty building the driver jams on the
brakes, so that the car stops with a jerk. I run up the
steps. Two senior staff officers are standing at the door
of the Chief, and make a dash at me. Captain von Bülow,
head of the Central Department, tears open the envelope.

He concentrates on the letter for a moment, then turns
half left and calls to the Commandant of the Nauen
Wireless Station, standing behind him :

" Commandant ! Get Nauen going ! "

The Commandant runs to his room, and snatches up
the receiver of the telephone which communicates direct
with Nauen.

Two seconds later the High Seas Fleet knows, and in
another second all the torpedo-boat flotillas :

" War with England ! "

The stations in the Baltic and the North Sea, the
cruisers in the Atlantic and our squadrons are warned
within a few minutes.

.   .   .   .   .

We had all expected that after the British declaration of
war the High Seas Fleet would immediately put to sea.
We had thought that the Admiralty would become a
centre where the threads of great naval movements would
be gathered together ; we had thought that the Navy too
would intervene in the fight for Germany's existence.

But what we so confidently expected did not happen : the High Seas Fleet remained where it was, and, instead of taking part in the fighting, the Admiralty Staff became involved in passionate political conflicts. Just when we expected that the Naval Command would give the order to attack we were summoned to a conference of officers. We were informed :

" The Imperial Chancellor's view may be summarised as follows : We must not provoke England ! We are assured from authoritative British quarters that England is only taking part in the War for appearances and in fulfilment of purely military agreements of which the Foreign Office has been kept in ignorance. Energetic action on the part of the German Fleet would inevitably bring about a change of feeling in England ! "

That was the view of the Chancellor. It was not, however, the view of the Admiralty ; and it was certainly nothing new that differences should arise between the politicians and the admirals on the question of the interpretation of Britain's intentions prior to and at the outbreak of the War.

Even shortly before the War there yawned an abyss between the opinions of the two parties as to whether England would participate or not. These opinions were very sharply divided in the first days of August, when hostilities were already in full swing on the Continent, but England was still maintaining her attitude of reserve.

Whenever a telegram came from Lichnowsky, the Ambassador at the Court of St. James', to say that England thought neither of breaking with her tradition of

not mixing in continental quarrels, nor of taking up
arms against Germany, regularly and simultaneously there
came a telegram from the Naval Attaché in London,
Captain von Müller, to the effect that England, to all
appearances, was on the verge of opening hostilities at
sea. This state of things at last became grotesque. Dis-
patches, representing the two opposing standpoints, were
coming in every day, until at last war broke out and
England proclaimed that Germany was her enemy.

It was on the morning of August the 4th, the day
when England was to declare war on Germany through
her Ambassador, Sir Edward Goschen, that a telegram
arrived from Captain von Müller, which ran as follows :

"Stand firm by the conviction, in spite of the
Ambassador's different opinion, that trouble is brewing for us here."

On the morning of August the 5th, twelve hours
after the formal delivery of the declaration of war, when
nobody expected any further telegrams from the German
Embassy in London, there arrived a wire from Prince
Lichnowsky. It ran :

"The old gentleman [Asquith] has just declared
to me, with tears in his eyes, that a war between
the two peoples, who are related by blood, is impossible."

The Kaiser annotated it in his characteristic large handwriting. In the margin of the Ambassador's message he
wrote :

" What an awakening the man will have from his diplomatic dreams ! "

So we were now no longer surprised at the view taken by the Imperial Chancellor. It so happened that a few hours later I had to see Admiral von Tirpitz. Owing to family friendship he had occasionally made me the recipient of his confidences. I found him in a mood of utter despair. He sat in his chair, looking years older, and told me repeatedly that he had not the slightest desire to go with the " confounded General Head-quarters " to Coblenz. He feared that there he would be checkmated ; and as he said all this, as though to himself, I suddenly perceived an abyss before me. At this tremendous hour, at a time when everything had to be subordinated to the one purpose of saving the Father-land, which was threatened with enemies on every side, the situation was dominated by intrigues, malice, and motives of a petty and personal kind. When Tirpitz should have taken over the command of the High Seas Fleet and concentrated its units in the North Sea against England, the chief of the Naval Cabinet, Admiral von Müller, and some of his immediate entourage, were making efforts to frustrate him. The Chancellor had represented to the Kaiser that Tirpitz was too old to discharge an important war-time function.

It goes without saying that in the war which had now broken out we younger officers were not inclined to place political above purely military considerations. That was all the less to be expected since we had for years been taught that our numerical inferiority to England at sea

THE DARK INVADER

was only to be compensated by the success of a quick attack which should take the enemy by surprise. The tactics now employed against England, of merely waiting to deal with whatever move the enemy made, were not at all to our liking. So we had, however, to turn our longing for action into some channel, and we put all our energies into furthering the activities of our cruisers abroad.

Our ships of the Mediterranean Squadron, the battle-cruiser *Goeben* and the light-cruiser *Breslau*, had attracted unwelcome attention off the coast of Algeria and had naturally drawn down strong English and French fighting-forces upon themselves. They shook off the pursuing ships by a bold stroke: they ran into Messina, where they applied for coal from the Italian Navy.

Admiral Souchon, the Commander of the German squadron, at once saw the Commander of the *Diffesa Marittima* at Messina, to urge upon him the absolute necessity that Germany's Ally should not leave her in the lurch. In view, however, of the fact that a Royal Decree had just been issued forbidding coal to leave Italy, he could only telegraph to the Admiralty in Rome for instructions. It so happened that the Minister of Marine in Rome was Admiral Millo, who during the recent Italo-Turkish War had been brusquely prevented from taking his squadron into the Dardanelles by a stern protest from Whitehall. Admiral Souchon's need proved Millo's opportunity; and, giving loyalty to Italy's Ally as his motive, Admiral Millo at once ordered Admiral Souchon's squadron to be supplied with " best quality Cardiff coal " in the Royal Dockyards.

24

ADMIRALSTAB

Having thus succeeded in replenishing their bunkers, the *Goeben* and *Breslau* put out from Messina under cover of darkness and made for the Eastern Mediterranean.

Meanwhile, a poor, unfortunate Italian steamer, about to enter the Adriatic, was taken by the lynx-eyed British for a German warship and furiously bombarded, though luckily without success.

The Nauen Wireless Station permitted us in Berlin to listen to the exchange of courtesies between the British and French Squadron Commanders—cursing over the German Squadron having made its " get-away."

Admiral Souchon brought his two ships, twenty-four hours ahead of their pursuers, into the Dardanelles. As the Dardanelles, however, since the Berlin Congress of 1878, had been neutralised, and the passage of the Straits was barred to warships of all nations, Turkey was threatened with international complications and with the protests of Germany's enemies, if she allowed the two ships to remain where they were. All these difficulties, however, had been foreseen by Admiral Souchon, who had already wirelessed a pressing request to the German Ambassador in Constantinople to prevent any such complications. The Ambassador, Herr von Wangenheim, had a brilliant idea. When the two ships reached Constantinople they were transferred immediately to Turkish ownership. The Admiral put on a Turkish fez instead of his naval cap, and fired a salute in honour of his new Sovereign. The British Ambassador in Constantinople raised a furious protest, but the ships remained Turkish. They were in the Imperial Ottoman service, which meant that, financially at any rate, they would very soon be on the rocks.

On Saturday evening, the 15th of August, some days after hearing the welcome news of their arrival, I was descending the staircase in the Admiralty building at Berlin, when I met my departmental Chief, who took me into his room and showed me a dispatch from Admiral Souchon, which had just been received. It ran as follows :

> " Turkish tradesmen and contractors refuse German paper money. Immediate dispatch five million marks in minted gold absolutely necessary."

My departmental Chief looked at me and said :

" We can't leave Admiral Souchon in the lurch ! But where are we going to get the gold ? Who's *got* gold ? No more is being issued. But something must be done, and pretty quickly."

" The regulation should not, of course, apply to cases of this sort," I said. " I'll try my luck with the Reichsbank."

" Good ! " he replied. " Do what you like, but see to it that Admiral Souchon gets his gold."

As I stood in the street and looked round for a taxi, a private car stopped in front of me. The wife of the Spanish Ambassador beckoned to me.

" Good evening, Captain ! " called the Marquesa. " Can I give you a lift anywhere ? "

" To the Reichsbank ! "

ADMIRALSTAB

In front of the Reichsbank, on the Hausvogteiplatz, Landwehr reservists in shakos had taken the place of the Infantry of the Guard in their spiked helmets. They were marching up and down according to regulations and presented arms to us. The gateway to the Nibelungs' Hoard was, however, locked and barred, and Alberich, its keeper, disconcerted by the visit at so late an hour of a representative of the armed forces, declared simply that it was after business hours. Fortunately, however, Herr von Glasenapp, the Vice-President, lived in the building. The porter took me to him, and His Excellency at once realised that he must help and was prepared to hand over the required gold.

The strong room, however, was shut, and could only be opened by putting two keys in the lock together—two keys which were in different hands. Geheimrat von Lumm had one of them, and the Chief of the Trésor the other. It appeared that Geheimrat von Lumm lived on the Kaiserdamm and the Chief of the Trésor in the Schönhauser Allee, at the other end of Berlin.

A Reichsbank attendant was immediately put into a taxi and given strict orders to bring the latter, dead or alive, with his key to the Reichsbank, and as quickly as possible. I myself got into another taxi and drove to the Kaiserdamm, to the house of Herr von Lumm. At my first ring nobody answered. I rang again in desperation, and at last an old housekeeper came shuffling to the door and said :

" Yes, yes, but it's so late ! The Herr Geheimrat ? The Herr Geheimrat is out, of course."

" Where has he gone ? "

" Oh, he never tells *me*. But I expect he's taking his evening drink now."

Undeterred by the housekeeper's ignorance, I seized upon a ludicrous idea. I decided, quite simply, to put the police on the trail of the Herr Geheimrat, because, as I said to myself, if the police could manage to find a man who had stolen silver spoons, then they would certainly know how to lay hands on so well-known a person as Herr von Lumm.

So I rushed back to Police Headquarters.

" Where is the office of the C.I.D. ? "

The Commissioner on duty was quite excited by such a late visit from a naval officer.

" Whom are we to arrest, Captain ? "

" Geheimrat von Lumm of the Reichsbank."

" Whom did you say, Captain ? Geheimrat von Lumm of the Reichsbank ? "

" It's not quite as bad as you think, my dear Commissioner, but Herr von Lumm, who is very probably at this moment in some wine restaurant in Central Berlin, must be found before midnight, whatever happens, and taken to the Reichsbank."

" Very well," said the Commissioner ; " I'll send a few C.I.D. men out immediately."

There was no object in waiting at Police Headquarters till Herr von Lumm was found ; so I drove back to the Admiralty and awaited events. At ten o'clock at night I was rung up by the Commissioner on duty.

" The Herr Geheimrat von Lumm has just been

found at Kempinski's and is being delivered at the Reichsbank."

Now we could get to work. When I appeared at the Railways Department of the Great General Staff in the Moltkestrasse and asked for a special train to Constantinople, they showed blank amazement at my naïve ideas of railway management in war-time, but I harangued them for all I was worth, and finally succeeded in convincing them that by the following morning we must have a train to transport our millions in gold to Constantinople. I could not get the through train to Constantinople that I wanted, but they told me that the train could go as far as Bodenbach on the Austrian frontier.

"Farther than Bodenbach we cannot guarantee, and the Austrians will have to arrange for the rest of the journey."

The Austrian Embassy was opposite the General Staff building, and the Counsellor, Count Hoyos, promised that the War Office in Vienna would provide a train from Bodenbach through the Balkans to Constantinople.

"I must, however, point out," added Count Hoyos, "that there are unlimited possibilities of trouble in connection with the transport of gold right through the Balkans."

I had no time to think of all these possibilities; I had to return to the Admiralty. The Reichsbank explained over the telephone that all was going well: the officials were already assembled to count the gold, and the boxes would be packed in an hour's time.

The young lady at the Admiralty telephone exchange then proceeded to tumble a number of important gentlemen of the postal service out of their beds, and was able to announce half an hour later that six big postal vans would arrive at eight o'clock next morning in front of the Reichsbank.

From now on the telephones worked incessantly.

Telephone message from the Reichsbank:

> " The Admiralty must provide an escort for the gold through the streets of Berlin ! "

Telephone message from Police Headquarters:

> " Our bicycle patrols will be before the Reichsbank at half-past seven."

Telephone message from the Railways Division of the General Staff:

> " The train for Bodenbach will be waiting in the Anhalter Bahnhof at nine o'clock."

Telephone message to the Deutsche Bank:

> " The Admiralty would be obliged for the loan of an official familiar with conditions in the Balkans and in Turkey."

Telephone messages to the Turkish and Rumanian Legations for visas.

Telephone messages that the Bulgarian Minister, who also had to give a visa, could not be found.

A call for help to the police !

" Herr Commissioner ! You've done so splendidly in

finding Geheimrat von Lumm, will you be good enough now to find the Bulgarian Minister ? "

The police found the Bulgarian Minister as well. He was much surprised when he suddenly found detectives standing before him, being at the time in pyjamas. The official, who had been impressed with the necessity of bringing the Minister to the Legation as quickly as possible, helped him into a dressing-gown, put him into a taxi, and took him home.

Having on previous occasions asked Dr. Helfferich, the Director of the Deutsche Bank, for his advice about monetary matters of a technical nature, I now rang him up too. This transport of gold interested him keenly, and he turned up early in the morning at the Admiralty to drive with me to the Reichsbank. As we drew up we were filled with alarm. The bank premises were surrounded with most suspicious-looking persons. Slowly it dawned upon us that they were detectives in disguise doing their job.

The boxes were lifted into the vans, and the column moved off. We drove so slowly in front, that Helfferich remarked :

" We look just like a funeral procession."

The same afternoon at four o'clock I was rung up from Bodenbach by Dr. Weigelt of the Deutsche Bank, who had been lent to me by Helfferich to take charge of the transport.

He explained that the train promised by the Austrians to make the connection was not there, and that, as it was Sunday, he was unable to dig out any officials of the Austrian military administration, but that a solution had been found. The Austrian Automobile Corps had declared its readiness to take the boxes to Vienna.

As there was nothing else to be done, I told Dr. Weigelt that I agreed to this course, and that I should be able to arrange for a train from Vienna onwards.

On Monday, the 17th of August, a gentleman from the Austrian Embassy appeared at the Admiralty in a state of great excitement. He waved a telegram from Vienna in his hand, reading as follows :

" We have just succeeded in making an arrest in Vienna which has apparently frustrated enemy plans. A number of motor-cars have reached Vienna, and the unusual conduct of their occupants awakened the suspicions of the police. No time was lost, and the occupants of the cars were arrested ; in the cars were large boxes, one of which was opened. It was filled to the top with gold, which is apparently intended for Serbian propaganda in Austrian territory. The astonishing thing is that the gold is in German currency. On examination, the arrested men gave contradictory explanations, so that it is quite evident that it is an affair of Serbian agents, who, strange to say, are provided with German passports. They are all held in prison for inquiry and await sentence."

When I had read the telegram, the gentleman from the Austrian Embassy was astounded to see me start foaming

at the mouth. Then I began to laugh, and rushed to
the telephone.

In the afternoon the Austrian Embassy telephoned :

> " Your consignment of gold has been dispatched
> by special express train to Budapest. With regard
> to the mistaken arrest of your men in charge, we
> ask a thousand pardons for the misunderstanding
> that has arisen."

By Saturday, August the 22nd, a telegram from Constantinople lay on my table :

> " Gold consignment just arrived safely. Will be
> handed over to Mediterranean Squadron to-day."

.   .   .   .   .   .

In the meantime Admiral Souchon's appeal for help
had gradually worked its way through official channels.
By this path it eventually reached the appropriate department in the course of the week. On Thursday, August
the 20th, Corvette-Captain Oldekop stepped into my
office.

" I say—we have just received a wire from Admiral
Souchon. He seems to want a few million in gold. Can
one do that sort of thing ? Who could put it through ? "

" It was sent off from the Anhalter Bahnhof last Sunday
morning, sir, and we have just been informed that it
has already crossed the Rumanian-Bulgarian frontier."

" Oh, really ? Thanks most awfully ! "

.   .   .   .   .   .

THE DARK INVADER

The consignment of gold had safely reached Constantinople and the enemy's hunt for Admiral Souchon's squadron had ended unsuccessfully.

· · · · · ·

When war broke out, German cruisers were scattered all over the world, and the news of mobilisation reached them in the most unlikely places. The most important unit, apart from the Mediterranean Squadron, was the Cruiser Squadron in the Far East, consisting of the *Scharnhorst* and the *Gneisenau*, accompanied by the four light cruisers *Leipzig*, *Dresden*, *Nürnberg*, and *Emden*. Even the Admiralty in Berlin was uncertain where Count Spee was with his squadron at the outbreak of war. He had last been heard of in Tsingtao. Naturally Count Spee was not unaware of the storm brewing over Europe while he cruised in distant seas. His wireless officers intercepted the messages of cruisers which were soon to become hostile, and Admiral Spee was quite conscious of the fact that the movements of his squadron were being followed with particular interest by the Admiralties in London, Paris, and St. Petersburg. When hostilities began, he succeeded for a long time in concealing his aims and intentions, and in harassing the Allies and their Admiralties with the weapon they had most to fear—uncertainty!

The German Admiralty, whose duty it was to work out the general lines of active naval operations, and to transmit instructions to the squadron and individual commanders, was compelled by the suddenness of the

34

conflict and the precipitate course of events to give *carte blanche* to all cruisers in foreign waters, wherever they might be. They were left to make their own plans, since they were completely isolated from headquarters. In some cases it was impossible even to instruct the cruisers to act independently, as some of those warships, sailing alone, had been veiling their movements for some days.

Count Spee still possessed one line of communication with Berlin — through the Naval Attaché in Tokio, Captain von Knorr. Some days before the outbreak of war, when hostilities appeared to be imminent, the latter cabled that it was essential to send two million yen to Admiral Spee immediately, so that his movements should not be restricted. This money had to be sent to Tokio by the quickest possible route, for if it did not arrive soon the squadron would have to allow itself to be interned, as it could only pay its way in foreign harbours in wartime with cash. The telegram which Captain von Knorr sent to Berlin arrived by the usual route, via New York and London. I was ordered, on August the 2nd, to arrange that Count Spee should receive his money as soon as possible, and I cabled to New York giving instructions that a German bank in that city should wire two million yen to Captain von Knorr in Tokio.

It would be more correct to say: "I tried to give instructions," for my telegram was returned to the Admiralty from the telegraph office in Berlin. It could not be dispatched, for the cable station at Emden reported a "breakdown." Inquiries had been made in London whether there was a breakdown on that side too, but London, for some unknown reason, had not yet replied.

At first there was no explanation of the breakdown. The German cable to New York ran from Emden to America along the bottom of the ocean, and it had never yet failed. The apparatus in Emden showed, however, that there was something wrong with the line, for telegram after telegram had been sent to America, but in no case had the official signal from the other end been received. The telegraph authorities in Emden assumed that they would soon hear from New York again, so we had to wait ; but after forty-eight hours of waiting, with the cable still not functioning, we did not know what to do, since as yet there was no wireless communication between the two countries. The American station in Sayville, near New York, was not yet completed, and it was only in midwinter, 1914, that we were able to send wireless messages from Berlin to America.

We thought out a subtle way that might still be available, namely, to try to get into communication with the Deutsch-Asiatische Bank, which had branches in the most important ports of the Far East. Since the cable no longer functioned, we could not reach this bank by wire either. What we did was this : we paid in the required sum of money at a Danish bank, which instructed its branch in Tokio, by means of a carefully composed and apparently quite harmless business telegram, to provide itself with the necessary funds and place them at the disposal of the Deutsch-Asiatische Bank in Tokio. In a further telegram, which we likewise set up very carefully, we directed the Deutsch-Asiatische Bank to pay the money to our Naval Attaché in Tokio. Both the telegrams went first of all to St. Petersburg, though Russia was already at war with Germany. The unsuspecting officials in St. Petersburg transmitted the telegrams to Vladivostok, whence they reached Tokio, and so Admiral Spee received his two million yen.

Meanwhile, however, it was essential to send further consignments of money abroad, and the German cable to America was still not working. Suddenly we received a report from London which enlightened us as to why we could no longer wire to America. This report, which came to us from a confidential quarter in the British capital, contained astounding information. During the first days of August an unpretentious flotilla of fishing-boats had sailed from the Thames in the direction of Emden-Borkum and the Dutch islands in the vicinity. They were manned chiefly by experts from the department of cables and telegraphs. Under cover of night and fog this flotilla took up the German deep-sea cables, and joined them up with their own lines in London. Instead of going to New York the telegrams we sent from Emden went to London. This was the " breakdown " that Emden had reported !

After the successful dispatch of the two million yen to Count Spee it was my duty to provide and transmit the money required by our other cruisers in foreign waters. At first I met with grotesque difficulties in Berlin, owing to the fact that the authorities obstinately insisted on everything being done in the regulation way. The official procedure was as follows : A formal request had to be made to the Treasury, this request itself also having to go through " official channels " ; the Treasury had to approve the request according to its own system of minuting, and to issue instructions, through " official channels," to the department involved, and this department had then to make the requisite sum available at the Reichsbank, which again had to be officially instructed. The money could then be drawn by one of the big banks and the payment transferred to the payee.

No one knew exactly where our cruisers were, and since it was impossible to foresee whereabouts in the world they might suddenly appear and demand money, I had to have money available as soon as possible at every single large port in every neutral country. Both official and unofficial quarters had, it is strange to say, to be " convinced " first of all that Germany was *at war* and that " official channels " must be short-circuited. At last I managed with great trouble to deposit stocks of foreign currency for our cruisers throughout the whole world, from New York to New Orleans, from Venezuela to Uruguay, from Tierra del Fuego to Seattle, along the whole west coast of South, Central, and North America. We transmitted very large sums to confidential agents in these ports, who had been appointed in peace-time. In the middle of it a very inconvenient incident occurred. A Berlin bank was instructed by us to send half a million dollars to our agent in New York for the purpose of chartering a collier. The honest bank official who had to carry out the instruction innocently took up his pen and, as though we were still at peace, wrote in the letter which was sent to New York :

> " On the instruction and for the account of the Imperial German Navy we transmit to you herewith five hundred thousand dollars."

When I received a copy of this document next day I nearly fainted. Our agent in New York was, of course, compromised.

.   .   .   .   .   .

The next event to rejoice our hearts was the fall of Antwerp, where, for the first time in war, the Zeppelins had given a good account of themselves. In consequence, there arose a strong movement in favour of using them for raids over enemy territory.

One morning I received a welcome visit from my old friend, Kapitän-Leutnant Ostermann, who had lived for many years in London and had succeeded in slipping through the nets which the British Naval Intelligence Department had spread the moment war was declared. Both he and I knew every hole and corner of that great city, and in consequence we were given the task of surveying such centres as London and Liverpool, with a view to drafting plans, based on photographic enlargements, for effective raids from Zeppelins. Being, like everyone else at that time, totally unfamiliar with the military possibilities of this new weapon, we laboured

THE DARK INVADER

under the delusion that bombs could be dropped from the air with practically the same accuracy as shells could be fired from howitzers ! Large-scale maps were printed for us in the Admiralty's own presses, and our immediate business was to mark on them with large red circles the so-called "vulnerable spots." To our astonishment, however, we learned, at a conference held in the presence of Captain Strasser, the commander of the Zeppelins, that no guarantee whatsoever could be given as to where projectiles launched from airships might land.

Bluntly we were told that the bombs, if dropped, could only be dropped haphazard. Ostermann and I thereupon sent in a report stating that, in our firm opinion, the change in England's supposed temper which such a policy would bring about would far outweigh any success of purely military value.

Neither Ostermann nor myself was summoned to any further conferences on this subject. Yet, when a final consent to this questionable policy had been wrung from the Kaiser, he accompanied his Order with an auto-graph Minute to the effect that, in all circumstances, Buckingham Palace must be spared. Reading this, and remembering Captain Strasser's views on accuracy in bombing, I realized what a responsibility had been laid on the Zeppelin commanders.

．　　．　　．　　．　　．

About this period an unenviable task was laid upon all the officers of the various Headquarter Staffs in Berlin. They were instructed to counteract, wherever they could, and in every possible way, the impressions that were being produced by the first great setback on the Western Front, the Battle of the Marne. To us in the Admiralty, out of touch with those responsible for the conduct of the war on land, it was far from clear that this serious reverse was, in fact, the turning-point of the whole war. Yet, from neutral countries, despite the closely-watched frontiers, kept coming the most disquieting reports, whose evil effects it became our duty to minimise as far as we were able. Chance lightened our labours. The tremendous victory of Tannenberg, the triumph of Hindenburg, Ludendorff, and Hoffmann, came as if in answer to our prayers; and in the jubilation which it called forth, the disaster on the Marne lost its depressing grip upon all but the handful of those "in the know." Just as the Allied peoples knew neither the significance, nor perhaps even the name, of Tannenberg until victory was assured, so the meaning of the Marne was kept hidden from the masses in Germany until long after all was lost.

. . . . .

From Berlin we followed the movements of our cruisers, especially of Admiral Spee, with the greatest suspense. Our hearts beat quickly when he destroyed a British squadron off Coronel. We did not know whither he would turn after this battle. We received the news that he had put into harbour at Valparaiso and assumed that he would stay there for some time, to chase English merchantmen along the South American coast, but we were amazed to hear that he had left Valparaiso again at full speed.

The unexpected news of the battle of the Falkland Islands threw us into deep depression. We heard that Count Spee's squadron had been destroyed and that his proud ships lay at the bottom of the ocean. They had run straight into a superior British squadron. Deeply moved and saddened, we sat in our rooms and wondered what on earth could have induced Count Spee to steam round Cape Horn towards the Falkland Islands, but we could find no explanation. We could not imagine why such a prudent and cautious admiral should have attempted to attack the Falkland Islands when he must almost certainly have known that he might attract superior enemy forces. It was a mystery to us !

Not so very long afterwards I was unlucky enough to have dealings with the man " behind it."

.   .   .   .   .

In the midst of this depression we were involved in other anxieties. A Naval Corps was organised for service in Flanders, and we were faced with a situation, which we found at first difficult to believe, that arms were not available in sufficient quantity for the new troops. We had already learned, after the first weeks of the War, that every branch of the Army was beginning to lack the most essential munitions. When the Naval Corps was in being, and somehow had to be supplied with arms, the situation suddenly came home to us. We received orders to provide the corps with machine-guns, and we were told that it did not matter how we got them or where we got them from—that we had to procure them even if we had to fetch them from the moon. A few hours' telephoning to the remotest corners of Germany convinced us that there was no possible way of obtaining machine-guns at home. We commissioned confidential agents in the neutral countries to find out where machine-guns could be bought, and soon received the news that there were three hundred weapons of the most modern construction in a shed in Copenhagen, but that they had already been sold to Russia and were to be shipped in the next few days. We got busy on the telephone. We spoke to Copenhagen, and a little later the German Minister in that city called upon M. Scavenius, the Danish Foreign Minister, pointed out that Denmark was a neutral Power, and protested against the shipping of the machine-guns. The protest was successful, and the firm which had manufactured the weapons was forbidden to export them. As the Russians had long since paid for them the Danish firm was not much affected. The machine-guns remained in their warehouse in the port of Copenhagen, and repeated attempts to load them secretly on a Russian steamer were frustrated by our own agents.

The German and Austrian Legations had posted " guards " round the shed, and every time an attempt was made to get the precious guns on to a ship, one of the Ministers addressed a flaming protest to the Danish Foreign Office.

THE DARK INVADER

We now made an attempt to transfer the weapons to
our own possession. We came to an agreement with the
firm which had already sold them to the Russians but had
no objection to selling them again to us. When, however,
we prepared to load them on to a German ship the
Russian and French Legations came into action, and
we in turn were prohibited from taking the guns on
board.

This little game went on for some time. The agents
of the Allies kept an eye on our people, and our agents
kept an eye on them.

While we were unable to obtain arms and munitions
on a large scale from any neutral country, the Allies
could buy from the whole world; so we had to direct
all our thoughts to procuring by stealth the small
quantities which were still available in Europe. We
were therefore determined that these three hundred
machine-guns must belong to us, and I was ordered to
" fetch them."

I began my scheme, which I had carefully worked out,
by providing myself with a British passport. We had
a large quantity of these, taken from Englishmen who at
the outbreak of war had decided, on their own authority,
to transform themselves into Americans and try in that
way to pass the German frontiers. I put one of these
passports in my pocket, stuck a number of English hotel
labels on my suit-case, prepared a handsome packet of
English business correspondence, and started on the
journey. My name was Mr. William Johnson, I came
from London, and was a typical English business man.

ADMIRALSTAB

A few fellow-travellers noticed, though, that I had no difficulty in passing the German guards at the frontier in Warnemünde.

Upon reaching Copenhagen I took a room at the Hôtel d'Angleterre. This hotel was the headquarters in Denmark of all the agents of the Allies, and the lobby swarmed with them. I had not come to Copenhagen alone, but was accompanied by a man who knew the capital well, having carried on a business there for some years before the War. He had the advantage of me in speaking Danish, and his job was to assist me with his advice and active co-operation. We sat peacefully in the bar of the hotel or drank coffee in the restaurant, but every once in a while someone came sniffing round us. After a couple of days, however, we succeeded in becoming rather friendly with some Russian agents, and one evening I startled these gentlemen by telling them that I was a British agent, was furnished with plenty of funds, and that I had instructions to aid them in conveying the machine-guns to the Russian Army. The agents thought that this was *awfully* decent of me. But a few days later a Russian vessel steamed into the harbour. It had originally been a Swedish boat, but we had purchased it and disguised it skilfully as Russian. On its arrival I summoned the Russian agents. I told them that the German and Austrian agents were bribed by me with large sums, that a Russian boat lay in the harbour under orders to receive the machine-guns, and that the shipment was to take place on January 27th. I informed them that this day had been chosen because it was the

Kaiser's birthday, when the German agents would consider it a matter of honour to get completely drunk. Our agents, of course, had been told to stay away on that day, as the plan was that the Russians should help to transfer the machine-guns to the alleged Russian ship. This scheme had the advantage that the Russians were paying for weapons which we intended for use on the Western Front.

Everything was working smoothly, and merely for the final arrangements my companion and I had a meeting with the Russian agents in my room at the hotel. The Russians had already wired to their War Office that the machine-guns were at last about to be shipped to Russia, and we sat and drank coffee varied with numerous liqueurs. The waiter listened to everything we said, but that did not matter, since he was a French agent, and our conversation could only meet with his approval. When the Russians had had rather a lot to drink—we had to keep up with them of course—something dreadful happened. My friend, the merchant, who had come with me to Copenhagen, and who was a lance-corporal in the Prussian Reserve, must have had a little too much to drink and so lost his presence of mind. He suddenly made to me—to Mr. William Johnson—a respectful bow, clicked his heels together, and said in the purest German:

" *Darf ich Herrn Kapitänleutnant eine Zigarre anbieten?* "

The Russian agents were not so drunk that they did not immediately realise what a trap they had fallen into. They started up from their chairs, but I did not enter into tedious explanations. I found some sort of apology, let the agents say and think what they liked, and returned to Berlin.

The scheme so carefully thought out had come to grief, but we found it too good to drop altogether, so shortly afterwards I was ordered back to Denmark. avoided this time the Hôtel d'Angleterre, lodged in a remote corner of Copenhagen, and approached the French agents, who fell into the trap originally laid for the Russians. One day, when the German agents did not turn up because they had apparently been bribed by me, the Frenchmen put the machine-guns on the Russian steamer, which, however, still belonged to us. When it reached its destination the company of marines, which had remained hidden on board throughout the voyage, felt disappointed. The vessel might easily have been challenged by a British destroyer or submarine then in the Baltic, and a boarding-party might have expressed doubts concerning her nationality and her precious cargo. It would then have been the duty of the company of marines to disperse these doubts.

.   .   .   .   .

I returned to my daily routine at the Admiralty Staff. There was nothing exciting, no work to lift me out of the rut of my duties, and I came to realise more clearly with what embittered tenacity a war was being waged far away from the field of battle, a struggle between the Naval War Staff and General Headquarters.

THE DARK INVADER

On the side of the Naval War Staff Tirpitz fought, with a doggedness which can hardly be described, for the employment of submarines, for the inauguration of intensified U-boat warfare. On the other side, the Chancellor, Herr von Bethmann Hollweg, was ranged with General Headquarters in opposition to this plan. Bethmann Hollweg had the ear of the Kaiser, which gave him the opportunity, of which he made full use, of preventing the Naval War Staff from having its way. Bethmann Hollweg took the standpoint that the " confounded Navy," as he called it, was out to ruin his policy towards England. We in the Service were often told at the time that the Chancellor was firmly convinced that England's share in the War was only to be a " skirmish," which diplomatic cleverness would soon bring to a " nice, peaceful " end. He fought desperately, therefore, against the plan of Grand-Admiral von Tirpitz for the building of submarines and still more submarines, and offered a passive resistance which was not easily overcome. When, however, Great Britain began, by word and deed, to show herself increasingly hostile ; when the scale and the scope of Kitchener's plans for mobilisation became known to the Central Powers, and the London Treaty, binding the Allied Powers to conclude no separate peace with an enemy government, was signed— then the most optimistic of diplomats could no longer ignore the reality of England's participation in the War, nor doubt that England " meant to see this thing through." Borne down by the march of events, Bethmann threw in his hand and exclaimed,

ADMIRALSTAB

"Nun ist meine ganze England-politik zusammenge-
brochen!"[1]

At this time I received orders to go from Berlin to
Wilhelmshaven and communicate to the High Seas Fleet
the arrangements for the active carrying out of the
U-boat campaign. At the same time, incidentally, was
issued the famous order to the Battle Fleet to operate
with increasing activity in the North Sea, but to avoid,
as far as possible, contact with the enemy.

No one was aware that in a few days submarine warfare was to begin in an extreme form. The German
public had not the slightest suspicion of what was afoot,
and confidential warnings had only been given, in the
greatest secrecy, to the official representatives of certain
neutral countries.

At noon one day the Admiralty was startled by a piece
of news which exploded like a bomb. It was reported
that the *B. Z. am Mittag* (*Berlin Mid-day Journal*) had
printed on its front page in large type an announcement
of the impending submarine campaign. How did it
happen, we asked? How did this decision, which had
been "kept" a strict secret, reach the *B. Z. am Mittag*?
It had certainly not been communicated to the Press,
and so inquiries were made as to how the information
had found its way to that newspaper, and they resulted
in the discovery of the following astonishing facts:

Grand-Admiral von Tirpitz had been asked for an
interview by the representative of the American Hearst
Press in Berlin, Mr. Wiegand. He had had a long

[1] "There goes my whole English policy!"

4
49

conversation with this journalist, and had revealed to him
the fact, hitherto guarded with such rigorous secrecy,
that the German Government had formally and irrevo-
cably decided on the employment of submarine warfare. Mr. Wiegand rushed at once to the telephone
and cabled the sensational news to America, where it
was published, and put the whole world in a state of
excitement.

It happened that the New York correspondent of the
B. Z. am Mittag read this news one morning on the first
page of the Hearst paper, the *New York American*. From
the wording of the announcement it could be inferred
that it had not yet been given out officially to the German
papers ; so the *B. Z. am Mittag's* representative naturally
went and cabled the New York paper's news, word for
word, to his newspaper in Berlin.

It was then apparent what had moved the Grand-
Admiral to commit such an indiscretion. Tirpitz did
not believe that the Government would " stick " to its
decision to begin submarine warfare. He, however, was
convinced that it was essential in view of the whole war
position, and he wanted to force Bethmann Hollweg to
carry out the decision which had been wrung from him.
In giving the news to the American journalist he knew
that it would be blazoned forth to all the world, and he
was convinced that it would be impossible for Germany
to go back without being accused of weakness, which
would mean a perceptible loss of prestige.

Now that the intention was known, the coming
submarine campaign was being discussed by the whole

world. The Naval Attachés of the foreign powers came
to the Admiralty to ascertain how it would be managed in
detail. And, of course, the American Naval Attaché,
Captain Gherardi, came too. He was affable and conde-
scending, and talked about the " dangerous situation "
like an indulgent father to an unruly child. At the end
of his talk he did not omit to invite me to dinner the
following night. I was not altogether comfortable about
this invitation. I informed my superior officer, therefore,
and asked whether I ought to accept. I was told that I
must, of course, go, but that I should listen carefully to
the grumblings of the ill-humoured American.

When I went to Gherardi's house the following night
I was received with accustomed kindness. His wife
talked about a Red Cross Dinner, but he himself was
rather embarrassed in his demeanour, and we conversed
at table about unimportant matters. I made a great effort
to keep an interesting flow of talk going, but all the time
he was muttering something incomprehensible, and for
some obscure reason was even more out of sorts than
usual. So I thought we might introduce more dangerous
matters into the conversation, and I asked him straight
out what the American Navy was saying about the
proclamation of submarine warfare.

Gherardi lifted his moody countenance, raised his eye-
brows, wrinkled his forehead in astonishment, leaned
back in his chair, and said :

" Submarine warfare ? Submarine warfare ? What do
you mean ? There isn't going to be any warfare ! Nothing will come of it ! Our Ambassador has already been

so informed by the Imperial Chancellor. He has been officially notified that the order for the commencement of submarine hostilities has been revoked."

Then he became red in the face and boiled over.

"You are congratulating yourselves a bit too soon! We won't put up with anything from Germany."

I found it difficult to master my excitement. I am certain that I talked at random for the rest of the evening, and I was glad when a chance came to say farewell. Outside in the street the pure night air cooled my head, and I thought things over.

When I had left the Admiralty that evening the final orders for submarine hostilities had gone out, and the U-boats must by now be on the high seas. At that time submarines carried no wireless receiving apparatus. They had, however, received the clear and unequivocal order to attack the cargo-boats of all nations which were on the way to enemy countries, and no one could bring them back. Perhaps at this very moment the first torpedo was being launched, possibly sending to the bottom an American steamer—a few hours after the German Chancellor had told the American Ambassador that no such thing was going to happen.

I stopped a taxi and drove to the Admiralty.

Some senior officers were still at work in the building. I met two chiefs of departments in their rooms, and informed them of what I had just heard. Both stared at me in amazement. They could not believe what I told them, and one of them said :

"You must have misheard!"

ADMIRALSTAB

" No, certainly not, sir! Gherardi expressed himself in the exact words that I have just used."

The two captains grew agitated. They pointed out that as the submarines were already at sea it was extremely probable that the news of the torpedoing of an American steamer might come in at any moment.

It would have been the simplest and most proper thing to do, so far as it was possible to judge, to ring up the Chancellor the same night in order to ask him the truth about the matter. At that late hour, however, it was out of the question. Besides, the jealousy of the individual Services, the constant intrigues, conflicts, moves and counter-moves, rife even in the highest places of the Empire, ruled out such a simple course.

I had then, on the Kaiser's birthday, just been promoted lieutenant-commander. I was a small pawn in this fantastic game which those who controlled German politics were playing with one another. But I was full of fight; and as I was walking home that night I decided that I would venture a move on this dangerous chessboard. I knew a large number of people who were mixed up in the game as a matter of routine, and I began in the morning to ring them up, one after the other.

I first telephoned to Count Westarp and to Erzberger, both members of the Reichstag. Half an hour later they were sitting on the red plush sofa in my office at the Admiralty.

It was a Sunday morning.

" Bethmann is becoming impossible," Count Westarp

said. " I will see if I can collect a few more members, then we'll go and ask him what this is all about."

Erzberger broke in indignantly :

" I can tell you ! *Eine Mords-Schweinerei !* "

When they had gone I rang up Walter Rathenau, who was just beginning to organise the War Materials Department, and Dr. Salomonsohn of the Disconto-Gesellschaft. Both declared that they would go immediately to the Chancellor and ask him what had really happened. I then got hold of Helfferich, who also said he would call on the Chancellor. Next I hurried to the Reichstag, where I had a talk with Herr Südekum, the Social Democrat member. He was one of the few " field greys " among the members, and was in uniform, with the short bayonet of a non-commissioned officer at his side. He opened his eyes wide when he heard what I had to tell him, and despairingly said, as a " trooper " would :

" *'rin in die Kartoffeln, raus aus die Kartoffeln !* " (" Heavens ! Another order ! ")

Things now began to develop as I wanted them to. Each of the members of the Reichstag, everybody to whom I had given the information, promptly went to Bethmann. But what happened was astounding. The Chancellor told everybody most emphatically that he was unaware of any statement having been made to the American Embassy that the U-boat campaign had been countermanded.

Late that evening I was rung up by Count Westarp.

" Listen ! There's something wrong. Are you sure

your information is right? Bethmann denies everything, and complains that more than a dozen politicians
have called upon him during the afternoon to ask him
the same question. Mum's the word! But if it should
be discovered that it was you who started the ' run,' I'm
afraid, my dear Captain, that you must be prepared for
squalls ! "

I did not get much sleep that night. I was not worried
about myself, though I felt my head in the noose, but
because everything was so unfathomably mysterious.
Next day my fears were realised. Somebody had told
the Chancellor that I, Captain Rintelen, had started a
rumour to the effect that he, Bethmann, had informed
the American Ambassador that the U-boat campaign
would be called off.

That afternoon I had to report to my Admiral, who
reprimanded me officially at the instance of the Chancellor, and was given the most unusual order to call at the
Imperial Chancery during the evening in order to
vindicate myself. When I arrived at the Wilhelmstrasse
I was shown in to Herr Wahnschaffe, the Under-Secretary
of State. I told him that I was still definitely of the
opinion that I had *not* misunderstood Gherardi. Wahnschaffe grew annoyed ; but Herr Rizler, Bethmann's
secretary, joined us, and he also declared that no such
communication had been made, either verbally or in
writing, to the American Ambassador. I was completely dumbfounded, and asked myself if I were going
mad. But whom should I meet the very next day on the
steps of the Admiralty, but Wahnschaffe ! He returned

my greeting in a somewhat embarrassed manner. An hour later I was called to my Chief's room.

" Please take note that the copy of the Chancellor's letter to the American Ambassador has been found in the Chancery."

There ensued terrific confusion, for the Admiralty was now in possession of the official communication that the Americans had been informed of the countermanding of the U-boat campaign. The Government had even made this statement in writing to the American Ambassador. On the other hand, we were faced by the fact that the U-boats had for some time been at sea and that no power in the world could prevent them from torpedoing American ships.

A few days later a message arrived. An American freighter had been sunk, and we were powerless to prevent a repetition!

From the strategic point of view as well, what now ensued was calamitous. The U-boats which had already left remained without support, had no parent ships to return to, were completely isolated and exposed to every danger.

Some time later we learned how Bethmann had come to write his letter to the American Ambassador. After Mr. Gerard had had a stormy interview with the Chancellor, representing to him that America simply would not tolerate it, Bethmann went to the Kaiser, who immediately, without wasting much thought on the matter, cancelled the decision which had already been taken. Yet nobody had possessed the courage to inform the naval authorities of this complete change of policy !

The situation had swiftly come to a head. The American Ambassador, of course, also had heard that an American freighter had been torpedoed, in spite of the declaration that he had received in writing from the German Government. He inwardly foamed with rage, but outwardly remained impassive. He deduced from the whole incident that it would be practical policy never to believe anything that the German Government told him, even when he had it formally in writing !

About this time it was that everybody in Germany was raging. Large packets of newspapers had been received from America, and there was not a word of truth in the reports that were being made about the military situation. We were particularly indignant at the numerous stories of atrocities which had found their way into the American papers. With this kind of journalism it was inevitable that not only the mass of newspaper readers, but gradually also official circles in America, would assume an anti-German attitude. The accounts in the American Press describing conditions in Germany were equally disgraceful. Unimportant successes on the part of the Allied armies were inflated in the American papers to the significance of outstanding victories, while news of German victories was not printed at all. The Americans were being given a completely false picture of the real situation in Europe.

Since the beginning of the War attempts had been

made by Germany to influence the international Press, or at least to supply it with correct information. The German military authorities in charge of this matter, especially the Intelligence Department of the Supreme Army Command, was learning all too slowly how to win the confidence of the editors of the great German newspapers ; so how was it possible for them to influence foreign journalists ? Some more experienced officers at the Admiralty tried to repair much of the damage and to put things right, and the American correspondents in Germany soon got into the habit of obtaining their information from them. I too was frequently the centre of a whole group of foreign journalists. Eventually we succeeded in making it clear to them that the military situation was not unfavourable for Germany at all. When they were finally convinced of this they were honest enough to cable impartial reports to their papers in America. But no sooner had these articles appeared than our rooms were veritably stormed by the foreign correspondents, who protested that the British were no longer transmitting their wires. The British controlled the international cables, and were naturally exercising a strict censorship in their own favour.

An idea occurred to me, and I must confess that I was unscrupulous enough to exploit it. I was on good terms with Major Langhorne, the American Military Attaché in Berlin, who too had his difficulties owing to the English control of the foreign cables. He was in search of a way to send his telegrams to Washington without

London reading or intercepting them. They were, of course, in code, but the Attaché had no illusions about England's practices in this connection. He was positively convinced that the British would succeed in deciphering his code. So I proposed to him that he should give us the code telegrams and that we should have them sent via Nauen to the American wireless station, which had just been completed. In this way they would speedily reach his Government at Washington. The Yankee was startled for a moment, but then accepted my offer with gratitude, although he insisted that his telegrams should be in code.

He arrived with his first telegrams, which were sent off immediately via Nauen. I had copies made of them and called on a celebrated cipher expert, who shut himself up with the texts, and the Fates were favourable to us. It was to be presumed that the American Attaché had included in one of the telegrams, which was very long, an extensive official report from German G.H.Q., and this conjecture turned out to be correct. The expert substituted the German text for the code letters and figures, and everything fitted in. We were now in possession of the Attaché's code, and preserved it as though it were sacred. From now on we were " reading in " Langhorne's telegrams. When we gained those great victories against Russia I cabled " my own text " to America. I re-wrote Major Langhorne's telegrams so that they gave a clear account of our military position, and added the whole extent of the enemy defeats in such a way, of course, that the American Government was bound to believe that these telegrams came from its own Military Attaché.

Things went on well for weeks. When the next batch of American newspapers arrived a certain change of view was already noticeable in the more serious journals. Germany's strategic position was regarded and criticised more favourably, and I rejoiced at this success. Suddenly, however, I myself smashed my instrument of propaganda. I overdid matters by sending a telegram which allowed a certain pro-German attitude to be apparent between the lines, and the end came soon. Without warning and without reason Major Langhorne received laconic instructions from Washington to return to America.

His successor did not hand me any telegrams for transmission. He exercised great caution, for when Major Langhorne was shown his telegrams on his arrival in Washington he of course immediately denied that he had ever sent them, and little acumen was required to realise from whom they had come.

I was pricked by conscience at the way in which I had acted, but I consoled myself with the thought that Germany was facing a world in arms, a vastly superior force, which would perhaps crush her if she did not use every means in her power to defend herself.

Every means in her power!

.   .   .   .   .

At the beginning of 1915 the German armies, after the great battles of the previous year, were waiting to hurl themselves once more against the enemy. They were still faced by the same opponents and the same forces. The German Supreme Army Command knew approximately the number of troops they were able to send against the enemy on the Western and Eastern Fronts, and the generals in both camps began to prepare their great moves on the chessboard of war.

At this time there emerged a new foe, raining destruction upon the German troops both in the East and in the West. It was spreading disaster everywhere, and that so terribly that the Supreme Army Command, then in Charleville, wired to the Government in Berlin :

> " We are at our wits' end to defend ourselves
> against American ammunition."

So this was the new and dreadful enemy : American ammunition !

It was all the more to be feared, since it was being manufactured at the beginning of 1915 in a way that was still unfamiliar to the munition factories of Europe. The American shells, which were suddenly being hurled in great quantities against the German trenches by French, British, and Russian guns, were not made of cast-iron like the European shells, but of steel. These steel casings were a diabolical invention : they were ribbed and grooved, and when the shell exploded the casing burst into thousands of small pieces and came down with terrific force upon its victim. Its explosive effect was tremendous. At the time that these shells first appeared the German Army was suffering from a very serious lack of munitions. The batteries of field artillery in the West were hardly able to get the range of important enemy positions, since they had to economise their shells for emergencies. At the beginning of 1915 there was hardly sufficient ammunition available to keep down enemy battery positions which had at last been discovered. Even shooting at targets whose range was known must only be undertaken on special orders from Corps Headquarters. In the case of attacks which took the infantry forward, artillery preparations could not be anything but scanty.

The German munition factories, in spite of enormous efforts, were far from being in a position to supply even approximately the quantity of shells required by the Army.

The French, English, and Russian factories were in exactly the same position and were unable to turn out an adequate supply of ammunition. The factories in the whole of Europe could not produce as many of these death-dealing missiles as were needed in this war.

Then America appeared on the scene. There existed at this time in the United States half a dozen large powder and explosives factories. There were also numerous great industrial undertakings which had hitherto manufactured cast steel for the needs of a peaceful world. They were now ready to adapt their machinery to the production of war-materials, thus yielding many times the ordinary profits for their directors and shareholders. There was no law in America forbidding the manufacture of munitions by these firms, and no law to prohibit their shipment. British, French, and Russian agents had, as early as 1914, entered into negotiations with American concerns. There were at first doubts and difficulties, but these were soon removed by the cheques of the prospective customers. Money appeared upon the scene of war and began to exercise its decisive influence.

The American industrialists who were prepared to adapt their works made it quite clear to the European agents that they would have to invest vast additional capital if they were suddenly to start manufacturing a different class of goods. It would be necessary to install new machinery, to make experiments. When the industrialists approached the banks, after conversations with the Allied agents, and requested credits for the purpose of adapting their works, they met with very little sympathy. Their offers of high interest rates were of no avail, for the banks realised that the manufacture of munitions involved considerable danger, and, in addition, the bankers drew the attention of the industrialists to a factor which made it impossible for American banks to employ to advantage their capital in this way. This factor was American public opinion, which was opposed to the European War. At this stage of the conflict the citizens of America were convinced that their Government could not do better than keep as far away as possible from the military events in Europe. They took the standpoint that the warring countries would some time, perhaps very soon, have to lay down their arms, and when this juncture should arrive they were anxious to resume their ordinary profitable commercial transactions with all Europe. If America should now intervene in any way it might eventually come to pass that Germany, for example, would boycott American goods when peace were declared if American favour had been shown to the Allies only. These considerations were further influenced by the fact that it was still impossible to prophesy which side would come out victorious ; and even then there existed in America organisations which were very influential and neglected no opportunity of representing to the Government that it must avoid doing anything which one of the European Powers might be able to regard as an unfriendly act.

These were the factors which induced the American banks to refuse credits to the factories which wanted to produce munitions. The cheques of the European agents first exerted their influence among smaller manufacturers, who began to install lathes for the making of shells. The Allies, however, realised that ultimate victory could only be assured if American shells were shipped to Europe in vast quantities. But the American banks still declined to furnish the money for the turning of large factories into munition-works, because they were afraid that the Government, urged by popular opinion, might one day prohibit the export of arms and ammunition, so that they might risk the capital invested. Now the Allied agents took a step which abolished at one blow the hesitation of the bankers. They drafted contracts which led to the immediate production of vast quantities of munitions. In these contracts they undertook to

receive at the factories any quantity that might be manufactured, and to pay for it on the spot. They took over
the whole risk of transport as well as the risk that the
munitions might not become available at all for the
Allied armies by the prohibition of their export. They
deposited at the banks letters of credit for large sums,
and the bankers now had no reason to refrain any longer
from manufacturing munitions. Soon both large and
small banks were treading on each other's heels in their
anxiety to advance money on Allied contracts, and a
munition industry was in being which had veritably shot
up overnight. Enormous profits could be earned without any risk whatever, and American industry did not
hesitate. Steel was turned into shells and nose-caps, the
railways carried explosives from the powder factories to
the new munition-works, and the dollars began to flow.
Ships sailed from European ports for America, after
having been swiftly adapted to the transport of munitions, and soon they lay in American ports, while great
cases, guarded by Allied agents, but under the mistrustful eyes of American dockers, were piled up on the
quays. After these ships had returned and had unloaded
their cargoes in their home ports in Russia or in France,
and when these cargoes had reached the guns on the
battle-fields, to scatter destruction over the German lines,
the Supreme Army Command would probably again
telegraph to Berlin :

" We are at our wits' end to defend ourselves
against American ammunition."

THE DARK INVADER

The German Military Attaché in New York was ordered to report on the situation, and in his reply painted a picture which revealed the daily growth of the American armament industry. He wrote that the harbours were full of Allied transports waiting to take munitions on board. He continued :

" Something must be done to stop it."

In a despairing mood General Falkenhayn wrote on one of these reports :

" Not only must something be done, as the Attaché says ; something must *really* be done."

And a hasty meeting with General, then Lieutenant-Colonel, Hoffmann, Chief of Staff on the Eastern Front, whom I had known for a good many years, convinced me still more deeply that " something must *really* be done " ! We sat but a few hours together, at dawn on a dreary day of March, in a room of the Hôtel Kronprinz at Dirschau, on the Vistula. After he depicted to me the situation on the Russian Front, and especially in Galicia, I was inwardly certain that the dice were cast, that America *had* to be attacked !

American capital had flung itself upon an opportunity to make immense profits. It was thrown into the scales of war and began to send up in a dangerous manner the balance which held Germany's fate. That was what was happening in America.

In Berlin and at the General Headquarters this new

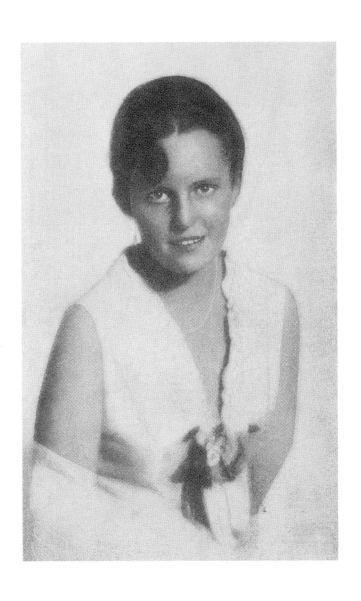

MY DAUGHTER : MARIE-LUISE

" MEINEN DANK FÜR FREUNDLICHES GEDENKEN ! "
August 13th, 1932. Haus Doorn

THE AUTHOR IN IMPERIAL NAVAL UNIFORM

THE AUTHOR
October 1932

AN HISTORIC MENU
The Guests of the evening
CAPTAINS BOY-ED AND VON PAPEN

AN HISTORIC MENU

A page of Signatures

AN AERIAL VIEW OF THE NEW YORK RIVER FRONT

WRECKAGE IN THE NEIGHBOURHOOD OF "BLACK TOM"
THE FOUNDATIONS OF A WRECKED WAREHOUSE CAN BE SEEN IN THE FOREGROUND

invisible enemy was the cause for the deepest gloom. It was no opponent who could be faced in the open field, it was no foe whose trenches could be taken by storm; it was a spectre, an intangible phantom, against which strategy, tactics, and all the courage of the German soldier were helpless. These shipments of American munitions were the ghost which haunted the corridors of the Army Command in Charleville. A powerful and sinister hand was raised against the soldiers of Germany and hurled them back with ghastly wounds.

The Supreme Army Command, in view of the situation, made grave and resolute appeals to the Government in Berlin to stop the transport of armaments. The Government moved along the ordinary legal and political channels and remonstrated officially to the Government of the United States. Army leaders interviewed the editors of the great German newspapers and requested them to discuss America's attitude publicly in their columns. The American Government replied in the same manner as had the American Press to the German newspapers. America took up the standpoint that she was distinctly neutral, that the shipments of munitions did not violate the laws of neutrality. It is true, declared America, that we are supplying the Allies with munitions, but we are equally prepared to supply them to Germany: " Send us orders and you will see that we shall execute them promptly."

This reply from America could be regarded in Germany only as irony. The seas were dominated by British, French, and Russian cruisers, and it was impossible for a munition transport from America to reach a German port. It was therefore impossible to place orders for munitions in the United States. German General Head-quarters were appealing to the Admiralty in Berlin to use submarines for the purpose of waylaying the transports ; but the Admiralty, however, was compelled to reply that the attitude of the Government at the beginning of the War had prevented the building of submarines in sufficient quantities to prove a serious menace to the Allies' shipments of munitions. Besides, those trans-ports mostly took the route north of Scotland, round Spitzbergen to Archangel, when the munitions were destined for the Rusian Front, and they unloaded in the Atlantic ports of France when their destination was the Western battle-fields. It was difficult in either case to attack the transports with submarines, though this would have been possible if an adequate number of U-boats had been constructed at the outbreak of hostili-ties. This, however, had been prevented by Bethmann Hollweg.

When it was realised that it was not possible to strangle the export of munitions from America by the usual political means deep pessimism settled on all the military and civil authorities in the country. The attempt had been made to transfer the initiative to the Admiralty by persuading it to use U-boats, but the Admiralty had been in the unhappy position of declaring that this method was not available. But it did not content itself with this, for we officers of the Admiralty Staff spent our days and nights trying to think out schemes for stopping the mischief. Suddenly an idea emerged which it seemed possible to carry out with success.

At the time when the Supreme Army Command was renewing its urgent appeals to the Government to take action against the transport of armaments, the Americans sent a request to Berlin that they might be allowed to bring into Belgium such quantities of provisions as they wanted. The German Government had hitherto resisted this demand. General von Bissing, the German Governor of Belgium, came to Berlin, and I had an interview with him, at which it was decided to make a bargain with the Americans. The latter emphasised their extraordinary anxiety to be allowed to feed the Belgian civil population. Good! We would agree to their request, but in return they should bind themselves to stop the munition shipments. I was put in charge of these negotiations because, among other reasons, the chairman of the Belgian Relief Committee, Mr. Lindon W. Bates, was a personal acquaintance of mine. I was to proceed to America and discuss the matter with Mr. Bates. The Foreign Office gave me a letter to Mr. Gerard, the American Ambassador in Berlin, asking him to obtain for me a safe conduct to the States from the British Government. I called at the Embassy to hand over the letter from the Foreign Office and gave reasons why I should be allowed a safe conduct. He replied that it was impossible, and that he could not and would not do what was asked of him.[1]

[1] This interview is referred to briefly by Mr. Gerard in his book, *My Four Years in Germany.*

So our plans seemed to be going wrong. Further anxious days were spent in discussion, and yet we had not come to a decision when G.H.Q. warned that things could not go on like this any longer. It was imperative to take some definite step.

My work in providing money for our cruisers abroad had gradually earned me the reputation of a man who knew his way about the world in the matter of financial transactions. I knew America, had numerous connections there, and spoke English without a noticeable accent, and the authorities became convinced that I was the man to go to the United States and take action against the shipment of munitions.

The wrecking of the plan with regard to the Belgian Relief Committee had proved a serious hitch, and no one could think of any other method of tackling the job. When it was definitely arranged that I was to go, and I had accustomed myself to this idea, a new channel presented itself to our minds.

Herr Erzberger, a member of the Reichstag, had then taken the first steps in organising an international propaganda service for Germany. His international intelligence service, which ran parallel with it, was beginning to furnish exceedingly good results and considerably surpassed the purely military service of the Supreme Army Command. Herr Erzberger's Bureau had discovered a man named Malvin Rice who claimed to be closely connected with an American powder factory, the " Dupont de Nemours Powder Company," of which he said he was a shareholder and a member of the Board. He stated that this firm held a large stock of explosives which was used for the filling of the shells which had hitherto been manufactured in America. It appeared that we might, with his help, make thus large purchases of that product in the American market, sufficient in fact to jeopardise, for some time at least, the delivery of munitions for the Allies.

It naturally occurred to me that Malvin Rice's magnificent plans might come to nothing ; but there was no time to lose. Either we had to believe what Malvin Rice had held out as a hope, namely, that large purchases of powder and explosives were possible, or to drop the idea then and there. I could neither brood over a possible non-success of this extraordinary journey before me, nor doubt as to whether Mr. Rice was an altogether reliable person. " Orders were Orders ! " ; and when the War Minister, General von Wandel, put the question to me : " You cannot give us a No ! " I did not hesitate a second. I replied : " Your Excellency, my train will leave on Monday morning ! "

This was on Saturday noon, March 20th, 1915.

. . . . .

I left Berlin with a sigh of relief. I was thoroughly disgusted by the terrible inertia over the question as to whether submarine warfare should take place or not. Indeed, I was congratulated on all sides in the Admiralty that a new field for energetic enterprise had thus presented itself to me. I was a man who meant business !

Personally, I was extremely anxious that my journey

to America should not turn out to be a mere pleasure-cruise in wartime, in view of the strong feeling aroused in Germany by the apparently one-sided comparison of two letters which I think I should quote here, and which spoke for themselves.

The Kaiser had sent that telegraphic protest to President Wilson against certain violations of the Hague International Agreements. In reply Mr. Wilson wrote:

> " WASHINGTON,
> " *September* 16*th*, 1914
>
> " YOUR MAJESTY,
> "I have received your telegraphic message through your Ambassador. . . . The day for deciding the merits of your protest will come when this war is finished. . . . It would not be wise, and indeed it would be premature, for any single Government of any particular nation to form a final opinion or to express such an opinion. . . .
>
> " I am, Your Majesty,
> " Yours truly,
> " (Signed) WOODROW WILSON "

Through the intermediary of a friendly personage in a certain Allied country I came into possession of a letter which the same President Wilson addressed, a few months later, to the President of the French Republic:

> " WASHINGTON,
> " *December* 7*th*, 1914.
>
> " MY DEAR MR. PRESIDENT,[1]
> " I feel honoured to be able thus to address you as a fellow-man of letters, and I desire to thank you

[1] Re-translated from the French.

very sincerely for the kind message which you have sent me through the medium of M. Brieux.

" I am sure I quite understand the circumstances which have prevented your visit to the United States, but I am anxious none the less to send you my regrets at your being unable to realise this project : and I should like to take this opportunity of expressing to you not only my own deep respect and admiration, but also the warm sympathy which all thinkers and men of letters in the United States feel for the distinguished President of France.

" The relations between our two peoples have always been relations of such cordial and spontaneous friendship that it gives me particular pleasure, as official representative of the United States, to address to you, the distinguished representative of France, my warmest sympathy for the citizens of the great French Republic.

" Believe me, dear Mr. President, my esteemed colleague,

" Yours very sincerely,

" (Signed) WOODROW WILSON "

So when undertaking my new enterprise I felt in my inner conscience that I had a good case for Germany.

It was accepted in all quarters in Berlin that something of a more forceful nature must be done than hitherto. Indeed, conferences took place in the War Ministry, the Foreign Office, and the Finance Ministry, in each of which I outlined my plans, in so far as I could gauge the situation from my post in Berlin. The impression of energy and determination which I contrived to make gave considerable satisfaction. Men of action, particularly men like Helfferich and Zimmermann, could not help smiling when I concluded one speech with : " *Ich kaufe, was ich kann ; alles andere schlage ich kaput !* " [1] One and all they resolutely agreed with me that sabotage was the only alternative.

As it had been arranged that I should travel under an assumed name, there was a risk that the German military police themselves might hold me up at the port. The Foreign Office therefore decided to issue me a " Kaiserpass " in my real name. A " Kaiserpass " was an altogether exceptional passport, which could only be issued with the knowledge and consent of the Foreign Office, and only to people on special Government missions, instructing all authorities, embassies and legations to render the bearer every assistance of which he might stand in need. " Thus provided, guarded, guided," I strapped my bags and set sail for America.

How badly indeed " forcible measures " were necessary was soon afterwards shown by Papen's letter to Falkenhayn, Chief of General Staff, thanking him that at last someone had come to America to act with every means possible.

It was arranged with Malvin Rice, who had since returned to New York, that I should sail on the Norwegian steamer *Kristianiafjord*, due in New York in the early days of April, 1915, while he was to meet me at the dock.

I had to start within a few hours. I provided myself

---

[1] "I'll buy up what I can, and blow up what I can't."

with an excellent Swiss passport, which had been cunningly printed in Berlin, with all the requisite stamps, seals, and endorsements, and the German Captain Rintelen became the Swiss citizen Emile V. Gaché. I chose this name because one naval officer in Berlin was married to a Swiss lady, who now became my sister, and coached me with information about numerous nephews, nieces, aunts, uncles, and other relations whom I had thus newly acquired. She gave me a photograph of my parents' house and of the little cottage high up in the Swiss mountains which we also owned, and furnished me with private lessons on the Swiss Civil Code and my army duties. My new initials were sewn on my linen, which was sent to a laundry in order that the letters should not appear too new. There was, in short, a number of small things to be attended to, and carefully attended to, because it was quite certain that I should have to submit during my journey to the inspection of keen-eyed officers of the British Navy.

A few hours before my departure I provided myself with the necessary " working capital," which I only succeeded in collecting when the train which was to take me towards my new duties was almost getting up steam, and it was high time for me to drive to the station. In the short time at my disposal I succeeded in arranging for a cable transfer of half a million dollars as a " starter."

The die was cast. While motoring in a service-car to the railway station I pondered over the contents of a letter which but a few days before, had been addressed

75

to me by Count Westarp and Dr. von Heydebrand, the leader of the then almighty Conservative Party—" the uncrowned King of Prussia " he was called—suggesting that I should become an M.d.R. (M.P.).

Admiral von Tirpitz narrates in his *Memoirs* how I was to replace a member of the Reichstag, recently deceased. The blue naval uniform was to make its first appearance in the Reichstag beside the many members in " field grey " ; and an " A. K. O."—an Allerhöchste Kabinetts-Order—had been signed by the Kaiser, giving the necessary permission for a procedure which, under the old conditions, was something of a quite unusual nature.

Well, I had now given my word to the Minister of War and there could be no going back on my word. But how different my career might have become ; for instead of about three months' absence, it was to take me nearly six years to reach " Journey's End."

What if I had even as much as thought of such a possibility then, leaving behind home, wife, and child, and of how cruelly Fate was to tear us asunder for ever !

The " little creature " of 1915 immensely enjoyed the ride to the station, sitting as she did by the side of the chauffeur ; in 1921 she did not recognise her returning father. . . .

PART II
SABOTAGE
The Manhattan "Front"

I STARTED from the Stettiner Bahnhof, on which the German flag was flying in honour of the birthday of the Emperor William I, on March 22nd, 1915. As soon as I was settled in the train I began a task which looked very funny but which had a serious purpose. I wrote post cards to all my acquaintances, dozens of picture post cards to my friends, particularly the Military and Naval Attachés of neutral States. These cards I sent to other friends, in envelopes, with the request that they should post them, so that the Attachés and all the people from whom I wanted to hide my tracks received cards from " Somewhere in Flanders," from Upper Bavaria, and from Silesia. Upon my arrival at Christiania I succeeded in obtaining at the British and American Consulates magnificent genuine visas for my Swiss passport, and I felt safe. When the steamer was on the high seas a British cruiser sent a lieutenant and a couple of sailors on board to see if the ship was harbouring any Germans. The lieutenant ascertained that there were no Germans on board. As we approached the American coast I grew a little uneasy, for the British cruiser *Essex* was stationed off New York—three miles and two inches off. She was commanded by Captain Watson, who had been Naval Attaché in Berlin until shortly before the outbreak of war. We had been friends, and he had been kind enough to give me occasionally a few hints on English naval expressions. This would have been a fine *rencontre* ! I was lucky, however, for the *Essex* was not inspecting the passenger boats on that day, but, as I could see through field-glasses, was engaged in target practice.

Once around these " dangerous corners," I at last landed, safe and sound, on the pier in New York.

I looked around, but in vain.

Where I should have been met by Malvin Rice, who was to take me by the arm and show me where I should find the powder ready for " spot " delivery . . . there was no Malvin Rice at all. The whole edifice which he had constructed before my eyes disappeared *fata Morgana*-wise.

So I stood there on that pier of New York, entirely alone, left to my own wits, but bent upon going through with what seemed ill-starred at the beginning. Single-handed I now ventured an attack against the forty-eight United States !

So more or less all the forebodings which I had prior to my departure from Berlin had been correct, and some of the difficulties, which I had then outlined, by no means on moral grounds or anything of that sort, but merely as an expert in " affairs American," had proved to be not without foundation.

Firstly, I might have been captured in the North Sea, or out in the Atlantic, by some mischievous British cruiser, and my Swiss nationality might have been doubted. In this case I had but one task—to swallow the two tiny capsules which contained in duplicate the brand new " secret code in miniature," which I was to bring over to America for the Embassy and the Attachés. In fact the question was afterwards raised in the House of Commons as to how it had been possible in wartime for a German Naval Commander to get through undiscovered; and, as usual, " no answer was given."

Secondly, it was highly doubtful whether weeks after this negotiation, Mr. Malvin Rice had the powder and explosives still available. It was an under-estimation of the Allies to expect them one and all to go to sleep in the interim. Indeed, the Allies had not gone to sleep!

Thirdly, could other measures be adopted in case the powder had been sold? Yes, they had to be—all the more so because at that time the Russians were gaining victory after victory in Galicia, and their actual invasion of Hungary was to be feared, with the result that Italy's entry into the war became a darker thought than ever before.

Fourthly, it was quite possible that my proposed mission to America, and the objectives I had in view, might quickly cause an international affray between America and Germany. For that eventuality I deliberately told Hr. Zimmermann, then Under-Secretary of State for Foreign Affairs, that he should serve out to the Yankees a flat denial of any complicity, and state that I was merely a " free-lance."

Fifthly, would not the Naval and Military Attachés consider themselves superseded in some way, and make my position a very delicate one henceforth? Indeed they did, and that was the worst of it all. But still, in spite of more cons than pros, I drove to the German Club in order to have a word with the Naval and Military

Attachés, for I had to hand over that important document, the new "Most Secret Code." I knew that they both lived at the German Club, where I had been a member for some years. I cannot say that they were very glad to see me. The Naval Attaché, Captain Boy-Ed, had a couple of gold stripes more on his sleeve than I was permitted to wear, which settled once and for all that his opinion was superior to mine. I tried my level best, as I had known him socially for several years and we had worked in co-operation, in Intelligence matters, for a long time too. He had already received a wire from Berlin that I was on my way. He felt aggrieved, for he thought that he did not need my help and that I might just as safely remain in Germany. The Military Attaché, Captain Papen, was likewise not pleased to see me, which made him side with Boy-Ed. As I had anyhow not expected either of them to burst out into whoops of joy when I made my appearance, I was not much worried at their ill-humour, which, as a matter of fact, I succeeded in dispelling somewhat by informing the Naval Attaché that I had been instructed to let him know that the Order of the House of Hohenzollern was waiting for him at home, and I rejoiced the heart of Captain Papen by telling him that he had been awarded the Iron Cross. Papen seemed elated—at any rate a day or two after he took great pains in writing a letter to General von Falkenhayn thanking him that " at last someone had come to America to take steps to hamper the shipment of munitions *by all means.* . . ." I personally felt that everything is fair, in war. Following my instructions I handed over the precious document that I had brought with me. It was the new " Most Secret Code." Berlin feared that the old secret code which the Ambassador and the Attachés used in their telegrams home, was no longer secret, and it was suspected that the British were able to read our cipher messages. The only code to be used in future was the one I had brought over. We then parted, the Attachés to pursue, as hitherto, the path prescribed by their official duties, while I disappeared into " obscurity."

Hardly a week after my arrival in the United States I received a letter from Captain Boy-Ed, the Naval Attaché, conveying the wish of Count Bernstorff, the Ambassador, to have a conference with me. After some hesitation, in view of the nature of my mission, I decided to go, and duly appeared at the Ritz-Carlton in Madison Avenue. Bernstorff at once asked me the object of my presence in America. In reply, I politely suggested he should not ask that question, since my answer might complicate his diplomatic duties. At that he drew his chair up to the sofa on which I was sitting and almost whispered : " Now, Captain, please understand that, although I am here as an Ambassador, I am an old soldier as well. You may tell me anything in confidence."

These words appealed to the officer in me ; and I not only gave a full account of how my mission had originated in Berlin, but also made it clear that it had a purely military character which lay in the general direction of sabotage. I told him that, as an officer, I cared nothing

for America's so-called neutrality, that the whole of
Germany thought as I did, and considered America
as "the unseen enemy." I had come, I told him, to
do what I could to save the German *Landwehrieute*—
our territorials—from American shells. Though I proposed to act with energy, I promised I would do so
cautiously.

The *Kaiserpass* though couched in the grand old
German of Frederick the Great's time made no bones
about the assistance to be afforded its holder.

> " Alle meine Behörden und Beamten
> " sind nunmehro gehalten . . ."

Even an Ambassador !

I moved into a modest but good hotel, the Great
Northern, in Fifty-seventh Street, and began to make
inquiries with a view to discovering whether it was really
possible to buy sufficient explosives seriously to damage
the manufacture of munitions for the Allies. I went to
several firms and told them that I was a German agent
anxious to purchase powder, but within a few days I was
satisfied that it would be quite impossible to buy up the
vast quantities of explosives that were by now available
in the American market. The daily production was so
great that if I had bought up the market on Tuesday
there would still have been an enormous fresh supply on
Wednesday. So during the first few days of my stay in
New York I went about and acquired wisdom. On one
of my visits to the firms which dealt in explosives I made
an odd discovery. One of the partners, a German-

American, drew me into a long conversation about the prospects of the War. I was optimistic and believed that the War might end well for Germany, but the merchant was of a different opinion.

" Yes," he said, " things are getting worse and worse, and if Italy comes in against Germany . . ."

" What's that ? " I exclaimed. " What did you say ? "

I remembered my last conversation with Erzberger, who showed me, shortly before I left for New York, a telegram from Bülow in Rome, in which the Ambassador said that he was convinced Italy would remain neutral.

When the merchant saw that I was incredulous, he opened his desk and took out a bill.

I made some joking remark, for I did not know what he meant by this, and said :

" No, no, I am not allowed to endorse bills. I was told that even as a sub-lieutenant."

The American laughed :

" I took this bill in payment. I do not accept bills endorsed by lieutenants—particularly when the amount is a hundred thousand dollars."

I looked at the bill. It bore the signature of the Royal Italian Treasury, had been made out about a month ago, and was payable on May 25th, 1915.

" A large number of these bills," the American said, " has suddenly appeared in the American market. They are exclusively in the hands of firms which manufacture explosives and army equipment, and they have caused a wild boom in the market for these materials. We think that these purchases, which have been made through French agents, but are certainly for the account of the Italian Government, can only mean that Italy intends to enter the War against Germany. This will reduce the prospects of a victory for the Central Powers and lengthen the War."

When I was outside again I thought over the significance of what I had heard and agreed with the merchant. On the next day I managed to photograph one of these bills which was in the possession of a friendly German-American. I cabled my information to Berlin and followed it up with the photograph. Berlin was at any rate now warned.

I became obsessed with one idea. If Italy came into the War, and American shells were to be hurled against the German trenches from Italian guns as well, it was high time that something was *really* done, and I could no longer content myself with running about and discovering that there was too much explosive material in America for us ever to buy up.

I began to lead a dual existence. In the evening I went about as "myself" in dress suit and white tie; I had decided that it was much more dangerous to go about New York under a false name. For, if one of the numerous English agents should find out anyhow who I actually was, he would know instantly that I had something nefarious up my sleeve. If, however, I did not conceal my identity, it would be assumed that I was in America on some peaceful economic mission. Otherwise, it would be argued, I should have kept behind the scenes. I appeared openly in the evening, and on one occasion I had the great pleasure of speaking at a lecture organised by a distinguished scientific club in New York, the Century Club. I listened to a lecture given by a very anti-German professor; and when he lamented that the Germans had burned down the cathedral at Louvain, I jumped up and told him that it was false, for I had seen the cathedral in all its beauty only one month before.

During the day I dressed unobtrusively and went first of all through the whole of the dock district, where I saw numerous English, French, and Russian transports waiting to take munitions on board. I watched them being loaded, and saw them steam out of the harbour and make for the East, their holds full of shells. I wished them at the bottom of the sea.

By way of comparison I could not help remembering what President Thomas Jefferson wrote to Pinckney, the American Minister to Great Britain, during the great European struggle of 1793 :

> " It is an essential character of neutrality to furnish no aid (not stipulated by treaties) to one party which we are not equally ready to furnish to the other. If we permit corn to be sent to Great Britain and her friends, we are equally bound to permit it to France. To restrain it would be a partiality which might lead to a war with France.
>
> " Were we to withhold from her (France) supplies of provisions, we should in like manner be bound

to withhold them from her enemies also, and thus shut ourselves off from the ports of Europe, where corn is in demand, or make ourselves party to the war."

And how did Woodrow Wilson act during the great European struggle of 1914 to 1917—until he did make his country a party to the War?

My own grim and sturdy resolution was only strengthened by the sight of those ships. But without wishing to be vainglorious, I felt " I want what I want when I want it."

Systematically I studied the conditions in the New York docks, and I soon became aware that a large number of German sailors, mates, and captains were hanging about the harbour with nothing to do. The merchantmen in which they would otherwise be serving lay in dock and were unable to leave, since they would be captured by the British on the high seas.

It occurred to me that a large proportion of the dockers consisted of Irishmen, who were far from friendly to England or those allied to her. Those men openly gave vent to their anger whenever they saw a transport leaving with munitions and did not care who heard them.

Who on earth could bring me in touch with these Irishmen? I went to see the German Consul-General, Falcke, a splendid man with vast knowledge and experience, who was firmly convinced—contrary to what the Embassy imagined—that America would soon join the Allied cause anyhow; so whatever I should suggest he would be only too willing to help. Unfortunately, his health was not of the very best then, and a few months later he had to return to Germany.

Then there was Dr. Albert. He had been sent from Berlin to make purchases of foodstuffs and raw materials, to be shipped, as far as possible, on board neutral vessels, to Scandinavia or Holland, and thence to Germany. Dr. Albert, Geheimrat as he was, did not care to go very much " out of his way " from the premises of the Hamburg-American Line, where he had an office.

Consul-General Falcke, however, had told me, prior to his departure from New York, that his Second-in-Command at the Consulate—Hossenfelder—was entirely at my disposal, and that this official had indeed already formed a connection with the Irish propaganda in America. Hossenfelder, too, was elated over my plans, which of course at that time had by no means matured, so that I could speak of them but in a rather vague fashion.

A few days later a nicely dressed, elderly gentleman presented himself at my office, giving the password which I had arranged with Hossenfelder, and introduced himself under the name of Mr. Freeman. I did not care twopence whether this was his actual name or not, as long as he proved to be of valuable assistance, which he did. Indeed, he overdid it ! In the course of time and events I had to discharge and otherwise " drop " some of his men, either for over-zealousness in duty or too great fondness for strong beverage.

Of course, the one man who should have been the first for me to apply to, and who had in the meantime received cable instructions from the War Ministry in Berlin that he should lay his plans before me, was the Military Attaché, Captain Papen. But no matter where or when I went, I heard so many almost incredible stories about how he was going about things, that I must say I was a bit frightened.

Already in Berlin I had been told that he might not be " quite up to the task " now incumbent upon him. Indeed, it was all too clear that too much was being expected of this young cavalry officer who had been sent to Washington to take a post of minor importance, at least from the viewpoint of the large standing armies of Europe. For whoever was sent to America as Military Attaché had to possess good horses, good address, and similar social amenities. And when Papen was appointed, I think in 1913, there was no thought that any bigger task might devolve on him.

I was told that originally he belonged to a provincial cavalry regiment, and having married a Miss Boche, the daughter of an Alsatian pottery manufacturer, his new wealth permitted him to be transferred to a Potsdam regiment of Uhlans, and thence to Washington.

Now he had to be a merchant, an engineer, a mechanician, a diplomat, a financier, an artilleryman, and an expert in rifles and explosives in one ! What else could the poor fellow be but an all-round dilettante ? His training in diplomacy led him to believe that the office which he most openly conducted on the premises of a well-known German-American banking firm was extra-territorial, so " extra-territorial " that this famous office was one morning raided by the American Secret Service. And Secretary of State Robert Lansing made the offer to Ambassador Bernstorff, who of course had vehemently protested against the " raid," that he would gladly return any document seized, if Papen or his men were willing to come and " recognise " their property. Yet Papen resented any suggestion which was bound to jeopardise his own position as much as that of others who came in contact with him, or saw him at his office.

The splendid helpmates which I was to find afterwards among the German captains and mates flatly refused to be under Papen's command. They all pointed to the case of that most unfortunate fellow, Werner Horn. This fellow, a fine and most patriotic man, whom I myself met much later under the most tragic circumstances, had been given a badge—black, white, and red—by Papen, to wear on his sleeve, and was told that he was now a soldier! Evidently an " Enlistment Act " of Papen's own! The poor fellow believed in Papen's creed to such an extent that he proceeded to try to blow up a bridge connecting Canada and the United States. The result had been that his bomb did not go off, that he was arrested by the American C.I.D., sentenced to several years " hard," then interned as an alien enemy, and afterwards handed to the Canadian authorities, who in turn gave him a further term of imprisonment. A completely broken man, whose mind had given way, he returned to Germany, I think, in 1924. At the time of my arrival in New York the Werner Horn affair was common gossip among the German reservists, both of the Army and Navy. Small wonder therefore that the ship captains and mates, who had after all, through their service, acquired some knowledge of things international, were definitely afraid of serving under Papen. Even my able assistant, Captain Steinberg, declined to have dealings with him and his crowd—with the " Kindergarten," as some called it—others the " lunatic asylum " !

Neither could the two Attachés agree among themselves. So confident of himself was Papen that he sent a telegram one day to Captain Boy-Ed, the Naval Attaché, warning *him* to be more careful ! Whereupon the latter, smiling cheerfully to himself, wrote back that " they in Washington " had no evidence against him, but had a whole heap of incriminating evidence against the Military Attaché Papen.

Boy-Ed showed me this bit of correspondence, and I was warned ; I decided to leave Herr von Papen the " glory," and gladly gave way in petty details.

So all this then did not appear to be a start under good auspices, as far as assistance might be forthcoming from the German officials or officers on the spot. Very well then ! As I said before : " Orders were Orders," and I set out to " pick my own way."

I soon found out that there was one man in New York who was trusted not only by the German seamen, but also by the Irish. This was Dr. Bünz ; he had formerly been German Consul in New York and now represented the Hamburg-America Line. I called on him, for we had known each other for years, and he had already begun to work for the German cause. He had instructions to charter ships, which were loaded with coal and reconnoitred the high seas in order to transfer this coal to German cruisers at certain given places. To render this possible, Bünz was in permanent telegraphic communication, in code of course, with the German authorities at home. When I saw him he told me that it would be useful if I could furnish him with detonators.

" Detonators ? What do you want detonators for ? "

" Well, you see," said Dr. Bünz, " my people want a change. I must tell you what my methods are. I charter a tramp steamer, the captain receives a couple of thousand dollars, and disappears. In his place I engage one of the numerous officers of the German mercantile marine who are compelled to hang about idle, and, as you know, these men generally belong to the Naval Reserve—that is to say, they are now on active service ; and they want to get into action. My men have asked me to provide them with detonators. When they are sailing about on the open sea, waiting for the cruisers in order to hand over their coal, they find that time hangs heavily on their hands, so they have thought out a neat plan. If they have detonators and meet another tramp taking shells to Europe, they will hoist the war-flag, send over an armed party, bring back the crew as prisoners, and blow up the ship with its cargo. So, my dear Captain, please get me some detonators."

I had no objection to Dr. Bünz's men sinking munition

93

transports ; but where in New York could I procure detonators without drawing unwelcome attention to myself? The Consul had, however, done me a very important service. He gave me the address of a capable man, an export merchant whose business had suffered through the War. This was Mr. Max Weiser, and I soon found that he knew his way about New York Harbour. I put him to a severe test and saw that he was not only a man who had had a finger in many pies, but was also thoroughly reliable. Though it was possible to stage my plans from my hotel room, we hit on the idea of setting up first of all as honest merchants. We founded a firm which we called " E. V. Gibbons Inc.," the initials being the same as those of my Swiss pseudonym. We rented an office of two rooms in Cedar Street, in the heart of the financial quarter of New York, and entered the name of the company in the Commercial Register as an import and export firm. I sat in one of our two rooms as a director of the concern, and in the other sat my " staff." While I was still wondering how to get hold of the detonators, and in fact how to further my plans at all, I happened to find the right man. I had by now established contact with all sorts of " shady " characters, some of whom had secret schemes, and one day I was visited by the German chemist, Dr. Scheele. I received him in my newly furnished office, in the first room of which sat Max Weiser dictating to the stenographer the most fearsome business letters. He was inviting all the firms of New York to send us offers of wheat, peas, shoe-polish, glassware, rice, and similar goods. We posted piles of letters, so that our firm might present the appearance of a flourishing concern.

Through this room came Dr. Scheele. He began by presenting a strong letter of recommendation from our Military Attaché, Captain Papen, and continued by saying that I was a man with varied interests, and that he was a chemist, with a new invention which he would like to offer me. I saw that he was rather hesitant, so I moved my chair nearer and told him that he had come to the right place and had only to reveal to me the purpose of his invention; if it were any good, he could be sure that I would acquire it; for the rest, I was the most discreet man in New York, and he could trust me. He plucked up courage, took a piece of lead out of his pocket, which was as big as a cigar, laid it on my desk and began to explain.

This piece of lead was hollow inside. Into the middle of the tube a circular disc of copper had been pressed and soldered, dividing it into two chambers. One of these chambers was filled with picric acid, the other with sulphuric acid or some other inflammable liquid. A strong plug made of wax with a simple lead cap made both ends airtight. The copper disc could be as thick or as thin as we pleased. If it were thick, the two acids on either side took a long time to eat their way through. If it were thin, the mingling of the two acids would occur within a few days. By regulating the thickness of the disc it was possible to determine the time when the acids should come together. This formed a safe and efficient time fuse. When the two acids mingled at the appointed time, a silent but intense flame, from twenty to thirty centimetres long, shot out from both ends of the tube, and while it was still burning the lead casing melted away without a trace : *spurlos !*

I looked at Dr. Scheele. I had hit upon a plan in which this " cigar " should play the chief part, and I asked the chemist to demonstrate his invention by an experiment. We went out into a little wood near the town. He chose a very thin copper disc, put it in the tube and laid the apparatus on the ground. We stood near by. If the detonator worked, I could put my scheme into operation. I knew what use could be made of this " diabolical " invention ; and all that was necessary was that it should function. Heaven knows it did ! The stream of flame which suddenly shot out of the confounded " cigar " nearly blinded me, it was so strong ; and the lead melted into an almost invisible fragment.

When I looked round I saw Dr. Scheele leaning against a tree. He was gazing with bemused eyes at the tiny piece of lead, all that was left of his fiery magic.

" That was pretty good, wasn't it ? " he said.

" I'll say it was ! "

We soon came to terms. He was first given a round cheque in return for allowing me to use the " cigar " in any way I wished. I asked him to return on the following day, and in the meantime I secured a few assistants—captains of German ships with whom I had already become good friends, and Irishmen whose " approval " I had won. The Irishmen had no idea who I was, nor

did they ask me. It was sufficient for them that I was
not very friendly towards England. I collected these
men together, and took them to my office. I was sure
that I could trust them, and they did not disappoint me.
I came straight to the point and explained to them that
I had found a means of stopping the hated shipments of
munitions, and one which would not infringe American
neutrality as far as I was concerned. The construction
of the " cigars " was explained to them, and I inquired
if it were possible to smuggle them unobserved on to
the transports which were carrying explosives to Europe.
They were unanimously of the opinion that this could
be very easily arranged, and had no scruples since the
incendiary bombs would not go off till the vessels were
outside American territorial waters. They were full of
enthusiasm for my plan, and wanted to take a few bombs
with them at once. They were very disappointed when
they heard that the things had to be manufactured first
of all on a large scale. We put on our hats and went to
the docks. We discussed the possibility of finding a
workshop in which we could manufacture our bombs
without being discovered. This presented great difficulties, and as we walked along we could think of no
way to overcome them.

We were faced with a difficulty. Where could the fire
bombs be manufactured ?

A great many things had to be taken into consideration.
In the first place, I insisted that under no circumstances
must anything be done on American territory proper.
Such things as docks and decks, tugs and trawlers, piers

and ports . . . all these, with my notions of what I
could put forward, in case of need, in an American court,
I could work on. But not American territory! I was
informed that a man named Boniface would be able to
overcome, by hook or by crook, such minor legal
obstacles as the definition of where American territory
ended and where the high seas began. Of course, there
was always the problem of "territorial waters." But
that was a small matter. It was my duty and my exclusive
task to see that these transports of munitions were
stopped, or at least impeded. It was not my job to get
around legal points which might be presented by the
American Secret Service, or to brood over such things
as Courts and District Attorneys. That could be done
by others. I remembered an instruction emanating from
the British Admiralty, and intercepted for once not by
the Naval Intelligence in London, but by one of our own
clever agents down in South America. A somewhat
timid British Cruiser Commander had, in December
1914, wirelessed a diffident and hesitating question to his
Admiralty from the port of San Juan Fernandez, where
he had found the German cruiser *Dresden*. He received
the required sop to his conscience, which was still trained
to peacetime considerations and conditions—and rightly
so. For if this had happened a few years earlier, he
would certainly have received a stern rebuke for not
knowing the first thing about international etiquette.
Etiquette! Etiquette! what did that matter now! There
were no longer such things as etiquette or Hague Con-
ventions. The people in London knew what they

wanted. To the Admiralty the news might have meant the concentration of a dozen warships off the West Coast of South America : for what mischief might a cruiser such as the *Dresden* have caused, with her energetic and enterprising commander and her enthusiastic crew ! A German cruiser was lying in wait on one of the main routes of British high seas trade, just off the coast of Chile, where all the saltpetre came from. After very little hesitation the Admiralty in London wirelessed back :

"You sink the *Dresden,* and we shall attend to the diplomatic side."

This splendid message, showing how to deal with neutrals, was constantly before my eyes. Had I not, about a year before the Great War, chosen the title : " Who is not for me is against me " for one of my examination compositions in order to enter the Naval War Staff ? Had I not been praised for the energetic way in which I had treated the subject ? And now the British Admiralty had set me an example of how to act in face of " petty considerations " such as the question of neutrality, or other matters ! What applied to South America might well apply to North America !

Mr. Boniface came strolling into my room—Mr. Boniface, who was always and at any time prepared to hear the most startling and daring suggestions. Serious and thoughtful elderly gentleman as he was, full of dignity and stateliness whenever legal points were presented to him, he became almost doubly bewigged in his importance. He shook his head, and once more shook his head.

"Well, Captain. . . . Let me think. . . . 231 . . . Article VIII of the Hague Convention speaks entirely against your line of thought. Grave doubts are in my mind as to whether your attitude could be absolutely approved of. I must state most emphatically, upon mature reflection, that such things as violating American neutrality should not enter your mind."

Thus spoke Mr. Boniface.

He noticed the perplexity in my face, and the consideration that something more " substantial " than the advice of learned counsel might yield him the harvest of a few attractive bills containing several noughts, deprived him suddenly of his dignity. He ran out of the room and disappeared.

Less than half an hour later he turned up again, disseminating as usual a slight odour of whisky. As always when he was in high spirits, his pince-nez were slightly off the straight.

"Why not manufacture your bombs on one of those interned ships?" he suggested. "I have brought you the right man to attend to it—Captain von Kleist, an old friend of yours."

Kleist was on the best of terms with a great many of the captains and officers of the interned vessels, and he developed without more ado a magnificent plan, a plan pregnant with unlimited possibilities.

We were to transplant ourselves, with all our schemes, devices, and enterprises, on board one of the German ships and thus place ourselves in a most admirable situation. Germany within American territorial waters! What possibilities!

Possibilities they were; but there were also facts to be attended to, the first of them being the provision of some American treasury notes for Mr. Boniface.

I had seen Herr Heineken, the Chairman of the North German Lloyd, a few days before I left Berlin. Throughout the winter of 1914–15 Heineken had proved a staunch friend and ally, a man who saw a little further than the general run of shipping people. He had been one of the first to express the fear that the War might last longer than was anticipated. There was naturally some hesitation as to what should be done with all the shipping tied up in neutral ports. Of the two schools of thought, one claimed that everything should be prepared so that immediately on the conclusion of peace, each and every merchant vessel could take her full load of cargo and speed towards the ports of Germany. The other school, a little more fearful as to the possible duration of the War, and consequently as to the state of these vessels on the cessation of hostilities, felt all the time that they should break out of their ports of internment, or at least should be made use of somehow or other.

And Heineken belonged to the latter school.

He was enthusiastic when I divulged to him the secret that, after so much shilly-shallying in official quarters, General von Wandel had put to me the definite question whether I was going to give G.H.Q. a " No " to their urgent request that someone should proceed to

THE DARK INVADER

America, and that I had as definitely replied : " I shall proceed."

" Take all our ships, take all our men, make use of everything you find in America, and go after those iniquitous munitions. What else are the ships for ! The Fatherland requires us to do our duty, and the British will have to pay the price anyhow." He almost embraced me in his rapture.

This all coincided wonderfully, and fitted in splendidly with Mr. Boniface's advice.

I can still see Herr Heineken standing before me, deeply moved by my resolve to tackle the job, which really meant making war against America on American territory. He, too, saw the dangers. He, too, fully recognised that diplomatic troubles, if nothing worse, might come to a head over such an enterprise. But it was then and there that I coined for the first time the phrase which so often in later times was to soften my own conscience, and that of my splendid assistants, the German captains, officers, engineers, stokers, and sailors over in America. And it was not merely an empty phrase. It was something full of meaning, something that must appeal to any German, no matter what position he held. Whenever things became dangerous, as they so often did, with the British Intelligence Service and the American Secret Service both on our heels, it had at all times a heartening effect upon each of us. " Never forget that the lives of so many of our splendid *Landwehrleute* will be spared if we hold on to our job over here ! " Our *Landwehrleute*—" Territorials " as they are called in

SABOTAGE

England—the fathers of families and defenders of their country's soil. The lives of our own Territorials, of our *Landwehrleute*, were at stake, and the thought of this in the ports of the United States served to strengthen the will to our task.

Here I now was, and here was Karl von Kleist. This was the first time I had met him since the outbreak of War, but I had heard a good deal about the energy and skill he had already shown. They were combined in him with the modesty of a man who, coming from one of the oldest aristocratic families of Germany, had yet decided to make his own way in life. He had started his career as a boy on board an old windjammer, gradually obtaining his mate's certificate, and finally that of captain. It would have been easy for him to join one of the crack regiments of the Cavalry Guards at Potsdam, but that would never have satisfied his ambition to prove to his family at home in Germany, that in those days one could make a career for oneself even outside the Army. He was now nearly seventy.

The matter was too delicate to be handled in the presence of Mr. Boniface; so we got rid of him, and over a drink we discussed what could be done and who might be the right men to do it in the right place.

Kleist knew all the interned German sailors. He could size them all up, and with a wave of the hand he gave me an estimate of the character of each man, from the General Manager to the youngest boy.

A few of them were weaklings. Some of them were

born underlings. But some—and it was a joy to hear it !
—the vast majority were men of steel. Men who did not
care for anything and would dare everything.

" Well, Kleist, this is going to be something out of
the ordinary. We must find a ship where the captain
will play the game, where the crew will abide by orders
given, and where, above all, the whole crowd will keep
their mouths shut."

Kleist reflected.

" Well," he explained, " you are asking a good deal.
Qualities like those are a rare combination to find on
board one vessel. Did you ever think of Captain Hinsch
of the Lloyd steamer *Neckar* ? He is made of good
stuff ; he has given ample proof of what a man can do if
once he is bent upon out-doing the enemy. He has been
out in the Atlantic for months, and the British have never
succeeded in getting hold of him. It was only after he
had some breakdown or other in the engine-room, that
he had to bring his ship into port at Baltimore. It has
almost broken his heart to have to give up the game.
That is the man you should get hold of, and also
Paul Hilken, the Baltimore representative of the North
German Lloyd."

" Baltimore ? Baltimore ? That would be all right.
But I am afraid it is too far away, and we must have men
on the spot ! What do you think ? Hinsch is too far
away, I am afraid. If we could get him here—— Or
what do you think of having him slip along the coast ?
It is not such a great distance from Baltimore to here.
Supposing we ask him to weigh anchor—— Oh, no,

that can't be done; he has engine trouble, and we can't get his ship repaired now. It would start too many rumours along the sea front down at Baltimore. No, that's impossible. But let's get Captain Hinsch here anyhow. He must be a good man, from what I hear from different sources. But, then, we must get a proper vessel right here in New York. I have had talks with Commodore Ruser, the Commander of the *Vaterland*, but I think she is too much of a floating hotel for our purposes. It would be better to hit upon one of the smaller vessels."

" Well, I know of one fine ship, where I am acquainted with the officers and engineers, and I am sure they will keep their mouths shut. They are just a wee bit more enterprising than a good many others, and it is an enterprising spirit that you are after, is it not ? "

" Of course ! Unless there are some daredevils on board, I have no use for the ship. You will soon see that the daredevil spirit is the only one that can enable us win the War. Look at the *Emden* ! Didn't she win almost as much admiration from the enemy as she did at home ? I must have men with ' pep.' That's the main thing ! "

Kleist banged his fist on the table. "I think I've got it ! It is the steamship *Friedrich der Grosse* you want ! "

" *Friedrich der Grosse* ! Splendid ! Splendid ! Do you know that the *Friedrich der Grosse* is the flagship of our High Seas Fleet in home waters ? "

" Of course I do—but what does that matter ? "

" It's the flagship"—my enthusiasm ran away with me—
"*Friedrich der Grosse*—what a wonderful combination !
Friedrich der Grosse! Der Grosse König! Our great
King!"

From her magnificent namesake I had seen only a few
months ago some excellent gunnery practice. It was on
board her that I had delivered to the Chief of Staff, as
recently as January, the message, so enthusiastically
received on all sides, that unrestricted submarine warfare
was to begin on February 1st, 1915. The rousing cheers
were still ringing in my ears. And now, here, thousands
of miles away, in the midst of all this semi-neutrality and
semi-hostility, I had found the same name, with the same
inspiration !

I was so elated at this development that I ran to the
trunk which I kept in my office, and where the flags, and
especially the war naval ensigns, of almost every belli-
gerent nation were carefully hidden in a double bottom.
They had been lying here for a good many months, ever
since we had prepared the plans for the outfitting of the
" Russian " merchant vessel that was to carry machine-
guns from Copenhagen. I unfolded the Imperial Naval
Flag and showed it to Captain Kleist. He slapped me on
the shoulder, and said with a smile :

" From what I know of you now, I think you would
be capable of hoisting our naval ensign right in the
middle of the port of New York, on the mizzen-mast of
the *Friedrich der Grosse.* That would be a sight ! "

" Of course, Kleist, you know that this is all my eye.
It can't be done. One has to hold oneself in and suppress

one's inward feelings. . . . I must remain what I am—
The Dark Invader! "

So the naval ensigns were carefully folded up again
and stowed away in the double-bottomed trunk.

During the following nights the great dark ship was
the scene of ghostly activity. I had purchased large
quantities of lead tubing through my firm, and my assistants carried it at night to the steamer, where it was cut
up into suitable lengths. I had likewise obtained the
necessary machinery through the firm, and after the lead
had been cut up, and the copper discs prepared in various
thicknesses, the little tubes were taken away again, under
cover, in darkness, to Dr. Scheele's laboratory, where
they were filled with acid. We had got to this stage
when one morning one of my sailors appeared in the
office, carrying a case of medium size under his arm.
I was sitting at my desk, and he said to me : " Excuse
me, Captain, just move your legs a bit ! " I removed
my legs, and he stowed the case in one of the drawers of
my desk. It was a disturbing neighbour to have !

The detonators were all fixed to go off in fifteen days,
so they had to be disposed of as soon as possible. I took
the man into the other room where Weiser was sitting
and asked him to summon the captains, the sailors, and
the Irish, whom I had meanwhile initiated into my
scheme, for the same evening, so that we might start our
dangerous work immediately.

" All right," said Weiser, " I'll round them all up."

·   ·   ·   ·   ·

THE DARK INVADER

For good or for ill, our decision had been taken. With increasing belief in my loyalty to them, and in my intention that something should be done, the captains and engineers, my helpmates and go-betweens, rallied round me. They were all agreed that the new " system " must be given a fair and thorough trial. All they needed was a guiding hand, and I was determined that it should be mine.

The saddest part of the whole story is that some of these fine officers, men of unswerving devotion, of unbounded patriotic zeal, who had volunteered for all and any service for their country, fathers of families as they were, never asking anything for themselves, had no sooner returned to Germany at the conclusion of the Great War than they were discharged. That was to be their reward! I felt humiliated and depressed when, years later, I received their almost imploring letters, and was reminded that in 1915 I had given them a guarantee, not only on behalf of their Companies, but also on behalf of the Imperial German Army and Navy, nay, of the Government that had asked me to undertake the task, that whatever they did was being done for their country, that nothing should be further from their minds than the thought, or even fear, that their actions might be disapproved! On the contrary, I had assured them over and over again that they were men deserving well of their country and their countrymen. After long internment periods, even terms of imprisonment, some of the finest and bravest of my helpmates, like Captain Wolpert and others, were dismissed and thrown on

108

their own resources by some " stay-at-home " Directors
of the German shipping companies—presumably as a
" fine " gesture to the United States, where, however,
personal courage and patriotism find more appreciation
and encouragement than that!—a disgraceful thing
altogether!

.   .   .   .   .

My occasional sojourns on board the *Friedrich der
Grosse* meant hours of rest and peace of mind. The
ship was an oasis in the desert of my hallucinations—
hallucinations that every knock at the door, during the
day or during the night, was an invasion of the Bomb
Squad of the New York Police, which had been formed
to capture the men who were directing their activities
against the Allied shipping. Two years afterwards I
learned that I had succeeded, thanks to Boniface and
Weiser and Uhde, and all the others who had volunteered for this particularly dangerous type of warfare,
in putting the Secret Service entirely on the wrong
track.

One night, as I was leaning over the rail of the
Friedrich der Grosse, gazing at the peaceful scene bathed
in brilliant moonlight, all of a sudden the thought
struck me : Why not go to the root of things ? Why
not go after the piers themselves, the piers at which the
munition carriers were tied up ? Gradually, this thought
became a desire, the desire a resolution, and the resolution an instruction !

THE DARK INVADER

And the instruction went out to my helpers.

A " War Council " was duly called for the following morning, at the Headquarters of the North-Western Railway Company of the State of Mexico—" the only peaceful place in the world," as Hon. James W. Gerard had so nonchalantly expressed it!

Mr. Boniface, as usual, shook his head, suggestive of long premeditation :

" Captain, I cannot possibly lend my hand to such enterprises."

Solemnly and gravely he took up the Penal Code of the United States of America, and adjusting his none too well polished pince-nez on his Roman nose :

" Paragraph No. 2345 of the Penal Code says——"

" Oh, shut up ! " one of the captains shouted. " What's the use of talking about the Penal Code of America? Are not the United States themselves violating their own Penal Code right and left, recklessly endangering their own free citizens, by permitting shells and shrapnel to be carried over the railway lines through their country right up to the Hudson piers ? "

But Boniface, unmoved by vulgar interruptions from minds not brought up in the lofty profession of the Law, turned again to Paragraph 2345 of the Penal Code of the United States.

" Now, Captain, I shall be glad if you will carefully listen to what I have to read to you. Paragraph 2345——"

" Oh, yes, we all know very well what Paragraph 2345

deals with, but never mind that! " came from all sides.
" To hell with the Penal Code! "

" Here are three hundred dollars as a fee for your
legal advice, and you know what I mean by legal
advice," I said to Boniface. " Legal advice to me in
our present situation means nothing! Help me to get
around the law—that is all you have to attend to! "

" Well, in those circumstances——" said Mr. Boniface, after having carefully inspected the notes, and as
carefully put them away in one of the many pockets of
his slightly shabby coat. He turned over half a score
of pages:

" Paragraph 678 of the Penal Code mentions mitigating
circumstances——" He then picked up another important volume, which had been well studied, as could
be seen from the many finger-marks upon it, " the
Commentary relating to the Penal Code of the United
States lays down in detail in just what circumstances the
guilt must be considered as proven——"

" Yes, that's just what I want you to find out. That's
the point, that's the paragraph I want you to read.
Tell me where the mitigating circumstances come in,
and where the 'proof of guilt' matter is explained.
Read that aloud, and very carefully, Mr. Boniface!
It's important to all of us! "

After careful deliberation, and after repeated and
thorough polishing of his pince-nez, Mr. Boniface came
to the final conclusion that his objections on legal grounds
might as well be ruled out.

Boniface, with all his sinister forebodings about

what might happen, had even gone as far as to warn me that the Piracy Act of 1825 might apply to me and to my doings, and in that case I stood to get "ten years"!

We had a really splendid legal adviser, and his advice was well worth 300 dollars!

.   .   .   .   .   .

I had first come in contact with Mr. Boniface through an almost farcical misadventure which befell us. One evening, when coming out of my room, I met Weiser, and we greeted each other as usual. But he bade me good evening in a tone of such gloom that it was clear something unpleasant must have happened. He followed me back into my room, and when I had closed the door he wrung his hands and said:

"Captain, we've bought some trucks full of whisky! What on earth are we to do with them?"

It appeared that Weiser, in an excess of zeal, had been negotiating so long for half a train-full of whisky that he suddenly found that he had bought it without having intended to do so. We would now have to take delivery and pay for it.

I did not quite know what to do, for I neither understood the whisky business nor was acquainted with anybody who could take the whisky off my hands. The worst of it was that Weiser, in spite of his comprehensive correspondence, could not find a purchaser for it either, and we appeared to be in the soup. Weiser thought that perhaps Mr. Boniface might be able to help us. I inquired about Mr. Boniface and learnt that he was a man of many parts. He dwelt in a small hotel, of no very good reputation, near the docks, and he had an extensive practice sweeping out the corners that the genuine lawyers had left for him. When Weiser told me all this I realised that we had long needed a man who could worm his way along the obscure paths of the American legal system. We needed, so to speak, a shady legal adviser for our " shady " business, so I sent for Mr. Boniface. He was tall and lean, wore pince-nez which kept on slipping down his nose, and gave one on the whole the impression of a mangy hyena seeking its daily prey on the battle-field. I had to rely on my instinct, and I was convinced that Mr. Boniface would rather let all ten fingers be chopped off than betray anyone who offered him the prospect of good fees. Future events proved that I had not deceived myself with regard to Mr. Boniface, for he never gave anything away.

I told him very cautiously about the affair of the whisky, and merely asserted a wish to get out of the deal. He adjusted his pince-nez, rubbed his chilly hands, and said firmly :

" Captain, it will cost you two hundred and fifty dollars. My fee is fifty dollars, and I need the other two hundred to kill the deal."

He received the money, and went and "killed" the deal. In the ensuing period we often had to call upon Mr. Boniface to " kill " a deal into which Weiser had been lured by his excess of zeal. When Weiser was dictating his letters he used to have visions of the happy past, when he possessed an import and export business, and then he would conclude a deal that had to be laboriously "killed."

Mr. Boniface could do other things as well, and his help became indispensable to us. He entered into close touch with the New York police, and many of the things he learned we found very valuable.

．　．　．　．　．

At the appointed time, as dusk was falling, a powerful six-cylinder car stood at the appointed place on the coast of New Jersey. A ferry-boat had brought it over from New York. I jumped in!

Through streets and lanes, across lines of railway track and ugly-looking spots, littered with rags and rubbish from the last loading or unloading of some tramp, occasionally crossing fields, meadows, marshes, and morasses, we finally landed before the gate of a shed, through the bars of whose doors a few inadequate lamps could be made out, indicating just how far the pier stretched out into the Hudson River.

One pier after another was inspected, and wherever a night watchman passed by, or took the liberty of objecting, a few dollar bills gently slipped into his hand by Max Weiser rendered him as silent as the grave.

Measurements were taken ; distances were paced out ; the possibilities were studied as to whether and where motor-launches could be comfortably fastened—and, if need be, quickly disappear and go into hiding.

Two or three evenings were taken up by these minute inspections, and our plans rapidly matured : here we were, at the root of the evil, and the evil had to be destroyed—no matter what happened—" *après nous le déluge !* "—come what might ! The War had to be won, and there was no room for other considerations.

Our trips along the New Jersey piers, made in a guarded and roundabout way, soon proved just where the most vulnerable, i.e. from *my* point of view, the most " valuable " spots might be. My general and especially my military knowledge showed me soon what could be achieved here, where trainload after trainload of munitions was discharged into the holds of the munition carriers.

One of our visits took us to " Black Tom," a rather curious name for a terminal station. It remains clearly in my recollection because of its quaint conformation, jutting out as it did like a monster's neck and head. I suppose that it was for this reason that it had derived the name of " Black Tom." To judge from the numerous railway tracks converging here, it appeared to be one of the chief points for the Allies' export of munitions.

I could not help urging upon myself the advisability of giving Black Tom a sound knock on the head—its mere name sounded so good to me : we could run little risk from paying Black Tom a compliment of this kind. Some peaceful summer evening — all arrangements properly made—a powerful speedboat at hand for us to disappear into the vastness of the Hudson River—it was all so remote from observation, from possible harm that might be done to human life !

About a year later, when I was a prisoner of war in

THE DARK INVADER

Donington Hall, one hot summer morning my eyes fell upon a large headline in *The Times* :

EXPLOSION OF CHIEF PIER

OF ALLIED SHIPPING

" BLACK TOM " BLOWN UP

BY ENEMY AGENTS

I had my own opinion as to how it had come about, and who were the men behind the scenes !

. . . . .

A great many rumours began to make the round about the *Lusitania*. Was she, or wasn't she, a munition-carrier ? One evening one of my most trusted captains was sitting with me sucking at a cigar and telling me a depressing story.

The *Lusitania*, he disclosed to me, had long been suspected of secretly carrying small-arm ammunition. It was thought that these were carried in flour barrels, and it was even rumoured that she had two heavy guns on deck so as to be prepared for anything that might happen at sea. We had heard this rumour at the time, but had soon convinced ourselves that there was no truth in it. It had, however, also reached the German Embassy, and Captain Boy-Ed was instructed to find out whether the boat was really armed. If it could be proved to the satisfaction of the Americans that there were guns on board, the *Lusitania* would be interned as a warship. Captain Boy-Ed hired a man named Stegler to investigate the matter, and after a few days this man reported that he had carried out his task. He had crept about the deck of the ship at night, unobserved, and had seen two guns hidden under a pile of miscellaneous objects. The Naval Attaché took him to a lawyer, to whom he made a sworn statement that he had seen both the guns with his own eyes. The Ambassador hastened with this statement to the Government of the United States and demanded that the *Lusitania* be interned. The Government immediately caused the ship to be examined, but could discover no guns on board, and so Stegler was hauled over the coals. He gave in and confessed that the story he had told Boy-Ed was a pure invention for the purpose of earning a reward of two thousand dollars. He had already received the money, but was sent to prison for a couple of years for perjury.

This story, which was not very cheerful, was told me by Captain Wolpert, and when he had finished I noticed that he had his hand bandaged. It appeared that the day before he had been crossing the Hudson on a ferry with one of our detonators in each of his pockets. He had his hand in his pocket and suddenly felt an excruciating pain, and knew that one of the detonators had begun to burn. He was able to seize it and throw it overboard before the full stream of fire shot out. Luckily no one on the ferry had noticed what was happening, but Wolpert had to rush to a doctor, for the skin was hanging from his hand in strips and he was badly hurt. Splendid fellow, he was, and nothing was so far from my mind at that time as that I should have to take the responsibility in the long run for such men losing their jobs.

THE DARK INVADER

All our plans were gradually laid and the right men were in the right places, when one afternoon early in May—this was in 1915—an upheaval of the first magnitude occurred—the *Lusitania* was sunk. Most unfortunately, and contrary to all expectations that the very construction of such a magnificent vessel would keep her afloat for hours, and thus give ample time for rescue ships to take on all the passengers, some internal explosion occurred, and down she went, taking with her so many human beings. Whether it is true or not that the American Customs Authorities had given her legal clearance papers, although she was not entitled to such legality—all this may possibly remain a secret for ever. Mr. Dudley Field Malone, the Chief of Customs of New York, was ordered to send all documents relating to the *Lusitania* to Washington, to the Department of State. What these documents really would have proved is an entirely different story.

There was reason enough for me to lie low, seeing that this tragic affair was bound to lead to endless complications and might even change the whole atmosphere in New York, especially along the water front, where all kinds of rumours got about. A great many Americans were of opinion that the whole affair was bound to lead to something entirely unexpected, and that the United States might declare an embargo on all shipments of munitions. One thing at least was certain. Mr. Bryan, the then Secretary of State, resigned because his opinion clashed with that of his superior. Bryan was said to be of the opinion that if there were no more shipments of munitions, the German submarine warfare might easily be brought to a standstill altogether, in return for such an embargo.

So why continue this destructive work of mine? Why stir up trouble and unrest, when there seemed to be a possibility ahead that there would be no more munition carriers? I had been sufficiently educated in matters political, especially during the winter of 1914-15, when on the Naval War Staff in Berlin, to realise that the smallest spark might in certain circumstances change the situation from one day to the next and give things a most unwelcome turn. For if there existed even the remotest chance that Mr. Bryan's viewpoint, which was supported by a strong body of public opinion, should prevail, then what I had been hoping for in my heart of hearts would certainly be realised, and the moment was at hand when I could wash my hands—not in innocence, but in carbolic acid, after so much " dirty work " had had to be done. No one would have been more exhilarated than I, after two months of outright sleeplessness, if the whole business had come to a standstill! So the general signal was flashed out from my headquarters all over the Port of New York, " Cease Fire ! " All plans were to be abandoned until further notice. . . . But, alas ! no such thing occurred. No embargo was placed on the export of munitions and we simply *had* to carry on !

· · · · ·

My assistants came in the evenings, and we discussed in my office what we should do next. The Irish had already thought out a plan. They knew their country-men who worked in the docks as stevedores and lighter-men and told me that these people were willing to plant our " cigars " on British munition transports. They had even chosen a ship, the *Phoebus*, which was to sail in a few days, and whose hold was packed with shells. I opened the drawer of my desk which contained the case of detonators, and it was soon emptied. Next morning the dockers who were in the plot carried their barrels, cases, and sacks on board the *Phoebus*, and as soon as they had assured themselves that they were unobserved, they bent down swiftly in a dark corner of the hold and hid one of our detonators among the cargo. When the *Phoebus* left for Archangel, with a cargo of high explosive shells on board, it carried two of these destructive articles in each of three holds.

I walked unobtrusively past the steamer while my men were at work, looked down the opened hatchways, through which the cases of shells were being lowered, and saw the British agents who were standing guard on deck, carbines slung across their arms ready to prevent anything suspicious from approaching their valuable cargoes. That evening my assistants came to the office. They were in good humour, and reported that the *Phoebus* was to sail on the next day, and that they had placed detonators in some other ships too, which were to leave harbour a few days later. We had now used up all our supply, and Dr. Scheele was instructed to prepare some more.

We sat in our office and waited for the first success.

SABOTAGE

We had subscribed to the *Shipping News*, which printed the daily reports of Lloyd's in London concerning everything to do with shipping and shipping insurance. We had calculated the date on which the accident was to take place, but a few days passed and there was still nothing about the *Phoebus* in the paper. Suddenly we saw :

> "*Accidents*. S.S. *Phoebus* from New York—destination Archangel—caught fire at sea. Brought into port of Liverpool by H.M.S. *Ajax*."

This was our first success, and everything had happened just as we had planned. Our dockers had of course only put the detonators in the holds which contained no munitions, for we had no intention of blowing up the ship from neutral territory. If we had wished to do so we could have used different means, but we achieved our purpose without the cost of human life. When the ship caught fire on the open sea the captain naturally had the munition hold flooded to eliminate the most serious danger. None of the ships reached its port of destination, and most of them sank after the crew had been taken off by other vessels. In every case the explosives were flooded and rendered useless.

On my visits to the offices of the brokers who dealt in explosives I had seen a large number of British, French, and Russian agents. At one of the large New York banks, which carried the account of " E. V. Gibbons Inc.," there was a manager with whom I soon became rather friendly, but who only knew that I was one of the partners of our firm and thought I was an Englishman. He had no idea of my real identity. I put in an occasional appearance at the Produce Exchange, in order to keep in touch with what was happening, and sometimes I was addressed by various people as Mr. Gibbons. As a matter of fact, there really was a Mr. Gibbons, whose name had been entered in a perfectly legal manner in the Commercial Register when we founded our firm, but who never appeared in his own office, was never seen, and whom nobody knew. These circumstances gave me an idea, which occurred to me when I was one day asked by my bank why I did not try to procure one of the contracts which the Allies were negotiating with American armament firms. These contracts were not for munitions alone, but also for military equipment of all kinds, from shoe leather to mules. With one of these contracts in one's pocket one could go to any bank and obtain an advance on it. They were the most desirable documents that an American business man could possess. I thought over a plan during a sleepless night and set to work next morning with the full realisation that the consequences might be strange and fateful. I went to see a family that I knew very well—German-Americans whose sympathies were so wholly with Germany that they were ready to do anything to help the Fatherland and injure its opponents. I required the help of the lady of the house, who had spent a long time in Paris and was particularly well acquainted with Colonel Count Ignatieff, the Russian Military Attaché in that capital.

Count Ignatieff played an important rôle in the

European War game. He was clever and energetic, and his post gave him influence and power. It was clear that he could be of great use to me. He was especially fond of the material pleasures of life and was celebrated far and wide as a connoisseur of claret. At my request the lady wrote him a letter conveying the information that an American merchant, Mr. Gibbons, desired to import claret into America, and she requested the Count to help him in the matter with his valuable advice.

A reply came by night-letter to the effect that the Count would be delighted to be of service to Mr. Gibbons. My firm now came into action. Weiser wrote the most convincing letters, was unsparing in telegrams, and we were eventually in possession of a large consignment of claret. Count Ignatieff had sponsored the transaction. We were a sound firm, and we cabled the purchase price to France. Weiser was quite excited when the deal was concluded, for I told him that we should undoubtedly be able to dispose of the wine. I did not see him for two days after this, when he turned up again completely exhausted but happy. The wine was sold before he was back in New York.

We now wrote another letter to the Count, suggesting that it would be advantageous for both parties if the Russian Army would employ our old-established and extremely well-capitalised firm for their purchases in America. We were in a position to supply everything that the Russian Army might need, and we inquired whether it would be possible for us to obtain a large contract for military equipment.

Ignatieff replied at once. He wrote that of course there was nothing to stop us from receiving large army contracts, but that we should first of all get into touch with the Russian agents in New York, who were there for the purpose of negotiating with American firms. He gave us full permission to use his name for reference, and made things easy for us by telling us to whom to go.

On my voyage over in the *Kristianiafjord* I had followed Ulysses' example and refused to stop my ears to the constant and compromising chatter of my fellow-passengers—many of whom were Russian emissaries of importance, hot on the trail of American munitions. I little thought how and where I was to meet with them again.

I set out, and soon found one of them who was living in a New York hotel, and who had come over to arrange for the supply of war material. I was Mr. Gibbons, and acted in a way that persuaded him that I was a hundred per cent American citizen. But the Russian was reserved. He had already given all the contracts that were available, and he invited me to return in six weeks. He then stood up to show me out, but I sat more comfortably in my chair and suggested that what he had just told me would sadden a very good friend of mine. The Russian only listened to me with half an ear and said that he was in a hurry. We were sitting in the lobby of the hotel, and in order to show me that the interview was really at an end he summoned a page to fetch him his hat and coat. I thereupon drew out Count Ignatieff's letter, played with it a moment, and asked him whether he knew his distinguished colleague in Paris, the Military Attaché Count Ignatieff. If so, I should be glad if he would give him my kind regards, when he happened to be passing through Paris, and explain to him why he had not been able to help me. I was sure that the Attaché would be interested. The agent looked at me in astonishment, and when I saw that I had made an impression I handed him Count Ignatieff's letter. He read it and was a changed man. It was clear that Ignatieff was too influential a person in the Russian Army for an ordinary captain of infantry, who had been sent to New York on account of his linguistic knowledge, to fall out with. He immediately begged my pardon, grew rather embarrassed, and we went up to his room. After some desultory talk I made things easy for him, and he confessed that he had, as a matter of fact, not yet placed all his contracts for the immediate future, and he declared his willingness to hand all those that remained to " E. V. Gibbons Inc."

I told him that I should shortly be going to Paris and that I would not fail to inform Count Ignatieff of the great courtesy and good favour that my companion had shown me. We went to a lawyer and put through an amazing deal. I received contracts to supply saddles, tinned meat, bridles, mules, horses, field-kitchens, boots, shoes, underwear, gloves, and small arms ammunition. I signed a dozen contracts, and the Russian called on his Military Attaché, after he had asked me, as a matter of precaution, to let him have Count Ignatieff's letter. The contracts arrived by post on the following day. They were signed by the Imperial Russian Embassy at Washington, and were worth good money. For anyone else they would have meant great profits, but the Russians would learn in good time with whom they had placed their contracts.

I left the papers in a drawer for some time, and then sent for Boniface to discuss with him the possibilities. He knew all the subterfuges for evading the American commercial laws, and declared at once that nothing could happen to us.

I took the contracts obtrusively and ostentatiously to my bank, so much so that all the inquiry bureaux in New York entered in their registers the fact that the firm of " E. V. Gibbons Inc." was carrying out large orders for the Allied armies. This was a distinct help. I obtained advances on my contracts for a magnificent amount, and deposited the money, about three million dollars, in a secret account at another bank.

I now awaited events. The goods were to be delivered in forty-five days, but a fortnight after the signing of the contracts the Russian agents telephoned to ask whether we could possibly deliver sooner. They were prepared to pay a bonus. I was sorry, but it was out of the question. Two Russians came to see me, and I learned that the man with whom I had conducted the original negotiations had gone to Archangel. They told me that it was of the utmost importance to fulfil the contracts at the earliest moment, and showed me telegrams to the effect that things were getting serious for the Russian troops, who were beginning to suffer a shortage of everything. I was promised a large sum for every day I could save.

I thought deeply. If I persisted in my refusal they might do something that would upset my scheme. They might hurriedly buy up everything they needed and send it across. So I compromised.

" What are the most important items ? "

The most important items were tinned provisions and infantry ammunition. I promised to give them an answer the same evening.

I had a hasty conference with Weiser and Boniface. Weiser shot out of the office, rang me up an hour later, and reported that he had succeeded in procuring the necessary tinned stuffs. He had purchased them in three different quarters, and I at once telephoned to the Russians that the provisions could be put on board as soon as they wished. Meanwhile I had myself looked round for ammunition, and eventually obtained as much as I wanted from brokers of all sorts.

The Russians were happy to hear my news. They came at once to my office and told me they had chartered a steamer so that the shipment could begin on the next day. I summoned my captains, and although I did not tell them exactly what I had done, I gave them to understand that we had been able to arrange for Allied supplies to pass through our hands, and that we should be handling the cases of ammunition and tinned foods on the way from the brokers to the ship. They knew what they had to do.

Next day Weiser rented a large store shed at the docks through which we sent the goods. I wanted to make quite sure, for I had a dreadful fear that my plan might miscarry, and I insisted on no less than thirty detonators being placed on the ship. It was quite simple, for we only had to put them in the provision cases. They were laid among wood shavings to ensure their effect.

The boat carried nothing but our supplies. I was given my cheque at the dock, together with a second one to cover the bonus, which was very high, for the days that had been saved.

I waited for four days in a state of fever. The Russians telephoned every day in their anxiety to obtain the horses and mules that I had promised them. I had no intention, however, of buying these. I sat in my office, with nerves on edge, until at last the *Shipping News* announced that the steamer had caught fire on the high seas, flames having broken out simultaneously from every corner of the vessel, that the crew had taken to the boats, and the ship had foundered. The crew had been rescued by an American steamer.

Half an hour later the Russians were wringing their hands in my office. I pretended to be overwhelmed and promised to help them. By the evening I had collected enough tinned provisions and infantry ammunition for two ships, and we carried out the same operation that had been so effective with the first consignment. This time I engaged numerous detectives from a reliable agency, and distributed them about the ships to see that nobody should sneak on board without authority. The cases were loaded without incident. I again snatched up the *Shipping News* every morning, and again the ships took fire on the high seas. I had promised to supply twenty-one shiploads in all, and it never occurred to the Russians that the conflagrations had been engineered by the contractor, since in any case ships carrying other people's goods often came to the same end.

The day arrived when I had to deliver the remainder of the supplies. I had been told by my captains some time before that another ship or two could be loaded with war materials for the Allies, and that it was only necessary to make certain it could be done from the Black Tom Pier. I should continue to arrange for the cases to be stored in barges, after they had been taken from the trains, and our barges would then come alongside the steamer. I knew that it was safe to follow the advice of the experienced old captains. By the appointed day I had again purchased enough materials for one shipload, and I went with the Russians to the dock, showed them the goods trains, handed over their contents, and demanded my cheque. The agents, however, had bought the goods f.o.b. and declined to pay until they were actually in the holds.

I shrugged my shoulders and pointed out that it was illegal to convey explosives through the harbour. For each case it was necessary to conduct long negotiations with the New York police, before a licence was received; but the grant of this licence was always bound up with so much red-tape that in practice hardly a single consignment of munitions which passed through the harbour in barges, was reported beforehand, or carried the regulation black flag to advertise its dangerous cargo. The Russians raged inwardly, but I stuck firmly to my refusal, and after some exchange of words, during which the Russians nearly had apoplexy, I received my cheque and gave orders for the loading to begin. It took place next day under remarkable circumstances. The barges were packed to capacity, and two little tugs came to tow them alongside the two steamers which were to take the cases on board. They did not reach the steamers, however, for one barge after another slowly but steadily heeled over, and finally they all lay peacefully together at the bottom of New York Harbour. The tugs had quickly hove to when the barges began to go down, and took on board the few men who had been on them.

Nobody was particularly excited about the disaster; the owners of the barges were not in a position to make capital out of it, for they had acted in defiance of the police regulations, and only the Russian agents appeared next morning with pale faces in my office. It had still not occurred to them that our firm had some slight connection with their misfortunes, but they anxiously demanded the immediate delivery of the rest of the supplies that they had bought from me. I spoke of *force majeure* and strikes, of transport difficulties, and everything else I could think of. I finally told them straight out that I had no intention of delivering the goods. The Russian officers were struck speechless. I shrugged my shoulders; they grew wild, I remained calm. They began to abuse me, so I took my hat and left them.

SABOTAGE

They sent their lawyers, and Boniface spoke to them. Meanwhile I went to the bank to pay back my advances; and the bonuses I had earned on the three sunken steamers sufficed to pay the interest. I went home with the conviction that I had done a good job. By the time the Russians were ready to take legal proceedings the firm of " E. V. Gibbons Inc." no longer existed.

After this success I extended my organisation. Dr. Scheele worked day and night to manufacture detonators, and results continued to be gratifying. The number of accidents at sea reported in Lloyd's *Shipping List* increased, and the *New York Times* published on its front page an item of news which cheered us. On July 5th the Russian Minister Prince Miliukov had delivered a speech in the Duma regretting that the delay in the transport of munitions from America was becoming more and more serious, and that it would be necessary to take firm steps to discover the cause, and trap the miscreants who were responsible for it.

We were greatly encouraged by this, for it showed us that we were successfully paralysing the transport of munitions to Russia and helping our troops on the battlefields; so we continued to place bomb after bomb. I founded branches in Boston, Philadelphia, Baltimore, and, gradually, in the southern ports of the United States. It was difficult to get our detonators to these towns, for they had to be hidden in the luggage of our confidential agents who travelled regularly round those ports. My most fanatical helpers in this way were the Irish. They swarmed about the various ports with detonators in

131

their pockets and lost no opportunity of having a smack at an English ship. They still did not know who I was, for they had been told that I was connected with Irish Home Rule organisations. I soon, however, had to refrain from employing them, for in their blind hatred of England they had begun to use their bombs in a way we had not intended. They were throwing caution to the winds, and when I turned up at my office one morning Max Weiser came rushing to meet me on the stairs.

"Captain," he whispered in agitation, "something absolutely idiotic has happened. One of our Irishmen has just boasted to me that he has put two of our 'cigars' into the mail room of the *Ancona*."

The *Ancona*! She was a large English mail boat, carrying passengers, and I was thunderstruck at the news. If a fire broke out in the mail room of this steamer, the passengers would be in the greatest danger, and a conflagration on such a well-known boat would attract the attention of the whole world. It might be guessed that there was a connection between this and the "accidents" on the munition transports, and if the New York police got on to our track our work would be rendered vastly more difficult, or even impossible. In any case, it was a senseless thing, for there were passengers on board the *Ancona*, but no shells.

Weiser left me standing on the steps and dashed out. Luckily the Irishman had given him details, and we knew that the "cigars" were in a cardboard box, made up as a postal package. Weiser knew the address that was on it, and after a long talk with the postal official on the *Ancona* and the exchange of some dollar bills of large denomination, he returned, out of breath but happy, with the dangerous parcel in his pocket.

.　　.　　.　　.　　.

I received cipher messages from all ports with the names of the ships in which my men were putting bombs, and I carefully examined the *Shipping News* to see what happened to them. In many cases a fire broke out and the munitions were rendered useless. Sometimes, however, the fire must have been rapidly extinguished, for about half the ships we were interested in came off unscathed, or else the bombs must have failed. I sent for Dr. Scheele to see if it might not be possible to perfect his invention, though I was in any case convinced that I must find other methods too ; but I could not think of any, and when the chemist called we discussed his " cigars " and various other matters. We had exhausted our subjects of conversation, but he still sat tight, and I suddenly had an uneasy feeling that he had come to the office with sinister intentions. I looked past him through the window, where darkness was beginning to fall, when all at once he stood beside me at my desk and snarled :

" If I don't have ten thousand dollars this evening I am going straight to the police."

I continued to gaze through the window. I had long realised that an attempt at blackmail was bound to come, since we had been compelled to initiate a number of shady individuals into our plans, but I was firmly resolved not to yield to any such threats, for if I did so I should be finished. I soon pulled my wits together and came to the conclusion that I could not take the immediate risk of telling the man to go to the devil. He still stood tensely at my side, so I turned to him and said :

" Yes, of course I'll give you the money. Will a cheque be all right ? "

I heard his breath hiss through his teeth with relief as he replied :

" Yes, Captain, a cheque will suit me."

" But the banks are closed."

" They will be open early to-morrow morning."

I gave him the cheque and he was perfectly content. I could see in his eyes that he believed he had achieved his purpose, and he struck me at the moment as being one of the greatest blockheads that I had ever met. He took his leave in a rather subdued manner, put on his gloves, and went out at the door. As he was waiting to enter the lift I called out and asked him whether he would like to drink a glass of beer, with some of the captains and myself, later on in the evening. He stood still in surprise. I observed him furtively and saw a gleam come into his eyes. I knew I had persuaded him that I was too afraid of him to dare to quarrel, in spite of the meanness of what he had done. He apparently thought that I wanted to get on better terms with him than before, and I found out afterwards that my instinct was right. At any rate, he agreed to meet me later on in a restaurant in the Woolworth Building. The door of the lift closed with

SABOTAGE

a bang, and Dr. Scheele departed with a vision of the long-desired little country house, on the heights of New Jersey above the sea, which he would now be able to purchase. At least he thought he would.

When I returned to my office, my assistants had gone, and I threw myself into a chair to work out a plan of action. I was still certain that it would not do to let the man get away with blackmail, for he would only return the next week to ask for twice as much, and in a month his demands would be increased tenfold. Besides, if he continued to receive from me the large sums he would demand, it was still possible for him to go to the police one day for some reason that might seem to him good. The first thing to do was to prevent him cashing the cheque, and thus crowning his first attempt at black-mail with success. I took up the receiver and telephoned to two of the captains. I gave the password " *Notleine*," [1] and they knew that there was trouble in the air. I made a hurried appointment with them and announced that " squalls were blowing up."

Dr. Scheele turned up as arranged, though I was sur-prised that he did so. We sat together drinking beer and talking about a variety of things. He apparently had an itch to show me what a valuable colleague he was, and without referring to his attempt at blackmail, he pointed out a number of things that might be done. I replied very politely, and about half an hour went by before the two captains turned up. Dr. Scheele was not acquainted with them, and neither of the sailors knew

[1] Alarm cord.

135

what I wanted, for of course I had not been able to discuss the matter on the telephone. They sat at a table not far away but did not greet me, so that Scheele had no idea that I knew them. When he left the room for a moment I quickly informed the captains how the land lay, and what I hoped to do with their help. In due course I took leave of Dr. Scheele in the street and went off to my hotel not far away in Manhattan. Scheele, like the captains, lived near Hoboken on the other side of the Hudson.

The chemist crossed on the ferry, followed by the sailors. He strolled to and fro, and when he reached a dark corner near one of the large landing-planks, one of the captains, a man of vast size, suddenly loomed up in front of him and said calmly :

" Give me the cheque you squeezed out of the Captain to-day, or you'll get a sock in the jaw that'll send you whizzing down this plank."

Scheele swiftly looked round, but there was not a soul in sight. He started back when he saw the resolute and angry face of Captain Wolpert staring at him in the darkness, drew the cheque out of his pocket, and handed it over. Wolpert continued to stand there, powerful and threatening, while the chemist clung to a plank with both hands.

" Of course," said Wolpert, " you can go to the police now, but I don't expect they'll pay you the same monthly salary as you're getting from the firm of Gibbons. In any case, we've still got a disgruntled Irishman or two who, if you'll pardon my saying so, would find it a pleasure to tickle your stupid head with a nice, thick, iron bar. Did you really think that men like us haven't our own ways of making sure that you don't show those gold teeth of yours again ? "

The ferry reached its destination, but Scheele did not move. Captain Wolpert turned sharply on his heel and walked off the ferry with an angry step and his hands in his pockets.

I received the cheque back the next morning. We realised that we had played a dangerous game, for though Scheele was apparently intimidated for the time being, we could not know what he would do next. Mr. Boniface had come in answer to my summons, and I asked him to keep an eye on things as far as the police were concerned, and to give us immediate warning if Scheele should denounce us. Boniface, who had just " killed " another deal for us, stuck his hands in his pockets, looked up at the ceiling, and said :

" Captain, there are a lot of wicked people in New York. But I am going to do something that will enable you to put a curb on Dr. Scheele."

He went away, and a few days later I knew what he had done.

Scheele had one weakness. He was fond of women, so fond of them that he was ready to make a fool of himself if they were only young and pretty. Mr. Boniface knew this, and drew up his plans accordingly. In order to understand his scheme, it must be mentioned that there is a law in America which can often be taken advantage of for strange ends. This law exacts high penalties for seduction, which is only just. But when an individual has a grudge against somebody else, the law can be exploited with an ease which renders it a farce, though a dangerous one.

Mr. Boniface had, as I have said, a varied clientele, which included a pretty young girl who was useful in more ways than one, and who was by no means unwilling to do Mr. Boniface a good turn. Mr. Boniface was also on good terms with the police, and was particularly friendly with a certain detective who had been of service to him on a number of occasions.

One day when Dr. Scheele was crossing by the Hudson ferry, this girl was also on board and happened to drop her umbrella. Scheele picked it up, and the acquaintance thus begun soon ripened into friendship. In a day or two he had to go on a journey, and he invited her to accompany him. He possessed a venerable Ford, in which he and the girl drove out of town. When he had left the skyscrapers of New York behind, he stepped on the gas and gave himself up to pleasurable thoughts of what was to come. Suddenly a man was seen standing at the side of the highway. As soon as the girl caught sight of him she began to scream and wave her arms wildly in the air. Dr. Scheele was astonished, slowed down, and asked the girl what was the matter. The man in the road put up his hand and stopped the car. Out jumped the girl, shrieking that her companion had tried to seduce her and she wanted to ring up the police. The man announced that he *was* a police official and that he had stopped the car because of the girl's screams. He also told Scheele that he was under arrest. Scheele was speechless. He argued with the detective, who at last let him go after he had used all his powers of persuasion and had handed over a note for a large sum in order to stop the matter going any further. He continued his journey, pondering on the wickedness of the world.

When he returned and appeared once more in my office, Mr. Boniface was also present and kept up the comedy. He told Scheele that it had come to his ears that a girl had consulted a *very* celebrated New York lawyer about an attempt made by a certain Dr. Scheele to seduce her. He, Boniface, was employed by this lawyer to find Scheele. The girl had also asserted that her would-be seducer had bribed a police official, and, to cut a long story short, it lay in Mr. Boniface's power to send Dr. Scheele to prison. Mr. Boniface, however, came to an agreement with Scheele : " If you don't say anything, I won't say anything either." So Scheele held his tongue and continued to manufacture his detonators.

The clouds, however, were gathering above our heads, and things were beginning to get awkward. The " cigar " business was getting too hot for us. I was rung up in the middle of the night in my hotel bedroom and I recognised the voice of Mr. Boniface at the other end. He did not tell me what was wrong, but gave me a rendezvous where I could meet him on the following morning before I went to the office. I turned up punctually and heard from Boniface that since the previous evening the New York police had been manifesting feverish activity. The docks were swarming with detectives, looking for a band of men who were placing bombs on ships. Boniface was sure of his facts, for he had got them from a confederate at Police Headquarters. We walked past the docks, discussing the possible reasons for these sudden measures, and my eye lit on the front page of the *New York Times*, which I had just bought. We were in for it ! The newspaper announced with large and sensational headlines that when the empty hold of the steamer *Kirk Oswald* was being swept out in Marseilles Harbour, a peculiar little tube had been found, which on closer examination proved to be an extremely dangerous incendiary bomb. This bomb must have been deposited while the boat was moored at New York, and it was at once obvious how the numerous conflagrations at sea during the last few months had been caused. The paper announced at the same time that the whole Secret Service department of the New York Police was at work to seize the miscreants, and that a clue was being pursued which offered good prospects of success.

I remembered that my men really had placed a bomb on the *Kirk Oswald*, but I also knew that the steamer was destined for Archangel. It was clear to me that she had received fresh orders on the way and had taken her cargo to Marseilles instead, and that the bomb had not gone off because we had timed it to explode at a later stage on her long journey to Archangel.

I had an appointment that morning in the lobby of my hotel, and, as I left, I saw that I was being watched. Two men, whom I had seen in the lobby, were following me. I drove to a remote quarter of the town and saw that I was not mistaken, for I was still being shadowed. As

I walked along, the two men kept on my tracks, at a suitable distance, and when I saw a taxi and had ascertained that there was no other car anywhere near I jumped in and drove off. I hastened back to my office by a devious route, " liquidated " E. V. Gibbons Inc., and shut up shop. It was necessary to disappear for a time, and after we had hurriedly arranged how to keep in touch my staff scattered in all directions. I looked out a quiet watering-place not far from New York and awaited events ; but nothing happened. Since no more bombs were being laid, the police had no opportunity of making a discovery. Still, I felt a " need of privacy."

My little retreat was not far from Stamford in the State of Connecticut, and I took up my quarters in a small hotel, where I enjoyed the sea and the sunshine and renewed my energies preparatory to returning in due course to New York. I had registered in the visitors' book as Mr. Brannon, from England, kept to myself and spoke to nobody, but received daily letters from New York, which kept me posted as to what was happening there. I was yearning to return to the scene of operations, but caution compelled me to keep away for some time. My agents wrote me that the man who had drawn the attention of the New York police to the gang which was supposed to be making the docks unsafe, was Captain G——, the British Naval Attaché at Washington. The investigations of the police, however, had only enabled them to report that it had not been possible to discover any proof of the truth of his allegations. Captain G—— had applied for a whole detachment of detectives to be sent out from England, who were to work on their own initiative and under his direction, for the purpose of capturing the conspirators. The Attaché himself intended to collect the proofs which would enable the New York police to intervene. The detectives had arrived and among them were officials from Scotland Yard who understood their job. Boniface had discovered that they were following a definite clue, and my men in New York were worried, for it was possible that the Scotland Yard men were on the right track.

As I lay on the beach reading this report, the problem began to give me a headache. If the police really had found something out, it was too risky to deposit any more of our incendiary bombs. We should have to liquidate our whole scheme, and others would have to finish what we had begun. The English detectives would be waiting for our next move in order to catch us, though, if they were not really on our track, we could continue with our work in spite of Captain G—— and his men from Scotland Yard.

That afternoon I drove along the coast to another watering - place a little distance away. It was more fashionable and elegant, and slightly less sleepy than the retreat in which I had hidden myself. I walked up and down in deep thought and finally landed on a terrace of a small hotel. A jazz band was playing, and I drank iced coffee while I racked my brains to find a means of discovering what Captain G—— did and did not know of our activities.

I suddenly looked up and saw two ladies standing in

front of me, who knew me. They were ignorant of my name and who I was, and their knowledge of me rested only on a chance meeting at a society function in New York. We had met at a late hour in the evening, and I remembered that only the host had known who I was, none of the guests having any inkling of my real identity. The two ladies recognised me and came up to my table. They were Mrs. James B—— and Miss Mabel L——. Mrs. B——, who was the older of the two, was the wife of a coal merchant in New York, and Miss L——, who was young and very pretty, was " her best friend." They told me that they were very glad to see me, for there were many more ladies than men in the place, and I gathered that they did not have any accurate remembrance of my name. I hastened to inform them that it was Brannon, and they remembered immediately that it was.

We discussed a variety of things : water-sports, the War, the new dances, the stock exchange, and religion ; and I then learned that they were staying at the hotel on the terrace of which we were sitting. They told me that a large party was being given in the hotel on the following evening for which invitations had already been sent out, and they asked me to come along. It appeared to be difficult to round up enough dancing men, and the ladies reckoned on my co-operation in the entertainment. I had no desire to go, for I had other things on my mind, until Miss L—— surprised me by saying :

" Some nice people are coming. You are English, aren't you ? You will be interested, Captain G——, the Attaché at your Embassy, will be there. He is a charming person. Do you know him? No? Well, *do* come. You will find him easy to get on with."

I looked out over the sea. The orchestra was playing softly. My two companions began to devour pastries in large quantities. On the spur of the moment I decided to take a great risk in order to find out what I wanted to know.

"Yes," I said, "I shall be very glad to come."

They told me that the hotel was small but very fashionable, and that you could only be accepted as a guest if you were recommended by a member of New York society. Most of the apartments were already booked for a long time ahead. All the visitors knew each other and they formed, so to speak, a private club.

I moved into this fashionable hotel on the following morning, having been recommended by both the ladies. We sat on the beach together and went for walks, and I may repeat that Miss L—— was really very young and very pretty, while Mrs. B—— manifested a tact which appeared to have been acquired from a familiarity with difficult situations. We passed the day in complete harmony.

In the evening, when the ladies were wearing their best gowns and the gentlemen appeared in all the elegance and dignity of swallow-tails, the moment arrived for which I had waited. Mrs. B—— introduced me to the British Naval Attaché. I was informed that I had the pleasure of meeting Captain G——, and the Attaché was informed that he had the pleasure of meeting Mr. Brannon.

SABOTAGE

After Mrs. B—— had left us, we stood at one of the large windows that opened on to the sea. The Attaché was obviously trying to think of some pleasant remark to make to his countryman. He was tall, broadshouldered, with a clever face expressive of great energy, and was leaning out of the window a little to breathe in the sea air.

I began to put my plan into action.

" I am Commander Brannon, sir, and have been sent to the United States to study a new torpedo invention. I heard something yesterday in New York that I wished to communicate to you personally, but you had already left, and I thought that it might wait until your return."

" Oh," said the Attaché, " I am glad to meet you out here, then ! "

" They only know here that I am an Engiishman," I put in hastily ; " but they have no idea that I am in the Navy, and it is not necessary for them to discover it."

" You are right," said the Attaché; " but tell me, Commander, what was it you wished to report to me ? "

I pulled myself together. Now was the moment.

" A certain Captain Johnson, in charge of an English transport, has informed me of the strange incident of which he was a witness. He saw five men carrying heavy cases through the docks a few days ago, and as their behaviour looked rather odd he followed them for a couple of hundred yards. They loaded their mysterious cases into a motor-boat and shot off into the harbour. It was a clear night and he saw them draw alongside a vessel which had been loading munitions, in order presumably to go out to sea next day. The strange thing was that these men, together with their cases, were taken on board by means of a crane. The vessel sailed, but in the morning, before it left the harbour, Johnson called on the captain to tell him what he had seen. And what do you think happened? Not a soul on the whole ship admitted having seen the five men—neither the officer of the watch, nor any of the crew, nor our detectives. Don't you think there was something queer about it?"

Captain G—— had listened very attentively. " Tell me," he said, " did your confidant see any of these five fellows sufficiently clearly to recognise him again? Was he close enough to notice how they were dressed, and did he describe to you what they looked like?"

I regretted that Captain Johnson, who had already gone off to sea again, had told me no more than I had imparted to the Attaché, and that I had no more helpful information to divulge.

" I thought it would interest you," I said. " We have heard so much in the last few weeks about acts of sabotage against our ships."

"Yes, of course," replied Captain G——; " of course it interests me. I suppose you have read that we have definite suspicions. There is a gang working in New York Harbour under the direction of a German officer. We even know his name. He is called Rintelen, and has been mentioned a number of times in wireless messages by the German Embassy. The strange thing is, however, that the American police stick to their statement that he is a gentleman who is not doing anything criminal, and yet my men have often seen him hanging about the docks. He even admitted his identity once in a tavern, when he was drunk, and hadn't a hold on his tongue. He did not give away any details concerning his activities, but it is certain that he owns a motor-boat, and runs about in it for days together selling goods of all kinds to the ships in the harbour. I cannot tell you any more, Commander, but I can promise you that he will soon be in our hands."

"Yes, that's not likely to be a difficult job," I said, laughing internally till it hurt. "A fellow who gets drunk and lets his tongue run away with him, and sails about the harbour openly in a motor-boat, must be easy to trap."

The jazz band broke into our conversation, and I had to dance with Miss L——. She found me a delightful companion, for I was very elated, and I had good reason to be.

It is true that I knew the English suspected me, though I had no idea how they came to believe that I was accustomed to getting drunk in waterside taverns, and that I was doing business in a motor-boat. Naturally I did not like being under suspicion, but it was inevitable sooner or later, and it did not matter so much since at the same time they believed such glorious nonsense about my character. It was obvious that they were not aware of the identity either of the instigators or the tools concerned in our plot ; in other words, that they were on the wrong track, chasing a phantom which they believed, for heaven knows what reasons, to be identical with myself. The ground began to burn under my feet : I could now return to New York and resume my activities.

Suddenly I saw the Attaché talking to a man who looked like a servant and must have just handed him a letter. The dancing continued, and when G—— and I met a little later on at the buffet he drew me into a quiet corner to consume a dish of herring salad. He asked me about a number of fellow-officers, and as I had been employed in the department of the Admiralty at Berlin which was concerned with British matters, and had met British naval officers in the course of numerous journeys and social functions, having indeed written a dissertation on the British Navy for the staff examination, I was able to relate a variety of stories about officers whom we both knew. We sat in our corner and talked shop to the great displeasure of the ladies. Captain G—— soon became more confidential and told me that he had just received a letter that would necessitate him doing a little work that very night. He had just heard that the captain of a small freighter had reported in New York having sighted the German cruiser *Karlsruhe* in the Atlantic. He gave the degrees of latitude and longitude, and it was evident that the *Karlsruhe* had some definite plan in view since she had not bothered the freighter at all.

The *Karlsruhe* ! I had had no news of her since leaving Berlin, and now she, or a raider of the same name, to mislead the British, was apparently cruising about the Atlantic in order to molest English merchantmen on their way from America to Europe. This was what I

thought to myself, but I only said : " The *Karlsruhe* !
Really, the *Karlsruhe* ! What are you going to do ? "

" It's very simple," replied Captain G——. " You can
probably imagine. In an hour's time I am going to cable
to the Admiralty in London, and at the same time I shall
inform the Bermuda Squadron, on my own initiative,
that this impudent little cruiser is sailing about our seas.
The Bermuda Squadron will send the cruiser *Princess
Royal* to put a stop to it. We shall see."

If the powerful cruisers of the Bermuda Squadron
should come upon the little *Karlsruhe* there was no doubt
what the end would be. This realisation was accompanied by the immediate resolution to try and provide
something else for the Bermuda Squadron to do instead
of going in chase of the *Karlsruhe*. If I could succeed in
holding up action for a few days, it might be possible to
warn the German vessel by wireless. I did not yet
know how this could be done, but hoped for a lucky
idea.

" I think," I said, " that the Bermuda Squadron ought
to keep an eye on the German auxiliary cruisers."

" The German auxiliary cruisers ? *What* cruisers ?
What do you mean ? "

" I mean, sir, that the Bermuda Squadron ought to
prevent the large German steamers, which are lying in
the North American harbours, from breaking through.
There are about thirty or forty of them and they are very
swift. It is rumoured that they would try to avoid being
interned if the United States broke off diplomatic relations
with Germany, and they are said to have guns on board

which the confounded Boches have managed to get hold of."

The Attaché bit his lip.

" Yes, yes, of course," he said ; " yes, of course."

I could see that this information had startled him. There was not a word of truth in it, though the idea had once been on the *tapis*. Attachés resemble each other all over the world. They would rather let their ears be cut off than admit that there is anything connected with their job that they do not know.

At last he said, " I thought this affair of the German steamers had been kept pretty quiet. How did you hear about it ? "

" I got it from the American engineer whose invention I am testing, and also—now, who was it who told me ? —yes, I remember, it was an oil merchant."

The Attaché grew distinctly pensive. " Yes," he said, " I must reconsider the matter. It would of course be more useful to catch the steamers than send our battle-ships chasing after the *Karlsruhe*."

I was called to take part in a game which the ladies had organised, and I was unable to get out of it. I then had to dance, but my eyes sought G——, who had dis-appeared. Shortly afterwards I was accompanying Miss L—— on a walk along the beach under a very romantic moon, when I saw a man in evening-dress crossing the promenade. It was G——. When he came up he took Miss L——'s other arm and we all three went back to the hotel. I cogitated as we walked how I could find out what G—— had been doing in the meantime. I decided to base my action on my "special" knowledge of the *genus* Attaché, and began to say flattering things to him. I gave vent to my regret that I should probably never become an Attaché myself, which, I said, had always been my ambition, though it was likely never to be achieved.

"You, sir, are a factor in the history of this great War. People will always say of you, 'Yes, he was Naval Attaché in Washington.' London acts on your advice, and things are done at your bidding."

Captain G—— listened attentively and was visibly pleased. He said something patronising, and as we stepped aside to let Miss L—— enter the hotel he held me back and whispered:

"Commander, you are an understanding sort of person, and will know how to keep a secret. The telegrams I am about to dispatch will prepare a surprise for the German steamers if they try to leave dock. So we will let the *Karlsruhe* alone for a bit. . . ."

Every ball comes to an end eventually, and when I was back in my room I felt very happy. I had achieved more than I dared to hope, for I knew that the English had no inkling of the shady paths that my agents and I had been pursuing in New York, and I believed that I had saved the *Karlsruhe* from the guns of the British battleships.

It had been a good evening.

Next morning all the king's horses could not have kept me in the place, and I left for New York as soon as I could. I put my luggage in the cloakroom at the station and tried to re-establish contact with my men. After

some vain attempts I found one of the German captains.
We met in the town and he was so brimful of courage
that I poured out my heart to him, and we decided to
resume full activity on the following day. We discussed
details, arranged to collect all our people, and made our
way to the office that had been the headquarters of the
firm of Gibbons. I wanted to see whether any mail had
arrived for me. On the way we considered how it might
be possible to warn the *Karlsruhe*, and thought that perhaps the Naval Attaché might have ways and means at
his disposal. I made up my mind to send a message to
Captain Boy-Ed late that evening to let him know what
I had heard.

When I opened the door of my office we both stared
in amazement. A veritable mountain of letters lay heaped
up on the floor. They were apparently offers of goods
which had been invited by the indefatigable Max Weiser,
catalogues, newspapers, samples and all sorts of things,
pushed through by the postman. It would have taken
a day to discover whether the pile contained a letter
that needed my attention, and I had to leave the task
to Weiser, for I had no time to look through them
myself. The captain and I were standing by the door,
pushing the letters aside with our feet, when we suddenly
saw a man outside scrutinising us. The captain banged
the door in his face. There was a knock, and I opened
the door again, to see the man still standing there. He
wore a shabby overcoat and the rest of his clothing was
also in a state of decay, but he was sunburnt and he
looked like a sailor.

SABOTAGE

"Excuse me," he said. "Is there anybody here belonging to the firm of E. V. Gibbons?"

He spoke broken English and appeared to be a German, or, it swiftly shot through my mind, perhaps he wanted to make us think he was a German. He looked suspicious to me.

"No," I replied; "we are only clearing up."

"Do you know perhaps where the gentlemen are to be found? I must speak to them urgently."

"I don't know anything about them," I growled. "Don't worry me about other people's affairs. Go and see the manager of the building."

"I've been there already. Can't you *really* tell me where I can find them?"

"Haven't the faintest idea," I said in an irritated tone, and closed the door.

"That young fellow looks very suspicious," the captain suggested. "Shall I follow him and find out what sort of a bird he is?"

"Yes," I replied hastily, "that's a good idea. Go after him quickly, but don't let him see you."

I told him where he could reach me and left the building. I had laid my plans on my journey back to New York, and I was anxious to give the impression that I was a man who had nothing to fear. So I took up my quarters at the New York Yacht Club. This was one of the most exclusive clubs of New York, and I had been a member since before the War. It had only three German members, the first being the Kaiser, the second his brother, Prinz Heinrich, and the third myself; so I was

in good company. I had my luggage fetched from the
railway station and sent for the rest of my things. I had
nearly finished unpacking when the telephone bell rang.
The German captain was at the other end and sounded
very excited. He would not tell me what was the matter
over the telephone, but begged me to come to the docks
as soon as I could. When I met him in the little tavern
which we had arranged as a rendezvous, he was still
agitated as he told me what had happened.

He had followed the man who had appeared at the
office that afternoon and made a strange discovery. The
suspicious-looking customer had taken him on foot
right through New York and had finished up at last in
a small pub by the waterside. The captain had looked
through the door and seen ten men sitting round a large
table, apparently waiting for the new arrival. They had
half-empty glasses in front of them and one or two had
fallen asleep with their heads on their arms. The man
had conveyed some gloomy news to them, and the whole
company seemed to have no idea what they should do.
The captain had telephoned to a sailor he knew, who
entered the tavern, pretended to be a little drunk, and
stood a round of drinks. The captain waited in the
street until his friend came out and said :

" I'll be hanged if they are not the crew of a German
man-o'-war."

Seamen have an unfailing eye for such things, and they
sent for me immediately.

The captain's excitement communicated itself to me,
and I had to find out what these people were doing.

They were still inside the tavern, and the captain suggested that he should go inside and fetch out the man who had asked for us. I agreed and waited outside.

The captain soon emerged, accompanied by the man. I stepped out of the surrounding darkness into the light of a street-lamp, and, following a sudden inspiration, said to the man in German :

" Whom are you looking for ? "

He looked at me rather startled, and hesitated a moment before he replied, likewise in German :

" I am looking for the Captain. I was told to go to the firm of E. V. Gibbons and ask for the Captain."

" *Who* told you ? "

" A sailor, but I don't know who he was."

My men always called me " the Captain," and never mentioned my name. The man really appeared to be a German, and when I inspected him more closely he certainly gave the impression of being a naval rating. I decided to rely on my instinct again, and in any case I was sure he was not an English agent.

" *I* am the Captain. What's wrong ? "

He looked at me dubiously, and I could see from his face that he was mistrustful. He hesitated, looked at me for a moment, and replied in English :

" It's all right, sir. I made a mistake."

My doubts were now cast to the winds, and taking him by the arm I said :

" Don't be afraid. I will help you. But tell me who you are, and who are those men with you ? "

He hesitated again. I looked at him and knew that I

could reveal my identity. Moreover, I had a feeling that he had something important to tell me. A prickly sensation crawled up my spine and I had a vague dread of what I was about to hear. I put my hand in my breast pocket and drew out a document which was bound to convince him, if he was really a naval rating, of my identity. It was the "*Kaiserpass*" with which I had been furnished in Berlin as my authority at all foreign stations of the German Empire. I opened this document and showed it to him. He looked at the photograph, examined me keenly, and was persuaded. Suddenly he clicked his heels together and stood stiffly to attention.

" Petty Officer, sir, reporting with ten men from the sunken *Karlsruhe*."

I felt as if I had received a blow on the forehead. The street went round and round and the lights swam in a mist before my eyes. The sailor loomed gigantic and unreal against the background of the dock.

I pulled myself together and swallowed hard. The sailor was still standing stiffly in front of me, and I seized him by the shoulder to draw him away from the light of the street-lamp. He then told me the fate of the *Karlsruhe*.

A torpedo had exploded for some unexplained reason inside the ship, and had rent her in two, without the enemy having anything to do with it. She had sunk some time ago, and the sailor, together with his companions, had got away in a boat, been picked up by a steamer, and been brought to New York. The steamer belonged to a neutral Power and they had begged her captain to conceal the fact that he had rescued them. They intended to try and find their way home from New York. Their ideas as to what would happen to them if they reported to the German Consulate in New York were vague, and they were afraid of being interned ; so some one advised them to come to me. When we had arranged for them to be looked after, I went home and spent a sleepless night. I was obsessed with the thought of the *Karlsruhe's* fate !

The next morning I cautiously began to resume contact with my other agents. I met them in different parts of the town, and the whole day, as I went about, I could not forget the absurd story that G—— had told me concerning my hanging about the waterside tavern and selling things from a motor-boat. I spent the evening at the restaurant in the Woolworth Building with a number of my best men, including Max Weiser and a couple of the German captains. They laughed uproariously when I told them the story and were genuinely amused, but were unable to suggest how to get at the kernel of truth which must certainly lie at the centre of it. There were so many gentlemen who drank too much in the dockside taverns, and there were so many gentlemen who did business in the harbour. We had no clue to the mystery. On the following day I had an appointment with Mr. Boniface, who was to report to me what news there was at Police Headquarters. We met at a little café, and he looked more glum than ever. His face registered suppressed wrath, and he dumbfounded me by severely taking me to task.

"It isn't my business, Captain," he said, "to tell you

what you ought to do, and I should never have thought that you could behave so. I should never have believed that you could be so careless."

I lost my temper.

"Don't talk in riddles, man. What have I done? What has happened? Out with it!"

"You got drunk," said Boniface gloomily. "You got very drunk, and said you were the German captain who sets the ships on fire."

This was beyond a joke.

"If you dare to tell me that I also sail about the harbour in a motor-boat, I shall get rude."

Boniface almost wept as he polished his pince-nez.

"What good will it do you, Captain," he complained, " to be rude to a poor old man who only wishes you well? What good will it do you? Take my advice and be more cautious. What do you want in the harbour, Captain? There's nothing for you to do there and you only attract attention to yourself."

"How do you know all this?"

"The whole of the police force knows it. At Police Headquarters they talk of nothing else. All the detectives are discussing it—morning, noon, and night."

"Mr. Boniface!" I said. "Mr. Boniface! Just listen to me. I have never been drunk in New York. I have never said that I am the German captain who sets ships on fire. And I have never sailed about the harbour in a motor-boat."

Mr. Boniface put on his glasses and adjusted his hat.

"It is a great pity that we have to part, Captain. You

have ceased to trust me. Why not honestly confess that you made a mistake that might happen to anybody, and we could then consider how to cover it up."

I was no longer angry. I began to laugh.

" But, Mr. Boniface, what shall I do to convince you ? I have never in my life . . ."

To my surprise Boniface grew very serious and said : " I have heard that gentlemen of your rank in Germany are accustomed in such cases to swear on their word of honour."

" All right : on my word of honour, Mr. Boniface."

I then heard the absurd story for the second time, and Boniface assured me that the whole of the New York police were looking for the German Captain Rintelen who rolled about the docks and sailed about the harbour. I questioned him carefully and learned that he had obtained the most exact information from a certain official who had himself seen the alleged Captain.

" You must find out, Mr. Boniface, what is known about him. Find out the minutest details, so that we can ourselves have a look at the fellow who has been trumpeting forth his activities."

Boniface grew thoughtful. " It will cost money," he suggested. " I shall have to knock the policeman down first."

" Don't be ridiculous."

" Don't worry, Captain. I'll knock him down with a thousand dollars."

It was worth a thousand dollars. I gave Boniface the money, and he knocked his man down the same evening.

THE DARK INVADER

He telephoned me to meet him, and I found him very excited and rather ashamed. What he had to tell me was indeed queer. The police had been after me since noon, when I had gone out in my motor-boat, and I was at this moment sailing about the harbour. The police wanted to catch me climbing secretly on board a ship to deposit an incendiary bomb.

I shook my head in bewilderment, and sent for one of my captains to come down to the docks with me and cross the Hudson to Hoboken. Boniface went ahead and we followed.

Boniface knew the exact spot where the detectives were waiting to shadow me when I should draw alongside in my boat. Their intention was to ransack the motor-boat for incendiary bombs. Even before we arrived we could see a couple of men in bowlers leaning against the railings of a jetty. We went round them in a wide circle and stole into the surrounding darkness to await events. First came a woman, who remained standing for a time on the quay near the jetty and then began to walk up and down, with her eyes fixed on the waters of the harbour. Then a motor-boat drew alongside. The two men had meanwhile disappeared, but we saw them crouching behind a railway train. A man emerged from the boat carrying a couple of heavy baskets, and the woman hastened up to him. The detectives crept round to bar his way, and though it was too dark to make out his face, it could be seen that he was tall and wore a roomy raincoat. After he had made his boat fast, the woman helped him to carry his baskets along the jetty

160

towards the quay, with the intention apparently of making for the town. Suddenly they were confronted by the two detectives, with whom they collided, so that the baskets toppled over and their contents rolled along the ground. The detectives apologised profusely, picked up the fallen objects and put them in the baskets again, and while the man in the raincoat shouted abuses at them, they raised their hats and disappeared.

From our hiding-place we saw two other detectives following the man and woman and we attached ourselves to the procession. It was dark and rain was falling, and we could only see the pursuers, not the pursued. Suddenly they ran round different corners and we came to a standstill, for the detectives had lost the trail. I was fed-up with chasing myself and had other things to do, so I went home. We knew where the man kept his boat and it would not be difficult to discover what he was up to. In fact, we found out on the following day as much as we wanted to know. His business in the harbour was quite harmless. He was especially interested in the sale of tobacco and spirits, and, as far as the sale of alcohol was concerned, he appeared to be his own best customer. He lived with a woman and seemed to be in fear of the law, for he frequently changed his quarters. He had got drunk one night in a tavern by the waterside and had declared in all seriousness that he was a German captain occupied in placing bombs on Allied munition transports so that they caught fire at sea. The whole affair was ridiculous, but it was a matter of great concern to us since all the British detectives swore positively that he was

THE DARK INVADER

Captain Rintelen in disguise. The New York police had ascertained that Rintelen was often seen in society in evening-dress and that he lived at the New York Yacht Club. But this did not influence the detectives, who declared that Rintelen was leading a dual existence, in one phase of which he appeared as the decayed individual with the motor-boat. They even succeeded in convincing the American Secret Police, or at least the minor officials, who soon believed this grotesque nonsense. The man they were after noticed of course that he was being pursued ; but as he had a bad conscience he disappeared and thus strengthened the suspicions of the police.

We hit on an idea which caused us considerable amusement, but which, when we carried it out, served us well to the end. One of my men who was less in the bad books of the police than the others, and who could not under any circumstances have been charged with an act of sabotage, bribed the eccentric stranger to enter our service, and we discovered that, as a matter of fact, he bore a certain superficial resemblance to myself. He had gone to the dogs and was constantly drunk. Our subsequent activities not only completely nonplussed the British detectives, and even some of the American police officials, but made them all the more certain that we were one and the same individual. My agent picked him up in the street one day, stood him a number of drinks, put him in a car, and took him to the little dockside tavern in which he had previously engaged a room. The man was in a state of semi-intoxication and allowed himself to be stripped of his dingy garments and dressed in a new suit and patent-leather shoes which were much too large for him. He was then taken to a large, fashionable hotel and the detectives lost all trace of him. It was a game which my men went on playing with numerous variations, and it not only amused us, but fulfilled its purpose.

We then let him return to his business, which he soon began to neglect, however, as he received plenty of money from us. He was in such a state that he never asked questions, but did blindly everything we asked of him. A few dollars in his pocket and frequent drinks kept him happy. He could not give us away, since he knew nothing about us, and we found him very useful. He began to take an interest in his clothes, and every morning he showed himself at a busy street-crossing not far from the Yacht Club. In the other part of the town, where our office was situated, he disconcerted both the lift-boys and the detectives.

When we had thus led the police on a false trail I began to spin my threads again. Dr. Scheele was instructed to resume the construction of detonators, and in spite of the increased risks we succeeded in placing them on transports. As before, we only put them on British, French, and Russian vessels so as not to violate American neutrality. We also rented a new office, rooms being put at our disposal by a German of half-Mexican extraction and of an adventurous disposition. We equipped our new quarters so that the rooms were divided into two parts by special doors and were connected by telephone and an alarm bell which rang very softly. I was thus protected against undesirable visitors and possessed an emergency exit to the corridor to ensure an orderly retreat. We were now called the " Mexico North-Western Railway Company," and this name appeared neatly on the door of our office.

The first act of the new firm was to acquire an idea, the father of which was a young German engineer named Fay. He declared that he had invented a machine which was capable of tearing off a ship's rudder while at sea. He made a good impression on me, and after discussing the matter with my captains I gave Fay money to prepare his experiments. He returned a week later and said he was ready. I sent him into the country with a couple of the captains to buy a piece of ground in a deserted region which was well hidden by trees. Here they constructed the stern of a ship out of wood and attached to it a genuine rudder. To this rudder was fixed a detonator, the tip of which carried an iron pin which was needle-shaped at the lower end. The pin was connected with the rudder-shaft itself ; and as the shaft revolved the iron pin turned with it, gradually boring its way into the detonator, until it eventually pierced the fulminate and caused an explosion which blew away the rudder.

When the model had been solidly constructed, Fay attached his apparatus and began to revolve the rudder. The captains stood at a respectful distance and Fay kept on turning for about an hour or so. Then there was a terrific bang, and bits of the model flew about the captains' ears. Fay himself went up in the air, but came down again in the wood with only a few injured ribs. The trees themselves were damaged, and a fire broke out which they had to extinguish. They then got into the car and returned to New York to report to me that the invention had functioned efficiently.

Fay was financed with enough money to carry on his experiments, until he succeeded in producing his apparatus in a handy form and was ready to make his first attempt. He took a motor-boat out into the harbour one evening and apparently had engine trouble, for he drew up alongside the rudder of one of the big munition transports and made fast. He actually managed in two cases to fix his machine, and we awaited results. They were announced in due course by the *Shipping News*, and the New York papers were agitated. There had been two mysterious accidents, and nobody could say how they happened. Two transports had had their rudders torn away at sea and suffered serious damage to the stern. One of them had been abandoned by its crew and was drifting as a wreck on the Atlantic, while the other had had to be towed into the nearest harbour.

When this success had become public knowledge, Fay could no longer venture to sail about the harbour in his motor-boat. He was young, but bold and resolute, and during the next few weeks he undertook adventures on munition transports which demanded iron nerves. He mounted his machine on a large platform made of cork, and swam out into the harbour under cover of darkness. When he reached the vessels that he had marked out, he fixed his apparatus to their rudders. A number of further successes were recorded, and numerous Allied shells failed to reach the guns for which they had been destined. With the help of Fay's new invention, which he used not only in New York, but in other ports, we were able to give our undertaking a new turn. What the incendiary bombs could not achieve was reserved for Fay's machines. The number of transports had, however, increased nearly tenfold since we first began our work, and as it was impossible to interfere with them all, we had to find a new inspiration.

I read in the newspaper one morning that some of the New York dockers had gone on strike. I knew that strikes had been breaking out periodically on account of wage demands, but that they did not last long, because they were not sanctioned by the unions. I made inquiries about the general situation and learned that the dock-workers of New York and the other ports in the United States were to a great extent Irishmen, who vented their hatred of England in occasional strikes in order to do what they could to hinder the shipping of munitions. They hoped that their country would be able to free itself from the domination of England, if the latter lost the War ; and to that end they were prepared to do everything that lay in their power. All the strikes which were started for this or other reasons were illegal and had no prospect of success, for Samuel Gompers, the President of the American Federation of Labour, was very pro-English and had no intention of sanctioning a strike which would injure England. For some time other trade union leaders had been attacking Gompers' attitude to the question of prohibiting the export of armaments, but they were unable to do any good, since Gompers adhered tenaciously to his principle that the export of armaments should not be forbidden. The American unions split into two parties on the question. Some of them supported Gompers, while others did not hesitate to stigmatise Gompers openly at their meetings as an agent in the pay of England, and gave him the nickname " The Fifteen Thousand Dollar Man." It was only the unions that possessed strike funds, and therefore they alone could proclaim a strike with any prospect of success. An idea occurred to me which struck me at first as being fantastic, and that was to found my own " union." A union which was properly registered could proclaim a legal strike, and the law could not interfere. If, in addition, we could pay strike benefits, it might be possible to achieve something, and I certainly had the money to do so.

I had to set to work very cautiously and get in touch with the workmen's leaders. The moment it was known that I was a German staging a strike for the sole purpose of injuring his country's enemies, my scheme was bound to come to grief. I could not hope that the leaders would follow me, if I explained my true reasons to them ; so I had recourse to a stratagem. I was already acquainted with a few of the less important trade union leaders, men of Irish extraction, and some who were German-American. They believed me to be an American, and I succeeded in carrying them with me in a way that did not arouse their suspicions. They were all of the opinion, in any case, that the sending of explosives to Europe was reprehensible, and held the point of view that it could not be to the interest of the workers in other countries to supply munitions with which their brothers were to be shot down. They swore by the Workers' International and disapproved, on moral and ethical grounds, of the export of arms. I must admit to having deluded these men, but I was an officer in the German Navy and could not be particular as to the means I employed in the situation in which I found myself. Therefore I did not lift my mask, but pretended to adopt their views and to speak their language.

The first thing I did was to hire a large hall and organise a meeting, at which well-known men thundered against the export of munitions. Messrs. Buchanan and Fowler, members of Congress ; Mr. Hannis Taylor, the former American Ambassador in Madrid ; Mr. Monnett, a former Attorney-General ; together with a number of University professors, theologians and Labour leaders appeared and raised their voices. I sat unobtrusively in a corner and watched my plans fructifying. None of the speakers had the faintest suspicion that he was in the " service " of a German officer sitting among the audience. They knew the men who had asked them to speak, but had no idea that the strings were being pulled by somebody else. On the following day I met the German-American and Irish trade union leaders, who took me for a wealthy American interested in the humanitarian aspect, and willing to make financial sacrifices for his ideals. We took a mighty step forward and founded a new trade union which we called " Labour's National Peace Council." Of course, I was not a member of the union, but I had brought with me to the preliminary meeting a trustworthy sailor of German origin who had become a docker for the sole purpose of being eligible for membership of the union. I managed to secure for him a position of authority; and the union, which as yet possessed leaders but no rank and file, set to work.

My intention was no less ambitious than to enrol a large proportion of the American dock-workers in the new union. If I could achieve this, I should have the power to declare a strike that would cause great damage to the Allies. My hope that members would stream in from every side appeared, however, doomed to disappointment. Not a single recruit turned up. Gompers and his people laughed hilariously at my union, with its office near the docks, and well-known men among its leaders, but only a few members. Though the subscription was unusually low, it seemed that it would be a fiasco. I began to despair of success, but one morning, when I was immersed in gloom, Weiser, who of course was co-operating with me, telephoned me from the docks to come to the headquarters of the union as soon as possible and bring money. He would give me details later. I rushed to the docks with the necessary funds, and when I got near the office I saw some groups of excited stevedores standing about. Weiser came to meet me and told me what was happening. It appeared that an unauthorised strike, provoked by a couple of Irishmen, had broken out among the men loading shells on a vessel that was destined for Russia. They demanded extra pay on account of the danger involved in their work, and insisted that the British agents, who were guarding the Russian transport and were carrying carbines, should be dismissed. Before the negotiations had concluded, the Irish had ceased work, and the men were standing about and giving vent to curses and abuse. They could not make up their minds whether to remain on strike or to resume. Nearly the whole of the rank and file of our little union was engaged on the steamer; and as it was part of our programme to oppose the munition shipments, the men came to the office and explained why they had struck. They asked for strike pay, but merely as a formality, and apparently without any expectation that they would receive it, or that the strike would be sanctioned.

When Weiser heard what they had to say, he immediately telephoned to me, while the agent whom I had managed to get on to the executive put the men off for the time being and telephoned to all the other leaders of the union. These arrived almost at the same time as I did, but I was no longer there, for I had handed over my money and disappeared, so as not to excite suspicion. Subsequent events became the talk of the docks that evening. The almost incredible news spread like wildfire among the stevedores. The leaders of my union had met, but were very pessimistic and declared that the strike was utter nonsense, for the treasury was empty, and our few members formed an insignificant minority. My agent took the floor, however, and assured that though, of course, our numerical strength was absurdly low, yet it was necessary to act logically if we were to carry out our

SABOTAGE

programme. We were opposed to the munition shipments and we must not expect our members to engage in
the work. The only reply was a pitying smile from the
other leaders, who asked where the strike pay was coming
from.

"I made a collection after the meeting, and soon I
had twenty-five thousand dollars," declared our agent,
and put the money on the table.

This was different, and the matter began to assume
another aspect. With twenty-five thousand dollars in
the treasury it was possible to sanction the strike and pay
benefits.

My agent proceeded skilfully. He seized control without the others noticing it, and after an hour's discussion "Labour's National Peace Council" declared an
official strike. Weiser ran to the nearest bank like a man
accustomed to changing such thousand-dollar notes, and
on his return addressed the stevedores and told them
to come into the office one at a time. My agent also
emerged and announced that the union recognised the
justice of its members' demands and sanctioned the
strike. Benefits, for the ensuing week would, of course,
be paid out immediately.

The workmen were overjoyed at the unexpected news.
They thought it a very fine union to belong to and came
in to receive their money. As they passed the steamer
where some of the men had already resumed work, they
sang the praises of their union in loud tones, and then
went to look for another job, as far as possible from the
docks.

That evening I had a long conference with my agent, Max Weiser, and Captain von Kleist, who took over the conduct of the " attack." The result of this conference appeared next morning, when a large placard was hung outside the office announcing that new members would be welcomed. The union had, of course, always been ready to accept new members, but they had been slow in arriving and the placard had a particular significance at this juncture.

Kleist and Weiser were busy in the vicinity of the pier at Hoboken, and the news was spread that " Labour's National Peace Council " was prepared to pay strike benefits to all men ceasing work on munition transports, even if they had only been members for a day ; and before many hours had passed, a flock of workmen poured in, who paid their entrance subscriptions and immediately disappeared. Next morning they came back and said they had ceased work because their employers refused to pay them the extra wages they demanded on account of the danger of their duties. They received their strike pay, and when I passed by later in the afternoon I saw an astonishing sight. A vast crowd was thronging the office, and I estimated that at least a thousand men were waiting to pay their subscriptions. I found Max Weiser, who was thoroughly excited and bellicose to a degree. He told me that all these men had come to join the union, so I went to my bank and got more money. I had sufficient to pay strike benefits for some time, and I knew that when my capital ran out, a cable to Germany would replenish my coffers. By the following day about fifteen

SABOTAGE

hundred dockers were on strike in New York Harbour, and a few days later not a single munition transport was being loaded. Victory was in sight, but I had reckoned without the defensive forces of American finance. At the moment when I had brought the loading in New York Harbour to a standstill, the members of my union executive were travelling in all directions. They established branches in other ports, organised meeting after meeting, and proclaimed strikes everywhere. I sat in my own office, and telegrams, of course in cipher, landed on my desk by the score. Those of my men who had formerly been engaged in placing bombs, a business which we were for the time being compelled to neglect, were now working for the union, and collecting information from the various ports. I wired money to all the centres, to be used for propagandist literature and the hiring of halls. A series of strikes broke out in the United States, which made the leaders of the older unions grow pale. Their members were leaving them in large numbers and coming over to us, while the American Press seized with amazement and indignation upon the strange phenomenon which nobody could understand. A movement had been started the end of which could not be foreseen. Boniface turned up again and hired a gang of wild characters, who pretended to be sailors and cried themselves hoarse at the meetings, where they grew pally with the dockers.

Our success in the other ports was instantaneous. Transport after transport lay idle and could not be loaded. There arose a state of affairs which, in the words of the American Press, cried to heaven. The newspapers began

173

to print cables from Europe to the effect that the delay in sending explosives would be catastrophic for the Allies, and I prayed that this might really come to pass.

At the same time the local leaders of my union began to bombard President Wilson with hundreds of telegrams, which came from all the cities and ports in the country and were financed by me, petitioning for a law against the exports of armaments. I heard that Gompers had hastened with his friends to Wilson and had been received. I therefore caused the President to be snowed under with telegrams from all sides, demanding that the leaders of our union should also be received. He at last agreed to see a deputation on June 15th, and our hopes ran high, for we had reason to expect that the President would bow to the power of our union. He telegraphed, however, on the day before the interview was to take place, that he could not receive our leaders, since he was staying in the country. The Washington atmosphere was getting "too close" for him.

The armament industry mobilised for defence at the same time that Wilson gave his evasive answer. I again had the feeling that I was being watched. The authorities were after me, but I took precautions.

More serious was the fact that we began to lose ground. The men were returning to work. Our union was still on strike, but the older organisations were managing to mobilise their members, and we were unable to persuade them to join our ranks, since they were being paid high bonuses as strike-breakers. We soon found out that the armament firms had poured millions of dollars into the treasuries of the older unions; and Gompers and his friends were living in trains and motor-cars, travelling about the whole country to organise the counter-blow. The fight cost me an enormous amount of money, but I was unwilling to capitulate to Gompers.

When our opponents had succeeded in getting work started once more, I surprised them with another stroke. I had so far only been engaged in staging these dock strikes, but I now extended my activities. We likewise went on our travels, this time at the suggestion of the Austrian Ambassador, Dr. Dumba; and at the moment when Gompers saw victory in sight, employees of the greatest armament factory in the United States, the Bethlehem Steel Works, suddenly laid down tools. They were mostly Austrians.

So the fight went on, and ground was lost and won again. Ultimate success would be a matter of money and nerves; and for the time being, at any rate, we were in good spirits.

Meanwhile I had another iron in the fire. I had studied the foreign political situation of the United States, and realised that the only country she had to fear was Mexico. If Mexico attacked her she would need all the munitions she could manufacture, and would be unable to export any to Europe. There was, however, no prospect of this, since Mexico was torn by internal dissensions. Huerta, the former President, was in exile, though I knew that he still hoped to regain his lost position. He ascribed his fall to the United States, which he suspected of having fomented the revolution which had brought him to grief. While he was still in power, American capital had made further attempts to gain possession of Mexico's oil, but had met with resistance from Huerta, which was only broken down when the revolution sent him into banishment.

This was the situation when I decided to take a hand in the game. I learned that Huerta was in the United States and made every effort to find where he was staying. He suddenly turned up in New York, and I went to his hotel, the Manhattan, to see him. On my way I pondered how to approach him, but could not think of any plan, and decided to rely on my instinct. He was sitting alone in the lounge and was surprised to be addressed by a complete stranger. When I looked into his eyes I realised at once the best way to approach him. I told him I was a German officer, mentioned the munition transports, and offered him my help there and then. I expressed my readiness to do all I could to bring his party into power again in Mexico.

Though I gave my reasons for visiting him, he was afraid of a trap and thought I might be an American agent. He remained silent, and I made every effort to convince him that I really was a German officer, and not in the pay of the United States. At last he believed me and was prepared to speak frankly. He told me that another revolution was being engineered by his friends, but that they lacked weapons, or, in other words, money.

The interview lasted a long time. I was in a position to offer him effective help, and we discussed what was to be done if the new revolution should be crowned with success. This was a matter of the utmost importance to me, and we came to terms. Huerta stipulated that I should procure the sanction of the German Government to the following conditions :

German U-boats were to land weapons along the Mexican coast ; abundant funds were to be provided for the purchase of armaments ; and Germany should agree to furnish Mexico with moral support. In that eventuality Mexico would take up arms against the United States, and Huerta would have his revenge. This desire for revenge, incidentally, seemed to me to be Huerta's driving motive. After the interview I sent a cable report to Berlin.

. . . . .

As I left the hotel I caught sight of two familiar faces. They were those of detectives who had frequently shadowed me in the past. I remained in the vicinity of the hotel until I saw Huerta come out, followed by two men, who were apparently guarding him. I went after them in order to make sure. Huerta entered a car, and the two detectives stopped a taxi and followed. There was no longer room for doubt that our interview had been observed. On the same day another disturbing incident occurred ; for when I returned to my office, still somewhat agitated at my disconcerting discovery, I found Mr. Boniface sitting there with his legs crossed and very depressed. I was by no means pleasantly surprised when he told me that he had extremely disagreeable news.

" Cut it short, Mr. Boniface," I begged. " I have already had enough amusement for one day."

My eyes grew wide with astonishment, however, when he told me a story that I was at first disinclined to believe. He had found out, with the help of his shady but very valuable connections, that the " Most Secret Code " of the German Embassy had been stolen. British agents had got a girl to make up to a young and badly-paid secretary on the staff of the Naval Attaché. The two had become very friendly, and she had persuaded him that it was absurd to exist on a wretched pittance, when he was in a position to earn a fortune with a single stroke. He had agreed to do what she asked of him, and had communicated the immensely important code to her, and therefore to the British. He was said to have made a copy and to have restored the original carefully to its place, which evidently was but poorly guarded.

This ' leak ' in the office of the Attachés was naturally reported to me at once from another source. It had become known at Washington and was actually under discussion at a Cabinet meeting.

I was very upset. It was the code that I had brought with me from the Admiralty in Berlin for the use of the Embassy, because it was suspected that the old code was in the hands of the enemy. I thanked Boniface for his information and sent him away. I then went immediately to the Naval Attaché, though it seemed to me unlikely that the code could have been accessible to a secretary, since there was a regulation which prohibited the trusting of a cipher to a lower official. When I was shown into the Naval Attaché, I said :

SABOTAGE

" Do you know that the ' Most Secret Code ' has gone, sir ? "

Captain Boy-Ed exploded :

" Who says so ? Impossible ! It is kept here under lock and key."

"*Always*, Captain ? "

" Of course, I haven't the time to lock up every code myself. That is done by one of the secretaries."

" In Berlin no one under the rank of captain is allowed to put away a secret code."

" Excuse me. That is my own concern."

This interview convinced me that really the code had been stolen. I had a presentiment of misfortune, but I could not yet know what the fateful consequences this was going to have for *me*. It was as well that I did not.

.   .   .   .   .

There ensued some weeks of waiting for the reply to my message to Berlin, and I was on tenterhooks to hear whether I could agree to Huerta's terms. I came into frequent contact with him during this time, and always found him in excellent humour at the turn his country's fortunes were about to take.

Meanwhile I was preparing a scheme of a very different kind. Sir Roger Casement, the Irish leader, had turned up in Berlin before I left, where he revealed the true situation in Ireland to the Wilhelmstrasse and to the public. They had hitherto believed that all the Irish were enemies of England and prepared to shake off her yoke, but they now learned that there was a very important

Protestant group in Northern Ireland, the so-called Ulster
Party, with powerful leaders, which was absolutely
loyal to Great Britain, and even desired the support of
English bayonets against the more numerous Catholics
of the South. The militant Irish, who were being supported to the uttermost, both morally and materially, by
the enormous number of Irish immigrants in the United
States, all came from the South. Sir Roger Casement
was one of their most prominent leaders, and it was their
object to detach Ireland as a whole from Great Britain
and force the Northern minority to come into a newly
constituted Free State. Casement's purpose was clear.
He had first of all to make it possible for the Southern
Irish to overcome the Ulstermen; for in the case of a
revolt against England they would have to reckon with
armed resistance from the North.

Though Casement was in Berlin, the German capital
was an unfavourable centre from which to spin the
threads of political intrigue; for Germany was surrounded by foes and was suffering the disadvantage of
the strict blockade which the latter had imposed.

I was by now acquainted with some of the Irish leaders
who had established an " Activist Committee " in New
York. I could not deal with them as I had dealt with
Huerta, so I pretended to be a wealthy man with a strong
personal dislike for England, and ready to help them.
I only played this rôle, however, at the beginning,
keeping it up until I had convinced myself that the
people at the head of the Irish Independence Movement in America were of a character to ensure that

something would be done. I dropped my mask when I thoroughly understood their aims and intentions. When they discovered that they were in league with a German naval officer they really did have scruples about accepting my aid, but these were soon dispersed since their hatred of England was so fierce, their rage so inflamed, and their desire to attack the detested country so irrepressible, that we soon came to terms.

A revolt in Ireland had only been prevented hitherto by the fact that insufficient arms were available, and the circumstance that Sir Roger Casement was away in Berlin. They did not think that they could afford to dispense with the advantages with which his popularity would furnish them when the rising took place. There was also justified anxiety about the intervention of English warships, which could easily land troops everywhere on the Irish coast.

I began to take a hand in the Irish question. After communication with Berlin I was able to make positive proposals to the malcontents. They lacked rifles and munitions. Very well! These were to be had in abundance in America. There were enough ships sailing to Ireland from American ports; and if the factories could pack rifle ammunition in barrels and declare it was flour, it could equally well be done in the case of vessels going to Ireland. This problem offered no great difficulties. The question of naval intervention on the Irish coast was much more serious, and constituted one of the chief anxieties of the Irish committee in New York; but at one of their meetings I put the German

Government's reply on the table. The Admiralty was prepared to send U-boats to the Irish coast which would lie hidden until the opportunity arrived to put a spoke in the British Navy plans for landing men. When my Irish friends looked up from this document, I saw in their eyes the desperate resolve to commence hostilities. They made their arrangements with their home country, and I made mine with Berlin, and a day was fixed for the rising to take place in Dublin, which was to spread throughout the whole of Ireland. Either one or two days before, I do not remember exactly, Casement was to be put ashore on the Irish coast from a U-boat, and Germany, in order to exploit the opportunity as far as possible, was prepared to land troops carrying machine-guns from an auxiliary cruiser sailing alone. So I had plenty to do in the meantime. I was still waiting for the answer from Berlin which was to sanction my conspiracy with Huerta. It arrived eventually, and informed me that money was being held for the day when Mexican troops would be ready to commence hostilities against America, and that German submarines and auxiliary cruisers would appear on the Mexican coast to lend their support. It appeared to be a matter of ultimate indifference to Germany whether the United States maintained her secret enmity by supplying munitions to the Allies, or came openly into the War on their side.

On receiving the German Government's reply I drove to the Manhattan Hotel, but Huerta was not there. I learned from one of his friends that he was expected back in New York at any moment ; so I waited. He had gone to the Mexican frontier to discuss matters with his party ; but though I waited and waited, he did not return. I sent my agents out to search for him throughout America, but they could not discover a trace. Though I mobilised all my forces, the difficulty of finding one man in such a large country was enormous. Boniface came to me one day, and I told him that Huerta must be discovered at all costs. He thought that the American Federal Police must know his whereabouts, since they were probably shadowing him as an enemy of the States. Some days went by without news, and I was very worried, since I was anxious to see the ripening of the seeds I had sown. One evening, as I was returning from a social function, I was walking along in evening-dress to find a taxi, when a man passed me from behind with a swift step. I took no notice of him, but suddenly heard the words :

" You are being watched. Look out ! Don't wait for Huerta. He has been poisoned."

I kept my control and followed the man with my eyes. I recognised the gait of Mr. Boniface. When I got into my taxi I was followed by a second car. Boniface was right. I was being watched. Later I heard that Huerta had been poisoned by his cook in a country house on the Mexican border, though no details of his death were ever made public. What actually became of him, I never found out.

Though I was aware that the police were on my track I resolved to hold out. I had always been so careful that they could have no direct and clear proof that I had

had a finger in so many " shady " transactions. When I entered my bank next morning, the official who always attended to my business—he was a German, knew my identity, and had often helped me—beckoned to me and gave me a letter. I read the address and grew pale. On the envelope were the words, " *Herrn Kapitänleutnant Rintelen, Hochwohlgeboren.*" The official whispered to me that the letter had arrived by post, and that there had been considerable excitement at the bank at the discovery that a German officer had a very large account through which enormous sums were being passed. Was the letter a trap ? I decided to open it nevertheless, and saw it was from the Military Attaché of the Embassy. I was furious at his thoughtlessness and stupidity in addressing me in such a fashion. Or was it done deliberately ?

I had not time, however, to yield to gloomy forebodings, for I was in the thick of activities whose threads met in my hands. Responsibility lay heavy on my shoulders. In spite of Huerta's death I tried to get the Mexican affair going again, and I was still absorbed in my plans when, on the morning of June 6th, 1915, an attendant came to me in the breakfast-room of the New York Yacht Club and gave me a message to ring up a certain number. The Naval Attaché was at the other end of the telephone, and he asked me to meet him at a particular street corner. When I arrived he handed me a telegram, which ran as follows :

" To the Naval Attaché at the Embassy. Captain Rintelen is to be informed unobtrusively that he is under instructions to return to Germany."

SABOTAGE

What was that? Had I not, but a few weeks ago, distinctly asked Headquarters in Berlin *not* to cable my name at all, but to send me in writing, in a carefully considered way, their reply to my most recent suggestion?—the suggestion that we should now proceed to buy up, in a guarded fashion, the majority of shares in such American corporations as were, under their own charter, not supposed to engage in the manufacture of ammunition or accessories. That appeared, after all, quite a good scheme, one which might have thrown a wedge into the machinery of Yankee munitions- and money-making.

Many years later—when I finally came home from this " Odyssey "—as late as 1921, *Anno Domini*, I learned that this suggestion had met with the approval of all and sundry in Berlin, even with that of the President of the Reichsbank, Dr. Havenstein, but was opposed by— Bethmann Hollweg !

I could not understand why this telegram had been sent to me, and only knew that if I obeyed it immediately, I should leave things in frightful confusion behind me. The Irish were relying on me, our strikes had begun to boom again, and we were still placing bombs on the transports. All this would now come to an end. I wondered whether I had fallen a victim to intrigues, such as were usually concerned only with the " big guns " at home, or possibly to one of the many intrigues which the Baronin Schröder of the Tiergartenstrasse was so fond of? She kept a political " salon " in Berlin, where everybody and anybody flocked : Falkenhayn, old Count Zeppelin and Police-President von Jagow, General

THE DARK INVADER

Hoffmann, Dr. Stauss and Erzberger—and I was a " pet " of hers too ; but who knows ? For some two years later she shot herself, after having been "found out " to have been an all-too-frequent guest at the American Embassy.

Or was I being recalled to Berlin in order to report how matters stood in America ?

At any rate I decided that " obedience ", in the loftier sense of the word, might still admit an appropriate interpretation of the recall-order, and I therefore wound up my business—unobtrusively, however, while I calmed my friends and helpmates with the assurance that within four weeks I should be " on the job " again, for I was convinced I could run the British blockade and pass to and fro at my convenience.

The word " fear " did not and does not exist in my vocabulary ; so danger or no danger, the journey *had* to be made, for I was a German officer and had to obey orders. I fetched out my Swiss passport and managed to obtain a letter of recommendation to Count Ignatieff, the Russian Military Attaché in Paris. He was, as I have said, a celebrated connoisseur of claret, and I soon had documents printed to provide evidence that I was a Swiss citizen travelling to France from the United States to purchase wines.

Now that I was about to leave the shores of America I felt like taking a carbolic bath.

PART III

BLIGHTY
A Guest at Donington Hall

I AGAIN became E. V. Gaché from Solothurn, and booked a passage on the *Noordam*, of the Holland-American Line. Accompanying me was a man whom I had engaged to help me during the crossing. He was a genuine American citizen and appeared in public as my friend.

I went on board full of despair at the thought of the work I had left unfinished; and as we left New York Harbour in the evening twilight I tortured myself with the mystery of the telegram which had ordered me to return. My companion pulled me out of the depression into which I had fallen, by announcing that he was hungry and it was time for dinner. He was powerfully built and had crossed the ocean more than once to give advice to the German Government. He had hit upon a splendid idea which gave him time to think when anyone addressed him unawares. He pretended to be stone deaf and always carried a gigantic ear-trumpet about with him. Every question had to be thundered into the trumpet, and this enabled him to prepare his answers. We descended to the dining-room and I ordered a bottle of wine to disperse my unenviable thoughts. As I looked round I received a dreadful shock. Sitting at a table opposite was a man whom I had known well in Berlin and had often met at dances, Count Limburg-Stirum, of the Dutch branch of the family. I must have grown pale, for my companion whispered:

" What's the matter ? "

Limburg-Stirum had already crossed over to greet me, and asked : " Do you think you are going to get across safely ? "

I registered astonishment and replied :

" Why not ? "

" Well, after all, you are a German ! "

" I ? A German ? Good heavens, I am a Swiss. In those days I was attached to the Swiss Legation in Berlin."

Limburg-Stirum looked at me in amazement. He hung round me during the whole crossing. He had of course seen my name " E. V. Gaché " on the door of my cabin and at my place at table, but he was certain that that had not been my name when he knew me in Berlin. Every time I saw him I had an odd feeling that he was going to remember just at that moment who I was, so I kept out of his way.

The good ship *Noordam* continued her voyage, and at last the chalk cliffs of England lay to port. I gazed at them with mixed feelings. It took a whole day to pass them, and I found it necessary to visit the bar at intervals to fortify myself. The chalk cliffs still lay on our left, when early in the morning, at seven o'clock on Friday, August 13th, as I was lying in my bath, a steward knocked at the door, and said :

" Some British officers wish to have a word with you."

This was the darkest moment of my life !

Nobody who had done what I considered it my duty to do in America, and was in possession of a forged passport, would have been anxious to converse with British officers opposite the white cliffs of England. Certainly not before breakfast. But I had no alternative. These gentlemen desired to speak with me, and there was no possibility of avoiding their welcome. I put my head outside and listened. The officers were not inspecting the other passengers, but had inquired exclusively for me, and I can truthfully say that it made an impression on me. I had an immediate intuition that I was discovered, and the only thing that could help me now was " bluff."

I went on deck in my bath-robe and found two officers and ten sailors with fixed bayonets waiting for me.

" You are Mr. Gaché ? "

" Yes. What can I do for you ? "

" We have orders to take you with us."

" I have no intention of disembarking here. I am going to Rotterdam."

" I am sorry. If you refuse, we have orders to take you by force."

" If you threaten me with force I have no alternative, as a Swiss citizen, but to follow you. Before I leave the boat, however, I demand the right to telegraph to the Minister of my country in London. In any case, I must dress and, above all, have breakfast. I am sure you will agree."

" How much time do you need ? "

" About two hours."

" All right. We shall return at nine-thirty."

Punctually at nine-thirty the British escort came on

board again and politely requested the Swiss gentleman to enter a steam pinnace. I was then taken on board a British auxiliary cruiser, where I was kept for three days. Morning, afternoon, and evening there was a bottle of champagne available in the captain's cabin, presented by the British officers to keep the Swiss citizen, whom they all pitied so, in a good humour. One evening one of the officers poured his heart out to me. He told me that he had been Consul in Karlsbad for seven years, knew all the German dialects, and could tell whether a man was justified or not in claiming to be a " neutral." He was tired of being the scapegoat every time a neutral traveller had to be put through the mill on his way up the Channel. He was completely fed-up. " But," he said, " there is a fellow sitting in London who never gives up, and when we capture a neutral, we have to carry out our job as best we can. Just imagine ! There's an old bear with a sore head in charge of the Department, and he's got a fixed idea that every neutral is suspect."

" Who is he ? "

" Admiral Hall."

.   .   .   .   .

On the last day of my stay on board the cruiser I was subjected to a surprise. I was confronted with my deaf American friend, who had also been taken off the *Noordam* as a suspicious character. He was being questioned on deck by an officer, who pointed at me.

" Wait a minute," cried my friend. With slow and deliberate movements he began to extract his great ear-

BLIGHTY

trumpet from his case. The electric battery failed to function at once, so he turned a few screws and said to the officer: "Excuse me just a moment." He then applied the trumpet to his ear and roared:

"What did you say?"

The officer saw his great confrontation scene ruined, and turned crustily away without deigning to reply. My friend shouted to me:

"What are these people saying?" and then proceeded to run about the deck, as he fiddled with his ear-trumpet, and to call out continually to the officers on the bridge: "What do you want of me? What's that you say?"

It was easy for him, since he had a genuine passport and nothing much to fear. My position was more serious.

We were taken ashore at Ramsgate. We were examined, our papers were inspected, we were re-examined, and our papers once more inspected, and in the interval we were taken with great courtesy by car to an hotel and invited to tea. In the lounge I saw a man, a waiter, whom I had seen before somewhere, and I suddenly remembered. He had been at the Hôtel Bristol in Berlin, where I used to be a frequent visitor. As we drank our tea I informed my deaf friend in a whisper of my disturbing discovery.

"That makes another old friend we've met," he complained. "Can't we go anywhere in the world without meeting somebody you know?"

We returned to headquarters.

"Please show your passports again for inspection."

"Yes, of course. Passport inspection."

We entered the room, and stationed in the corner I saw the waiter from the Bristol. I told myself to keep cool. The officer in charge, the Rt. Hon. Dudley Ward, M.P., a very eminent man, put to me the same questions that I had had to answer in the morning. Suddenly a shrill voice, full of hate and fury, broke in from the corner:

" Don't talk such rubbish ! You are Captain Rintelen from Berlin."

I did not move an eyelash, for I had caught sight of the man in time, but calmly replied to the officer's question. A man talking nonsense in the corner had nothing to do with me ! It was a pity there were such ill-bred people about.

The man roared again :

" You stop that ! You are the German Captain Rintelen. I've known you for a long time."

It would have been suspicious if I had continued to take no notice, so I turned round towards him and said in astonishment :

" What's that ? "

My deaf friend joined in and shouted, as he fixed his ear-trumpet :

" What's the man saying ? What does he want of me ? Or is he talking to you ? "

His trumpet being by now adjusted, I thundered down it :

" There's somebody saying that I am . . ." I turned to the waiter. " What was the name ? Will you spell it, please ? "

ADMIRAL SIR WILLIAM REGINALD HALL, K.C.M.G., C.B.,
D.C.L., LL.D.

FRESH FROM DELIVERING SIR ROGER CASEMENT

A GENERAL VIEW OF DONINGTON HALL

THE FAMOUS BARBED-WIRE FENCE

THE BRIDGE OF SIGHS : THE TOMBS, NEW YORK

THE "BIG ROCK," FULTON COUNTY, ATLANTA
SO CALLED BY APPREHENSIVE MEMBERS OF THE
BLACK POPULATION

OUTSIDE VIEW GRAND HOTEL, ATLANTA : MAIN ENTRANCE

INSIDE VIEW, GRAND HOTEL, ATLANTA : THE CELLS

BLIGHTY

An alphabetic pandemonium broke loose, and there was grotesque confusion between the English *a* and the German *e*. The name I shouted into the American's trumpet was one that had never existed. The sounds were all distorted, and we got thoroughly mixed up, until at last the American packed his trumpet into its case and said angrily :

" I've had enough."

To which I replied : " There are always ill-bred people in this world who insist on interfering with bona fide travellers."

The officer motioned the waiter, who was a Belgian, out of the room with an impatient gesture, then went to the telephone and reported that a mistake seemed to have been made. To our astonishment and my boundless joy we were allowed to return to the *Noordam*. Our luggage was already on board, and the Fatherland beckoned.

As the pinnace approached the ship, the British officer stationed on it called through his megaphone :

" Turn back ! "

When we were on shore again, I was separated from my companion and taken by train, under the escort of a detective and a naval officer, to London, where, to my amazement, I was driven to Scotland Yard. The storm was about to burst.

We entered a building like a castle, and crossed a courtyard to a mighty curved staircase. Through broad corridors instilling an atmosphere of peaceful dignity we came to a door which opened suddenly and admitted us to a room occupied by a group of naval officers in gold-encrusted uniforms. It was not long before I learned that two of them, who wore the *aiguillettes* of royal aides-de-camp, were Admiral Sir Reginald Hall, the Chief of the British Naval Intelligence Service, and his right-hand man, Lord Herschell. To the left of the fireplace stood a heavy table, behind which sat the Chief of the C.I.D., Sir Basil Thomson, wearing horn-rimmed spectacles.

This pleasant gathering in my honour offered exciting prospects. They all sat there and bored me through with malevolent eyes. Admiral Hall stood up.

" Do you know a Captain Rintelen ? "

" I am not obliged to answer you."

Sir Basil Thomson :

" You apparently do not know where you are ! "

" Wherever I am, I have been brought by force. I have no business here and I shall not reply to any questions until I have spoken with the Minister of my country. Or am I, perhaps, to be charged with a crime ? "

Sir Basil Thomson :

" You are a German and have to explain why you are on English soil."

" I did not land on English soil of my own free will. I was brought here by force in violation of all justice."

My reply caused a great uproar. Hall and Thomson grew irritated, while I pretended to get angry and, keeping faithfully to my rôle, began to shout that I protested against the whole proceedings and demanded to be taken to the Swiss Minister. I insisted on this right, until they actually became uncertain of their case.

But my faithful " A.D.C.," the Naval Officer who

had accompanied me from Ramsgate promptly bet me
a sovereign that I shouldn't even be admitted.   By the
way, he paid up like a gentleman—after the War !

The meeting broke up, and I was informed that I
should be escorted at once to the Swiss Legation.   The
Minister, M. Gaston Carlin, was a dignified old gentleman, tall and with white hair, and he spoke to me in
German.

" Now, tell me," he said, " what this is all about.
I was unable to do anything when your telegram arrived,
since I was away for the week-end.   What do the English
want with you ?   I have heard from my office that your
passports and military papers are in order, but the
English maintain obstinately that you are the German
Captain Rintelen.   Can you explain how they conceived
the idea ? "

I decided to risk a great bluff.

" I can disclose it to you, Your Excellency," I said.
" Captain Rintelen really was on the boat, but the British
have got hold of the wrong man.   The *Noordam*, as I
have read in *The Times*, has already reached Rotterdam,
and the German officer, whom I did not want to betray
to the English, is far away by now.   You see, Your
Excellency, my sympathies are with Germany.   I spent
my boyhood there, and you will remember that my father
was Swiss Consul at Leipzig."

" Oh, yes !   I remember your father.   Your attitude
has been quite correct."

He came from behind his desk and stretched out his
hand.

" Accept my thanks for your truly neutral conduct."

He telephoned in my presence to the Admiralty and communicated the disconcerting solution of the mystery, after which my escort took me back to Admiral Hall. Everybody was foaming with rage at having let the German captain slip through their hands, but the Admiral, who alone remained perfectly calm, came up to me and said :

" So you are not Rintelen ? "

" I gave all explanations to my Minister."

Nevertheless I was not immediately set at liberty. I was to be kept in custody until the evening of the following day, and should then be allowed to resume my journey. Two " adjutants " were attached to me, a naval commander and a detective, and I took up my quarters at the Hotel Cecil. I felt that the battle was won, and ordered a drink. Nothing could happen to me, and I only had to wait for the settling of a few formalities. I began to wonder how soon I could be in Berlin.

My two companions sat in the adjoining room, with the communicating door ajar, so that they might keep an eye on me and see that I did not escape. I walked to and fro and heard them conversing. Suddenly a remark was dropped which made me prick up my ears and listen intently :

" . . . a special inquiry in Berne by the British Legation ? "

" Yes. It isn't merely a consular matter. Admiral Hall has specially asked the Legation to find out whether it is possible that Emile Gaché is now in London."

BLIGHTY

I had heard enough to know that my position was serious, that I had lost the fight, when a minute before I had been convinced that I had won. I raged round the room. The Legation in Berne was bound to discover that the real Emile Gaché was living in Switzerland and could not now be in London. When the English knew that, I should be in a hole.

I reasoned as follows: as I had been the only passenger, with the exception of the American, to be examined and taken off the boat, they must be aware that I had embarked on the *Noordam* in New York, and if they knew that they must possess information concerning what I had been doing in America. That meant that a blow had been struck against us in the United States, which I had only escaped by my departure. When the answer arrived from Berne, I should be regarded as a civilian and sent back to America in custody, where a disagreeable welcome would await me. Whatever happened, they would not let me go, so it was better to be a prisoner of war than to be sent to an American jail. After I had rapidly reviewed the situation, I knocked at the door and said to one of my " warders " :

" Excuse me. Is it possible to have a word with Admiral Hall at once ? "

" I don't think so. What do you want ? Is it so urgent ? "

" Yes, it is. Admiral Hall will be highly interested in what I have to say to him."

" Well, tell me then."

THE DARK INVADER

" No. I cannot do that. I must speak to the Admiral himself."

He went to the telephone. It was already eight in the evening, but the Admiral was still in his office and prepared to receive me at once. Rain was streaming down as we crossed the courtyard of the Admiralty. Hall was standing in his room, and asked :

" What brings you here at so late an hour ? "

I stood to attention :

" I surrender."

" What do you mean ? We have just wired to Berne on your account . . ."

" That is why I have come. It is no longer necessary."

" What does all this mean ? "

" Captain Rintelen begs to report to you, sir, as a prisoner of war."

The Admiral dropped into his seat. He gazed at me, rocked a little in his chair, then sprang up and clapped me on the shoulder as he growled appreciatively : " That was well done." He tore open the door to the adjoining room, called in Lord Herschell and said : " Let me introduce you to our latest prisoner of war, Kapitänleutnant von Rintelen ! "

Herschell turned on his heel, went into his own office, and returned with a bottle and three glasses.

" Sit down," he said, " and let's have a cocktail to get over the shock. You are fond of cocktails, aren't you ? "

" What do you mean ? How do you know that ? "

Herschell replied :

" From New York ! "

BLIGHTY

It was growing late, and the two officers proposed that we should dine together before I was sent to a concentration camp. We drove to a club to which they both belonged, and entered the dining-room in which a large number of British officers were sitting.

" I wonder what they'd say if they knew who you were," Herschell remarked.

The Admiral selected a table in a corner where we could be alone and talk quietly. He and Lord Herschell naturally had a lot that they wanted to ask me, and in order to make me loquacious they told me things which gave me a thrill of horror as I listened. Certainly they did not reveal any important secrets. They were only, in their own view, giving me a few details of the world-embracing activity of the Naval Intelligence Service, yet it grew clear to me that during the whole of the War we had undertaken practically nothing without the British Secret Service having previously acquired information about our intended moves. I spent a long evening with the two Englishmen and learned much of which I had hitherto been ignorant.

" You need not have waited so long for that cocktail I gave you at the Admiralty, Captain," said Lord Herschell.

" So long ? "

" We expected you four weeks ago. Our preparations had been made for your reception, but you took your time. Why did you not leave New York as soon as you got the telegram ? "

What was that ? What was he saying ? There are times when one cannot trust one's own ears !

THE DARK INVADER

" Beyond a doubt, Kapitänleutnant," Admiral Hall went on, " it will hurt your feelings as a German officer, but it was not so much the work of our own agents that you fell into our hands! You may thank your Naval or Military Attachés for that—whichever of the two it may have been. I don't know. . . . Were you always in full harmony with—er—Captain von Papen . . . ? "

" What do you mean by that, sir ? "

" Still something unpleasant for you to hear. There must be a certain limit to human recklessness . . . he wired and wirelessed your name so often to Berlin in good honest straightforward German that he just played you into our hands. It seemed almost deliberate. . . ."

I was tongue-tied. I had been betrayed! They seemed to know everything—my sudden recall . . . everything. With an effort I harked back to the earlier topic of conversation.

" I don't get your meaning, Lord Herschell. Which of the telegrams were you talking about ? "

Admiral Hall bent over the table towards me. He pushed his spectacles aside, looked at me keenly, and said with pointed sarcasm :

" We mean the telegram which you received on July the 6th, that is to say, a month ago. Captain Boy-Ed met you at the corner of Fifth Avenue and Forty-fifth Street, where he handed you the wire and—just wait a minute—I'll read you the text."

He put his hand in his breast pocket and drew out a

small packet of papers, one of which he extracted and, to my astonishment, read out as follows :

" To the German Embassy, for the Naval Attaché. Captain Rintelen is to be informed unobtrusively that he is under instructions to return to Germany."

" What do you say to that ? " he asked. " Were we not right in saying that you took your time ? "

A certain macabre humour, which I had managed to retain up till then, began to desert me.

How had this telegram come into their hands at all ? Surely it must have been in cipher ? But to judge from the course of events it couldn't have been !

I sat back in my chair and thought of the day when Boniface had appeared in my office and gloomily reported that the " Most Secret Code " had been " borrowed " from the Naval Attaché by British " representatives."

The Admiral was watching me closely.

" The telegrams to Count Spee, the Admiral in command of the cruiser squadron . . ." murmured Lord Herschell casually, and as though absorbed in thought.

This was something new ! Admiral Spee had encountered the English battle-cruisers on December 8th, 1914 ; yet Herschell was apparently going to say that telegrams sent to him had also been intercepted, though the theft at the Attaché's office had not taken place until much later. I wanted to know the true state of affairs, so I said abruptly :

" But it was long after December 1914 that the code was copied ! "

Hall shot at me:

" When did you say we had the code copied ? "

This seemed a trap. He obviously wanted to find out if I knew when and how the code had been given away. I thought quickly. As a prisoner of war in England I was bound to get news through to Germany sooner or later, and I wanted to learn as many details as I could. It could do no harm if I told the Admiral that I knew how the code had come into their hands.

" Oh," I said, " you mean that affair in New York, when you put that young woman on to the secretary at the Embassy ? Every child has heard of that ! "

They looked at me a little dazed. Hall slowly ground out:

" Every child has heard of it, eh ? "

An uneasy silence ensued—and during this silence a hideous thought flashed into my mind. Why, why, why had they paused just then ? Could they be implying that the " children " at the Embassy itself had not ?

This was a shock. I had always been afraid of what would happen, even though I had sent a written warning to Berlin after my conversation with Boy-Ed, stating that the code had fallen into the hands of the enemy and urging that it should be changed as quickly as possible. I knew that my message had arrived safely in Berlin, but it had apparently been disregarded. The two Englishmen regained their composure and the conversation went on. I felt fully entitled to draw my own conclusions. Somehow or other they had got hold of the first code. My imagination ran riot. Perhaps they had recovered it from one of our early casualties . . . the cruiser *Magdeburg*, say, that went down off Kronstadt. Disastrous for us, but how, how, convenient for them! And then I had crossed with the new code, and they seemed to have been advised of the change over.

I looked longingly at the cocktails.

And then they had got hold of the new code as well.

And I poured myself out another glass.

It would be understating the case merely to say that I was horrified. What could the British not do to injure Germany if they could read the telegrams which were sent out all over the world from Berlin! It did not bear thinking of. I clung to a single hope—I must find a way to let them know at home that the code was no longer secret. I went hot and cold, for I had already sent a warning in those very terms to Germany, after I had learnt of the theft from Boniface, and what happened? They were still employing the same code on their wireless! If they had taken no notice of my first warning, it was only too likely that a second would also find its way into the waste-paper basket. I had just witnessed the dazed faces of the two British officers when they learned that I was aware of the theft of the code. They must have realised that I would not have kept the information to myself, but had passed it on to Berlin, and they could not conceive why the same code was still being used. I was in despair. There I was, a prisoner in a London club, with no opportunity to shriek into the ears of the German authorities :

"Are you bent on committing suicide? Are you blind and deaf? Haven't I already warned you? For God's sake, throw the code into the fire!"

It was ghastly, but I forced myself to keep calm. The mischief could not, for the time being, be averted and would have to take its course. In order to take my mind off it I said to Lord Herschell:

" What was that you were saying about telegrams sent to Count Spee?"

Herschell looked up and replied:

" Thank you for reminding me, Captain. We are the hosts and must do all we can to entertain our guest. You shall hear the story."

He then told me his story of Admiral Spee's defeat. Although, as I later discovered, he added quite a few trimmings not absolutely in accordance with the facts, his narrative was substantially true, and as such I recount it here.

Admiral Spee was cruising with his squadron some-where about the seven seas, and London could discover no reliable clue as to his whereabouts. The British Admiralty was, however, perfectly aware that the exis-tence of his squadron constituted a menace to Allied shipping, and it proceeded with stern logic to encompass Spee's destruction. In order to join battle with any prospect of success it was necessary to detach from the Fleet two battle-cruisers of the latest type. The splendid armament of the *Scharnhorst* and the *Gneisenau*, which belonged to Spee's squadron, could not otherwise be equalled. It was also essential to discover where Spee would be on a certain day, if the two pursuing cruisers were to have the opportunity to come into action, and a plan was formed for this purpose. First, however, two large cruisers had to be freed from routine duties.

This could only be done secretly, for if the German Naval Staff got wind of the fact that two powerful British battle-cruisers were steering for the Atlantic, it was bound to realise that their objective was Spee's squadron, and this had to be avoided at all costs.

Due weight was given to the fact that the German Navy must be fully aware of the presence of the majority of the British battle-cruisers in the North Sea, and that two of them had been detached for service in the Mediterranean, where they were stationed near the Dardanelles for the purpose of blocking the exit of the *Goeben*. They also took into account the probability that this German ship would try to break out and make for Pola, in order to strengthen the backbone of the Austrians. They could not simply send two cruisers to chase Admiral Spee, since their disappearance would soon be noticed by German agents, who were to be found everywhere. Their absence from their anchorage had to be camouflaged as an indispensable condition of success, and it could only be done by a stratagem.

Admiral Hall had a brilliant idea. He arranged for two new cruisers to be built secretly at an English dockyard, and they were ready in a few weeks. They were painted grey, and lay there with great funnels and heavy guns poking their muzzles threateningly from the armoured turrets. They were, however, only wooden

models, and as soon as they were finished two large tugs
appeared, which attached hawsers and towed the mon-
sters out to sea. Officers stood on the bridge of each
tug to keep a sharp eye open for signs of enemy ships,
and if anything of a suspicious nature hove in sight they
set smoke-screens in action ; for it was, of course, essential for the success of the scheme that the existence of
the models should be kept absolutely secret. They were
towed through the Bay of Biscay, past Gibraltar, and
through the Mediterranean to the Aegean Sea, where the
Invincible and the *Inflexible* were at anchor. These two
cruisers had been there for weeks, in full sight of the
inhabitants of the islands, among whom were agents
whose main duty was to make sure that they were still
there. Under cover of darkness the imitation cruisers
were drawn alongside, and to the eyes of possible
watchers on shore there was nothing to distinguish them
from the real men-o'-war they had come to replace. They
were surrounded by a numerous escort of torpedo and
patrol boats, which prevented them from being blown
up by mines or submarines and, which was of greatest
importance, kept curious strangers at a distance.

The wooden vessels were still rocking on the waves,
and had not yet dropped anchor, when the *Invincible* and
the *Inflexible* put out to sea. They ploughed their way
unobserved through the Mediterranean, and the German
Intelligence Service had no inkling of the fact that two
dangerous foes had set out to look for Admiral Spee.
After passing Gibraltar they set their helms sharply to
the south-west.

BLIGHTY

When Lord Herschell reached this point I interrupted him:

"Why did they turn to the south-west? They must have known where Spee was."

"We knew where he *would* be," replied Herschell, looking at Admiral Hall.

The Admiral continued to gaze in front of him. "I had telegraphed to him," he said softly, "to let him know where the British cruisers were to meet him—and he kept the appointment."

I pushed my chair back a little from the table and laughed.

"Excuse me, Sir Reginald, it is not very kind of you to pull a poor prisoner's leg in this way. You do not expect me to believe that?"

I looked into the Admiral's grave face and knew instinctively that what Lord Herschell had told me was true. But I could not conceive how he had been able to send a wire to Spee. What on earth did he mean? He began to explain, and I began to understand.

They never did anything by halves. Our people in New York were careless in regard to the code. They had taken precautions to ensure that the two cruisers should not miss their objective. They knew what they were doing. I suspected already that they were in possession of the German Secret Code. Bearing this in mind, I began to understand what they did. Spee and his squadron were bound to turn up somewhere, and most probably off the west coast of South America. The surmise was correct. On the evening of November the 1st, 1914, came the horrifying news that Spee had destroyed Admiral Cradock's squadron off Coronel. He had steamed away from the scene of battle in the direction of Valparaiso, and the news of his arrival was, of course, at once cabled in. They knew that he had gone ashore with his officers and had been welcomed by the German colony. So he was in Valparaiso.

Hall began to reconstruct his plan of action on the table with a variety of miscellaneous objects.

There was Valparaiso, a matchbox, here the two cruisers, and another matchbox for Berlin. There was Berlin. There Valparaiso and Count Spee. Here the two cruisers. Here was Berlin, and in Berlin was——

" Your man ? " I burst out.

" My man," he said calmly; " my agent. I had instructed him to find out how telegrams were sent from the German Admiralty to the ships which were still at sea. He informed me that the method was quite simple. When such a telegram had to be dispatched, a messenger was sent from the Admiralty to the chief telegraph office to hand it over. They used special forms, and the telegram had to be furnished with the stamp of the relevant Admiralty department and also the stamp of the censor's office. I do not know how my agent managed it, nor do I think that I should have been interested. All I know is that he possessed both stamps and forms, and I have no doubt that he used them.

" You will remember that Spee was at anchor with his squadron off Valparaiso. As soon as I was in possession of this information, I sent my agent in Berlin instructions to act. He had been carrying for some weeks a telegram that I had sent from London, set up in Boy-Ed's Code, and containing strict orders for Admiral Spee to leave immediately for the Falkland Islands and destroy the wireless station at Port Stanley."

"You have no need to tell me the rest," I said with profound emotion. "I know what happened afterwards, since I was serving at the Admiralty in Berlin at the time."

After Spee had had an interview with the German Minister to Chile in Valparaiso, he summoned his chief of staff and the commanders of his cruisers to a conference. They all tried to dissuade him from carrying out the plan he unfolded to them of steaming round Cape Horn and making for the Falklands. The Chief of Staff argued that this route might bring them face to face with great danger. The squadron might be rendered *hors de combat* and its value for any further operations of war destroyed. Spee kept to himself the fact that he had received a secret telegram, addressed to "The Admiral Commanding Squadron—*Personal*," and merely told his officers that he intended to carry out his original plan. The order he was obeying was, however, fictitious.

The end came as Hall had designed. Admiral Sturdee appeared with the *Invincible* and the *Inflexible*, on December the 7th, at the rendezvous which had been "appointed" for the German Admiral; and the two forces came to grips but twelve hours later. The death-struggle of the German squadron against a superior weight of guns lasted only a few hours, until about noon of December the 8th, 1914.

The Kaiser added a manuscript note at the time to the Report of the disaster :

" It remains a riddle what made Spee attack the Falkland Islands. See Mahan's *Naval Strategy*."

(That writer states in no uncertain terms that it is no business of a ship to attack land fortifications.)

. . . . .

The conversation, which was concluded at this point, was continued by Admiral Hall and myself many years later, long after the War. It was in 1925, and we sat in the same corner of the same club, where he received his former enemy in the most chivalrous fashion, to become, as years went by, a sincere and loyal friend !

I should like here to jump across the years, for both conversations have become woven together in my memory.

As we sat and exchanged War memories, the Admiral happened to mention the name of Huerta.

Huerta ! At that time, in 1915, it was from me that the suggestion to launch Huerta against the United States had come. The provision of arms and munitions and the dispatch of U-boats had been stipulated in the agreement. It had been an extremely risky project, and I had sent a reliable courier to Berlin with a letter which I was sure had not been read by anyone on the way. I could not then foresee that the negotiations with Mexico would later on be continued in a way which was to change the whole trend of events. My intrigue was taken up by others, with the eventual result that whereas Mexico did not enter the War, the United States took up arms against us. It was my intention that Mexico should attack the United States, if we definitely proclaimed unrestricted submarine warfare against all and sundry. We should, in that case, have to reckon with America's entry into the conflict, and we wanted to tie our new opponent to her own border. This could only be done if we could succeed in putting Huerta in power again, since otherwise there was no prospect of persuading Mexico to attack the United States.

Admiral Hall began the conversation by showing me a document. " There is no longer any point," he said, " in denying to me, your trusty old enemy, that you tried to get Huerta to co-operate with you. Your idea was worked out by others, but with the Mexican President Carranza, not with Huerta."

I picked up the paper, which lay in front of me.

" That is the Zimmermann telegram," I replied. " Of course, I know it. Everyone who is interested in the history of the War will remember that you intercepted it, when Zimmermann, who was at that time Under-Secretary at the Foreign Office, sent it to the German Minister in Mexico City, von Eckhardt. It is also a matter of common knowledge that this affair was the cause of America's entering the War on the side of the Allies."

At that moment Hall was called away by an attendant,

and I had leisure to recall everything that had happened in consequence of the famous Zimmermann telegram. I read the text once more.

On January the 16th, 1917, Zimmermann wired to Eckhardt as follows :

> " We shall commence unrestricted U-boat warfare on February the 1st. Nevertheless we hope to keep the United States neutral. If we should not succeed in this, we shall propose to Mexico an alliance on the following terms : We shall wage war and conclude peace in common. We shall provide general financial support, and stipulate that Mexico shall receive back the territory of New Mexico and Arizona which she lost in 1848. The details will be left to you to carry out. You are instructed to sound Carranza in the strictest confidence, and as soon as war against the United States is certain you will give him a hint to enter into negotiations with Japan on his own initiative, requesting her to join in and offering to act as intermediary between Japan and Germany. Draw Carranza's attention to the fact that the carrying out of unrestricted U-boat warfare will make it possible to bring England to her knees and compel her to sue for peace within a few months. Confirm receipt. Zimmermann."

That was the Zimmermann telegram.

I thought over the various ways in which the German Foreign Office was able at that time to send wires to America. There were four possibilities, each of which was taken advantage of. Every important telegram from Berlin to America was dispatched by four different routes.

BLIGHTY

In the first place, there was wireless, and messages transmitted directly across the ocean in this way were in code. Secondly, every telegram was sent to Stockholm, set up in the secret cipher of the Swedish Foreign Office, and either cabled or sent by wireless to the German Ambassador in Washington. Thirdly, every telegram was wired to Holland, and simultaneously, by one route or another, to Spain, whence the Attaché in charge of this duty cabled it to New York in the same cipher used when messages were sent direct from Berlin. Finally, the Foreign Office had thought of a fourth way, the consequences of which were particularly disastrous. It had accepted one day an offer from the Government of the United States, made through the American Ambassador in Berlin, to transmit German Foreign Office telegrams through the American Embassy. They would thus be cabled to Washington without an enemy Power having the opportunity to intercept or delay them.

The Zimmermann telegram was, in addition, sent by a fifth route. It went direct from Berlin by wireless to the newly constructed radio station on Mexican territory.

The Foreign Office, however, thought the matter over once more before it finally decided to use these five routes. In view of the extraordinary important contents of the telegram, it tried to think of an absolutely safe way, and resolved to entrust it to the U-boat *Deutschland*, which was to leave Bremerhaven for North America on January the 15th, 1917. War with the United States was, however, already threatening, and the *Deutschland*,

which was a mercantile submarine, was attached to the
Navy and her voyage cancelled.

. . . . .

I was smoothing out the document thoughtfully, when
Admiral Hall returned.

" Do you know," he asked, " how many routes were
used to send telegrams to America ? "

I did know, for there was nothing unusual in a
German officer who had served on the Staff at the
Admiralty being in possession of such information. But
it was extraordinary that Admiral Hall also knew. He
began by telling me that the Zimmermann telegram had
been radioed direct to New York, and I was not surprised
to hear that it had been intercepted and deciphered. It
was common knowledge, for its text had been published
in the United States. Hall told me, however, that the
Stockholm route had not been safe either, for the British
possessed the key to the Secret Code of the Swedish
Foreign Office as well. The third way, via Holland and
Spain, was no better than the other two, since England
had agents in her pay in the post offices of those coun-
tries, who passed the German wires on to the Naval
Intelligence ; and they were in the code that Admiral
Hall was able to read. A telegram handed in by the
German Naval Attaché at Madrid led eventually to Mata
Hari being shot at Vincennes !

Even the fourth route, through the American Embassy
in Berlin, was accessible to Admiral Hall, for I now
learnt that Mr. Gerard, even when the United States

were completely neutral, sent our telegrams by cable to the chief telegraph office in London for transmission to America. Since the English were in possession of the key, and Gerard let them know which wires came from the German Government, they had no difficulty in reading them.

Thus none of the five routes was secret, and they all led to Admiral Hall.

"When we first intercepted the Zimmermann telegram," he continued, "we said nothing."

The British kept their knowledge to themselves, but it was quite clear to them that they now possessed an instrument which could bring the United States into the War on their side. If the telegram were to be published in America, it would give rise to a storm of indignation against Germany which the United States Government would certainly not be able to ignore. It would not dare to fly in the face of public anger. If it did refuse to act, it would find itself in an extremely uncomfortable situation, since the United States had always been afraid of the danger which might come from both Mexico and Japan. These two countries were nightmares, the thought of which disturbed the comfortable beds of American citizens, and they would turn with fury on the Power which had the temerity to conjure them up.

"And what did you do then?" I asked. "It is obvious that you waited for a favourable opportunity. And then?"

Hall carefully picked up one of the documents lying before him, smiled, and turned it over. He pushed it towards me and I read the text. It was a telegram from Mr. Walter H. Page, the United States Ambassador in London, dated February the 24th, 1917 :

> " To the Secretary of State, Washington. Number 5746. In about three hours I shall despatch a telegram of the greatest importance for the President and the Secretary of State. Page."

Hall turned another sheet and showed me the telegram which Page sent three hours later to Mr. Lansing. It bore the number 5747 :

> " Confidential for the President and the Secretary of State. Balfour has handed me the text of a cipher telegram from Zimmermann, German Secretary of State for Foreign Affairs, to the German Minister in Mexico, which was sent via Washington and forwarded by Ambassador Bernstorff on January the 10th. You can probably obtain a copy of the text, as transmitted by Bernstorff, from the telegraph office in Washington. The first group of figures is 130. The second is 13042, and is the key number of the code. The penultimate group is 97556, and represents Zimmermann's signature. I will send you by letter a copy of the cipher text and its deciphering in German. Meanwhile I append the following translation into English. . . ."

Then followed a literal version of the Zimmermann telegram.

" Well, Sir Reginald, the telegram is now in America. What happened next ? "

The Admiral continued.

BLIGHTY

In spite of the fact that they had been given the actual details, with the key figures for the addressee, the text and the sender, the Government in Washington still would not and could not credit the bewildering revelation of their own Ambassador in London. It seemed incredible that such a grotesque telegram could actually have been dispatched from the Wilhelmstrasse.

" They thought it was forged," Hall said, with a smile.

Because they thought it was forged, they had no intention of making it public ; but in order to make sure, they inquired at the telegraph office in Washington, and there was found, after a short search, a copy of the wire sent by Bernstorff to Eckhardt in Mexico City. This nonplussed them somewhat, but they still needed a hundred per cent proof before they would incite the country to war. They were unable to believe that anyone could be so unintelligent as to send such a telegram, even though it was in cipher, but they had to probe the matter to the bottom, and requested Page to obtain the key to the cipher from Admiral Hall and send it to Washington as soon as possible, so that they could decode Bernstorff's message. Hall, however, had his own reasons for not complying with this request. He handed me another telegram, dated March the 1st, from the Ambassador in London to Washington :

> " In reply to your number 4493. I have taken up the question whether we could be given a copy of the key, but there are considerable difficulties in the way. I am informed that the key itself does not provide a solution, since it is only used together with a

frequent permutation of the groups of figures, and there are only one or two persons who are acquainted with the method of deciphering. These experts are unable to travel to the United States, since their services are indispensable in London. If you will send me a copy of the cipher telegram, the English authorities will set to work immediately and have it decoded. Page."

Washington forwarded the text of Bernstorff's wire, and a messenger came with it to Admiral Hall from the American Embassy in London. It was decoded in the presence of the Ambassador himself, and the groups of figures were translated before his eyes into the text of the Zimmermann telegram.

There was no longer any room for doubt that the telegram was genuine and had really emanated from the Wilhelmstrasse. The Americans were convinced that the British were right, and the text of the wire was made public. The ensuing storm turned the United States definitely against Germany, though pro-German opinion, at least determined opponents of President Wilson's pro-English policy, unanimously declared that the telegram was a crude British forgery. It was a heavy blow to the latter when Zimmermann, after the German public had also grown agitated, confirmed the authenticity of the telegram in a speech to the Reichstag, an occurrence which Page promptly reported to Washington on March 10th.

There could now be no holding back. Even the Southern States, which had been to some extent friendly to Germany, or at any rate hostile to England, were furious with indignation at Germany's attempt to help in the transfer of two flourishing American States to Mexico.

Admiral Hall leaned back in his chair.

" And that is the end of the story," I said.

" The end ? " he replied. " What do you mean, the end ? Read this ! It is a telegram from Eckhardt to the Foreign Office in Berlin. It was handed in on March the 1st."

The text was as follows :

> " The Mexican newspaper *Universal*, which is friendly to the Allies, has just published information that became known yesterday in Washington, according to which President Wilson appears to have had knowledge of our intention ever since the breaking off of diplomatic relations with Germany. Naturally I have not issued any communiqué here. Treachery or indiscretion here is out of the question, so there must have been a leakage in the United States, or else the Secret Code is no longer safe. I have denied everything here."

" How did you manage to decipher this telegram of Eckhardt's ? " I asked. " He says that he was afraid the code was no longer secret. What code did he use, in that case, for his own wire ? "

" I told you it was not the end of the story," the Admiral answered. " It is simpler, however, than you think. Though Eckhardt feared that the Secret Code was ' no longer safe,' he calmly continued to cable and radio with the same cipher. Just look at this."

This was a telegram from the German Legation in Mexico to Berlin, dated March 2nd, 1917:

" A visit to President Carranza in Queretaro would be inopportune. I therefore took occasion of calling on the Foreign Minister and sounding him. He was willing to consider the suggestion, and in pursuance of this he had an interview with the Japanese Minister which lasted an hour and a half, but the substance of which is unknown to me. He then left to report to President Carranza. Eckhardt."

Admiral Hall was right. The story was not yet at an end. The course it took was of so monstrous a nature that it took me some time to grasp it. I kept in mind certain facts. A telegram from the German Foreign Office to America became common property in spite of its having been in cipher. Although this leakage had been brought to the notice of every German authority at home and abroad by a scandal which was agitating the world, and even though the Minister to Mexico himself had expressed the fear that the code was no longer secret, this same diplomat continued to use an instrument which he assumed gave the enemy the power to read his confidential messages. This was one of the many incomprehensible episodes which occurred during the grim conflict of the Great War.

Hall interrupted my cogitations.

" We had of course assumed that the old code would be cancelled after this, and we were quite worried, since a knowledge of the cipher used for the most important State telegrams during the War was of almost decisive moment. We had already begun to rack our brains with a view to discovering the new code which we expected to come into use. Your Government, however, relieved us of all anxiety, for the old code was retained, and naturally we intercepted the telegrams which were sent after the first Zimmermann wire, and cabled them immediately to Washington. You can probably imagine the sensation they caused! Do you realise that you contributed to the eventual intervention of the United States in the War against Germany ? "

" Just a moment, Sir Reginald. Were there any other telegrams ? It must have occurred to some one in Berlin that the code was not safe to use. It *must* have occurred to *someone*."

" It occurred to no one. Here is the next telegram."

It was from Mexico to Berlin and was marked " Most Secret, No. 7 " :

> " Should we be in a position to supply Mexico with munitions ? Please reply. I have received offers of help for purposes of propaganda from several quarters here. Eckhardt."

Zimmermann wired to Eckhardt on March 7th :

> " Please burn compromising instructions. Your action is fully approved. We have publicly admitted that the telegram of January 14th was genuine. In this connection, please emphasise that the instructions were only to be carried out if America declared war. Zimmermann."

This wire was sent off in the morning. At noon the Japanese Under-Secretary for Foreign Affairs, Baron

THE DARK INVADER

Shidehara, issued a communiqué which was published simultaneously throughout Europe. It ran as follows :

> "Japan is very surprised to hear of the German proposal. We cannot imagine what Germany is thinking of when she suggests the possibility of our allowing ourselves to be entangled in a war with the United States. How can she impute to us a willingness to approach Mexico for such a purpose? I cannot find words to characterise the whole absurdity of the idea. It is unnecessary to say that Japan adheres faithfully to her pact with the Allied Powers."

This communiqué was, as I have said, issued at midday, and it was known in Berlin at that hour. Yet, the same evening Berlin sent the following wire, bearing the number 17 and addressed to the Minister in Mexico—of course in the same code as before :

> "Please ascertain the type of arms and munitions required, and in which Mexican harbours on the east or west coast a ship can discharge under a foreign flag. Mexico must try to obtain arms, as far as possible, from Japan and South America."

Hall saw that I was completely dumbfounded, and that I was trying to suppress a bitterness which I did not want to betray openly. He said :

"My dear Captain, please don't. Don't try to express what you feel now that you see all this before you. You cannot very well do so, since you are a German officer. Let me continue.

"This was the situation. A plot had been arranged;

all the participants and all the intended victims had been warned. The public had for weeks been occupied with the incident and nothing else. Opinion in America was roused. All eyes were turned to the Mexican frontier. The military authorities in the United States had been advised and were keeping a strict eye on everything that was happening in Mexico. Considering the relative strength, equipment, and military training of both sides, and the war material at their disposal, an attack by Mexico could only have a prospect of success if it were sudden. The factor of surprise, however, no longer existed, so her chances were nil. An attempt had been made to draw Japan into the plot, but she declared that the idea was absurd. It appears that the German authorities had been persuaded by the sole fact that there had been an interview between the Mexican Foreign Minister and the Japanese diplomatic representative, which had lasted an hour and a half—the substance of which they were ignorant of, that Japan would throw over all her existing alliances and join in the plot against the United States. There was thus in reality nothing, absolutely nothing, which could lead to the conclusion that Japan would be willing to change sides. Although the whole world knew what was in the wind, the intrigue, which had become completely inane, was continued. The only result, since I intercepted all Germany's telegrams and sent them to America, was that both the public and the Government of the United States were provoked beyond endurance.

" Here I have a bundle of telegrams which constitute

a bizarre interlude in this tragic affair. A satyric drama was performed while we listened in. We heard the German Foreign Office and its Minister in Mexico at loggerheads. They used the old code to inquire how this same code had been betrayed. On March 21st Berlin cabled to Eckhardt :

> " ' Extremely secret. To be deciphered personally. Please cable in this cipher who decoded cable numbers 1–11. Where were the originals and the decoded copies kept? Cable whether both were kept in the same place.'

" As the Legation in Mexico did not reply at once, Berlin wired again on March 27th, 1917 :

> " ' The greatest caution is essential. All compromising material to be burned. There are various signs which indicate that there has been treachery in Mexico.'

" But Eckhardt, who was quite innocent of the matter, was not very pleased to be told that the leakage must have taken place in Mexico. He replied to Zimmermann on the same day :

> " ' Telegrams deciphered by Magnus on special instructions from me. Both original and copy, as is the case with all political documents of a secret nature, were withheld from the knowledge of the office staff. Telegram 1 received here in cipher 13040. But Kinkel believes he can remember that it was forwarded from the Embassy in Washington via Cape Cod, like all telegrams received here in

cipher. The originals were burnt by Magnus and the ashes dispersed. Both telegrams were kept in an absolutely secure steel safe, which was obtained for the purpose and built into the wall of Magnus's bedroom. They remained there until they were destroyed.'

" Magnus was the Secretary of Legation, Kinkel was formerly at the Embassy in Washington, and Cape Cod is an American telegraph station. Berlin was apparently not satisfied with Eckhardt's answer and demanded further inquiries. The following telegram was received from Eckhardt on March 30th :

" ' Greater precautions than have always been observed here are impossible. The text of telegrams received is read to me at night-time in my private residence by Magnus in a low voice. My servant, who does not know a word of German, sleeps in the annexe. Apart from this, the text is never anywhere but in the hands of Magnus, or in a steel safe, the combination of which is known to us two only. According to Kinkel, even secret telegrams were accessible to the whole of the office staff in Washington, and two copies were regularly prepared for the archives of the Embassy. Here, however, there can be no question of carbon copies or of waste-paper basket. Please inform me as soon as we are free from suspicion, as no doubt will be the case. Otherwise, I insist with Magnus on judicial investigation.'

" This emphatic reply brought the desired vindication, for Berlin wired on April 4th :

" ' After your telegram we can hardly assume that treachery was committed in Mexico, and the signs

which pointed to it lose their force. No blame
attaches either to you or to Magnus. Foreign
Office.'

"So far so good," Admiral Hall went on. "Meanwhile,
however, the telegrams which were to organise the conspiracy with Mexico continued. On April 13th Berlin
urged Eckhardt as follows :

> " ' Please reply with statement of the sums neces-
> sary to carry out our policy. Arrangements are
> being made on this side to transfer considerable
> sums. If possible include amount required for
> arms, etc.'

"The curtain now began to fall : On April the 14th
Eckhardt sent a renewed warning to Zimmermann
against the use of the Secret Code, and continued :

> " ' President Carranza declares that he intends
> under all circumstances to remain neutral. If
> Mexico should nevertheless be drawn into the War
> we can discuss the matter again then. He says that
> the alliance has been wrecked by premature publica-
> tion, but might become necessary at a later stage
> of developments. With regard to Mauser 7 mm.
> ammunition and money, he will give his answer
> when he is authorised by Congress to make his
> decision.'

"Of course Carranza never gave the answer he had
promised, nor did he ask Congress for full powers. After
the dust stirred up by the first telegram, he never seriously
cherished the idea of taking up arms against the United

States. But yet they continued cabling from Mexico :
' No. 26040–612 ' :

> " ' For Captain Nadolny, Great General Staff.
> Have you sent 25,000 dollars to Paul Hilken ? He
> is to send me the money. With reference to this :
> Hermann claims to have instructions from General
> Staff to burn Tampico oilfields and proposes now
> to carry it out. But Verdy thinks he is English or
> American spy. Answer immediately. Eckhardt.'

" Quite a nice plan, wasn't it ? " Admiral Hall remarked. Then he put his papers together. He continued
to discuss the subject, and it became more and more
evident what this sort of telegram has meant for the
future history of the world. Germany's fate began to be
sealed when Admiral Hall got hold of the code.

As we sat there in our quiet corner of the club I had
a vision of the past. I saw myself standing in the Naval
Attaché's room in New York, and I heard myself
ask :

" Do you know that the ' Most Secret Code ' has
gone ? "

I heard his reply, grating, explosive :

" Who says so ? Impossible ! It is kept here under
lock and key."

" *Always*, Captain ? "

" Of course I haven't the time to lock up every code
myself. That is done by one of the secretaries."

I saw Mr. Boniface sitting in front of me, telling me
gloomily that the British had copied the Naval Attaché's
code.

" There is one thing about which I am not clear, Sir Reginald," I said. " From what you have told me, there can be no doubt that all the German authorities concerned kept on broadcasting their messages in this confounded code, but I fail to understand how nobody hit upon the idea of changing it. I witnessed many incredible episodes in the War, but I simply cannot realise that such a thing was possible."

Hall averted his eyes a little.

" Yes, that was a strange affair. Who would be interested to-day in knowing how it happened? I must, however, confess one thing. I was myself not altogether devoid of responsibility. I managed to convince the German authorities that it was only America which had had anything to do with the Zimmermann episode."

" I don't follow you quite, sir."

" Wait a moment, and you will. I had to prevent the Germans from believing that their code was no longer safe, so that I could continue to read their telegrams. When Eckhardt cabled his suspicions, I was rather startled ; so it occurred to me to suggest to the Germans that some one in America must have got hold of the telegrams after they had been deciphered. If I could succeed in doing this, Berlin would be bound to assume that the leakage had occurred either in the German Embassy at Washington or at the Legation in Mexico. I wanted them to think that it was the United States and not the British Intelligence Service which had discovered the story. You shake your head. I can assure you that

BLIGHTY

I also had good grounds for doubting whether I should be successful."

He then told me, with a friendly smile, what steps he had taken to delude the Germans. After Eckhardt had cabled his warning to Berlin, and the world was ringing with the Zimmermann affair, Admiral Hall invited a representative of the *Daily Mail* to come and see him, and said :

" Don't you think that we people of the Intelligence Service are very stupid ? "

The journalist looked at the Admiral, who was regarded by the whole of the British Press with awe, and laughed :

" Are you trying to pull my leg, Sir Reginald ? " he replied. " Do you seriously expect me to believe that the Intelligence Service is stupid ? "

" It's not a matter of pulling your leg. I admit it in all seriousness. You know the story of the Zimmermann telegram. Well, doesn't that tell you enough ? We have just seen how the Americans managed to obtain the decoded wire straight away, while we have been trying all over the world to decipher German messages and have not been successful in a single case."

The journalist looked at Hall very dubiously, and said, " Why do you tell me this ? What am I to do with this information ? "

" Publish it."

" I cannot do that."

" Why not ? "

" In the first place, because the story seems to me very

odd, and I simply do not believe that the members of the Naval Intelligence, with you at their head, are so unintelligent that it is necessary to call attention to it in a newspaper. Besides, there would be no point in writing anything against the Secret Service since it would never be printed."

" Why not ? "

" Because of the censorship."

" The censorship," said Admiral Hall emphatically, " you can leave to me."

The journalist looked at the Admiral, then stood up and laughed softly.

" I am very grieved," he said, " to see that you think me more stupid than I am. I can imagine more or less what you want, and you may rely upon it that the article will appear in the *Daily Mail* to-morrow. I shall use fine big headlines, I shall not be sparing with the heavy type, and there will be no lack of unflattering remarks concerning the Naval Intelligence. Good morning, Sir Reginald."

On the following day a sensational article appeared in the *Daily Mail*, to the effect that the British Naval Intelligence Service was making a pretty poor show and was very inferior to that of the United States. The Americans were clever people. They could secure German telegrams as soon as they had been decoded.

The sequel was as Hall had expected. The article convinced Berlin that the mischief had been caused through decoded telegrams being betrayed in America. The German Legation in Mexico was suspected, and, in short, the Germans fell into the trap that Hall had laid. He sat in his room at the Admiralty until the end of the War with his ear to all the wires. He snatched the German wireless messages out of the air, and listened to everything that a nation, fighting for its life, was thinking, planning and doing.

Yes, you British Admiralty, " You Were My Enemies ! " but one had to have respect for you for your energy of action and your circumspection !

They were guided in Whitehall by the one idea, " Nothing succeeds like success,"—at times, it must be said, ruthlessly falling in line with Lord Fisher's saying, " Sink, Burn and Destroy."

That saying I bore in mind throughout the War, and acted likewise : if Britannia ruled the waves, well and good ; if she waived the rules, well and good too ; but I was to be a good scholar of theirs !

" Rule the Waves "—that was the prime thought too of Winston Churchill, Lord Fisher's predecessor : " Rule the Waves "—to the exclusion of all others ! How often did my thoughts turn back to that master-stroke of his, political and tactical alike, prior even to the outbreak of the Great Conflagration : on July 30th, 1914, he went to see Asquith, the Prime Minister, and obtained his agreement to the Grand Fleet's units taking their war stations.

But that wasn't enough for him ! What else did he do ? Something more important almost, but at least as clever and far-sighted.

On August the 1st, I remember, a telegram from

Lichnowsky, our Ambassador at the Court of St. James',
was received at the Wilhelmstrasse :

> " Saw Asquith late last night: he pointed out to
> me that in the present tense conditions no demon-
> stration on the part of the High Seas Fleet should
> take place. Any movement, however slight, of any
> German naval unit might now arouse British public
> opinion with disastrous consequences for the whole
> political situation . . ."

and Bethmann Hollweg added in his own handwriting :
" Such an important hint should not be cast to the winds."
But the Kaiser wrote, after seeing both telegram and
annotation, " *Was für ein alter Fuchs der Asquith ist !* "

Still, Bethmann Hollweg forced the hands of the
Kaiser, and the strictest possible orders were issued. The
High Seas Fleet had to " stay indoors." The First Lord
of the Admiralty had his own way : the enemy-to-be was
carefully kept off the North Sea ; Britain's Navy had it
all to herself ! " Quietly and unmolested " did she take
war-stations, and on August the 4th the stage was set :
" No enemy vessel can be sighted "—that was the report
coming from all our patrol ships.

. . . . .

My readers must follow me back for ten years.

In my account of the conversation which I had with
Admiral Hall about the Zimmermann telegrams, I turned
the hands of the clock forward. I must now put them
back to that evening in 1915, when I had just been

captured and was sitting with Hall and Herschell in their club—the Junior United Service Club I think it was.

When we left we went straight to Lord Herschell's rooms, where we had a quick whisky, and Herschell sat at the piano and played Wagner. Hall then took me by the arm and said :

" I am afraid you must go now. There are two men waiting for you outside."

The two men were detectives, and they took me to the nearest Military Police station, where I was given a room which was partitioned off from the office. I sat down on one of the beds. I learned later that these beds were there to accommodate officers on leave who were found in the streets dead " tight." As I walked up and down, the officer in charge said to me :

" Why don't you go home ? Haven't you got any lodgings ? "

I pondered this remark and realised that he took me for an English officer who had been found in the street, and would be better off having his sleep out at the police station. It took me some time to think out the possible consequences of his mistake, and I came to the conclusion that it might be dangerous to leave at night when the streets of London were swarming with military patrols. Morning came at last, and as I lay on the bed I heard the officer who was being relieved say :

" There's another one at the back, but he'll soon be going."

I did not give him the lie, and prepared to take my

departure. I picked up my hat, said, " Good morning," and was outside.

I knew London like a book, and was familiar with the bus routes, so I waited for the next bus which went to the Mansion House, where I could change for London Bridge. I knew that there was a tram terminus on the south bank of the Thames, not far away, and that I could get a tram-car which passed alongside the docks. If I kept my eyes open, I was bound to see a Swedish steamer, and it would not be difficult to get on board. What happened then would depend on circumstances. Perhaps I should find some one who would help me to hide until we reached Swedish territory.

As I sat on the top deck of the bus which was to take me to freedom, I thought everything over, and suddenly a black, impenetrable wall seemed to interpose itself between me and my plan. I was done. I was in a state of nervous exhaustion after the last few weeks in New York, the crossing, and the struggle with Hall and his men. I was finished. I find it impossible at this late date to give a completely plausible explanation of my next action. I cannot give any details, or say what possessed me. I saw something from the top of the bus. . . . I think it was a stockbroker of my acquaintance walking down to the office this fine morning . . . and the sheer everydayness of the happening bowled me out. I just came to a sudden resolve, got out of the omnibus and went back to the police station! When I got there no one bothered about me. I sat down on a chair and read the *Daily Mail*. Only then did it occur to me what a chance I had missed. I tried to stand up, but fell back into my chair again and could not move. The officer looked at me once or twice disapprovingly. He appeared to be displeased that I was still there. All at once I saw a second officer in the guard-room, accompanied by soldiers with fixed bayonets. He came straight up to me and said :

" Are you the German Captain Rintelen ? "

" Yes."

" I have orders to take you to the railway station."

As we passed the officer in charge, he looked at me with his mouth wide open. There were more things in heaven and earth than were dreamt of in his philosophy.

·   ·   ·   ·   ·

I arrived in the concentration camp at Donington Hall on the evening of August 18th, 1915. To my astonishment I was cut by all the German officers there. At first I did not know why, but I gathered later that they took me for an English spy. Günther Plüschow, the aviator from Tsingtao, had recently escaped, and they thought I was stationed there to find out how he had got away.

I had a vague foreboding of what the future had in store for me, when Admiral Hall appeared one day with Lord Herschell and I was summoned to the Commandant's room. Hall's manner to me had changed, and he at once burst out :

" What did you discuss with the Irish leaders in America ? What have you been planning ? What plots have you been forging against England ? Do you realise that you have put yourself in an extremely dangerous position ? If you want to make things easier for yourself, you had better confess what conspiracy you have entered into with the Irish leaders."

So the Admiral knew all this ! Well, it could not be helped, and I determined that he should not learn anything from me, not even how I got my reports through . . . though he asked me about it twice.

"We searched the *Noordam* from truck to keelson," he said angrily, "and we couldn't find the damn things."

I couldn't resist the temptation.

"Look at my signet," I said ; "that, sir, has just been returned to me from Berlin as a proof of receipt. It went in the same parcel."

A silence ensued.

"But how did you get the reports through from America ? "

I didn't mind answering that one.

"Frankly, sir," I said with a smile, "I got the ladies to take care of them . . . and aren't all naval control officers—French or English—gentlemen ? "

But the battle of wits continued.

"And Irish leaders ? What Irish leaders ? " I went on. "I am a prisoner of war. Please leave me in peace."

A few weeks later I got a letter from him :

> " . . . I would not have you under a false impression, and your recent attitude gave me much food for thought. . . . The evidence that has been slowly accumulating regarding your actions cannot

BLIGHTY

be disregarded, and I am faced with a situation that leaves me few alternatives."

Booh ! That was some letter ! ! And soon afterwards an Army officer came to fetch me from the camp ; and before I had quite realised what was happening the door of a cell closed behind me. I sat down and mused over the fact that I was in the Tower of London, where Hans Lodi had been shot, the first spy the British had captured and convicted.

I remained there two days, and then there was a somewhat grotesque trial. During recess hours I was guarded by a picket of soldiers. One of them, in a mood of compassion, felt he had to make me " brace up " ; and this gem of a Tommy whispered into my ears : " Never mind, sir, five of our Queens have been executed in the Tower."
. . . So I seemed to be in good company at least !

I faced the court martial and was accused, as a German officer, of having landed on English territory in time of war. It was apparently the intention of the Admiralty to regard me as a civil prisoner, but they were frustrated by the court's strict sense of legality. When I proved that I had been brought into English territory by force I was acquitted and taken back to Donington Hall.

The next morning, about 10 o'clock, I was quietly sitting in a chair, when some one suddenly pushed a morning paper, I think it was the *Daily Mail*, in front of my eyes, and I read in large headlines a piece of news which interested me :

" Captain Rintelen Shot as a Spy in the Tower of London."

239

THE DARK INVADER

Below was my photograph, and the text stated that I
had been condemned to death by court martial on the
previous day and immediately shot. I turned round to
see a couple of subalterns standing behind me, who
expressed the view that I ought to invite them to the
" wake." The canteen overflowed that evening, and
the orchestra played Chopin's Funeral March : " *Weh'*,
*nun trinkt er keinen Rotspohn mehr, und keinen Champa-ha-
hagner.*" (" He's gone where they don't drink re-ed wine,
he's gone where there's no Champa-ha-hagne.")

I drank both red wine and champagne and praised the
Lord, surrounded by my German comrades, who were
now convinced that a man who had been shot by the
English could not at the same time be an English
spy.

On the whole, life at Donington Hall went along
smoothly enough. The Commandant, Lieutenant-
Colonel F. S. Picot, was a soldier and a gentleman, though
his temper was repeatedly put on trial by those of us who
began to suffer from " barbed wire insanity " or became
too acutely conscious of our nationality. The two
photographs of Donington Hall, very kindly lent to me
for reproduction by Lieutenant-Colonel Picot, show very
clearly the two sides of our life : the fine old house
clustered around with our wooden huts and the justly
famous barbed wire fence which kept us there. Naturally
there were certain incidents at this " Zoo," which arose
out of both Germans and English quarrels. These I wish
to forget.

But—*lest* I forget ! the Easter Rebellion in Dublin did

not come altogether as a surprise to me, though naturally, being by *force majeure* no longer in touch with America, I had no knowledge just when it was " timed " to come off !

．　　　．　　　．　　　．　　　．

British patriotism proved, for once in those dark days, a blessing to us. Of course, no one in England would care to drink Moselle or Rhine wines ; but a large London department store held, from times of peace, quite a stock of them. How quickly a deal—on the H.P. system for that matter—was put through with the store " flooding " a wet canteen in the heart of England ! I still keep, as a souvenir, labels with lovely sounding names in Gothic letters.

Though naturally it is neither a joy for anybody to watch enemy prisoners nor for soldiers and sailors to be condemned to idleness and boredom, yet, nothing really marred that enforced sojourn there. And I must say that those of the German officers who managed to escape and were sooner or later captured again, received fair trials before British courts martial ; and being asked to be " learned counsel " for them, I was given sufficient opportunity for pointing out the " extenuating " circumstances for my " clients." In most cases a pardon came soon afterwards.

I myself, however, was repeatedly " pestered " by American detectives and lawyers, trying to persuade me to " return " to the States voluntarily. If only those men had been a bit less silly in their argumentations that I

could certainly be shot by the British! Well, I had
" survived " this shooting once; and whatever hopes
these men held out to me for an early release, if once back
in—then -still neutral—America, I felt it was another
trap. Much later I was to learn, to my grief, what a
magnificent plan had been laid out by some personal
friends. Immediately after being arrested, once back
in America, I was to " go out on bail "; the bail was
to become a *cadeau* to the Department of Justice in
Washington, and all I had to do was to " smuggle "
myself on board the merchant U-boat *Deutschland*! She
had actually delayed her departure from Baltimore for a
day or two, as the Embassy felt that a public trial would
more than outweigh the loss of twenty-five thousand
dollars' bail.

What " eminent " lawyers those men had proved who
had come to see me!

The one tragic event that occurred during my " stay "
at Donington Hall was, I confess, the death of K. of K.
It by no means aroused enthusiasm among the German
officers and men interned there; unlike Jutland—our
Skager-Rak—or the Serbian and Rumanian routs, each of
which made our hearts thrill with joy, this time a feeling
of awe, of sullen sympathy spread over all of us. For a
soldier of his calibre merely to drown without a chance
to fight for it! K. of K., of all men!

Few of the German officers knew more about him than
that he was Kitchener, just Lord Kitchener, the Secretary of State for War. What lay behind these initials, of
that they were unaware, and in one of the lectures, as they

were being held regularly, I found an occasion to bring home to many of them what that great builder had actually done. K. of K.!

Here, I think, I should make mention that one day our Commandant, Colonel F. S. Picot, confided to me that K. of K. had sent for him, after " sinister rumours " had been making the round, that Donington Hall was " luxury galore." Nothing of the sort, of course : a dignified attitude was maintained on both sides, and a healthy spirit prevailed there. No " baskets laden with fruit," no " bunches of flowers " were ever sent. That was sheer humbug !

Mrs. Asquith, as she then was, had written to a young man interned there, a civilian by the way, who had been socially received at her house prior to the War, a letter to the effect that in view of his nationality and the exalted position of her husband she was unable to do more for him than express the hope that the War would not last all too long ! This letter, well befitting a lady, was the flimsy foundation of the monstrous edifice of rumour which grew round her—and Donington Hall !

While the one startling event of my twenty months at Donington Hall was when the Military Attaché, Captain Papen, passed Great Britain, after having left the United States as *persona non grata*.

His training in diplomacy misled him once more : whilst travelling, for his own all-important person, under British " safe conduct," his trunks did not ; and they were unkind enough in Falmouth to send to Whitehall whatever letters, codes, copies, documents, counterfoils the enlightened diplomat saw fit to carry across the seas. The results were : a trail of ruin and misery for dozens and dozens of Germans and others in America sympathetic to the German cause ; and a foaming with rage on the part of untold men interned in England, of the two hundred officers interned in Donington Hall. Our "senior," a Bavarian colonel, and a Front Officer, came to me to inquire how I might account for such monstrous stupidity, such punishable negligence.

" What regiment does that fool come from ? " he asked.

" First Regiment of Uhlans of the Guard, sir."

" That explains everything ! "

This incident, however—by far more serious than Geheimrat Albert's nap in the New York " Elevated," after which he found himself minus his attaché case containing " unpleasant " documents which the *New York World* published the day after—was soon to prove, for me personally, nothing short of a disaster. Whatever links were still missing, where proof, or at least alleged proof, was required by the American authorities, to bring me and my helpmates to trial, Papen had been graciously pleased to furnish them !

Days of worry followed restless nights for me. Had not Admiral Hall sarcastically remarked to me in London: " You fell into our hands through your Attaché's recklessness ! " A time, full of sinister forebodings, went on until the Zimmermann Note was published in February 1917. When the United States declared war against Germany I grew very depressed. Things seemed to be very black for me, and I was haunted by the ghost of Huerta as Macbeth was haunted by the ghost of Banquo, and he was accompanied by the shades of the men who had been my comrades across the Atlantic. It did not help to cheer me up when the Commandant of the camp came to me one day, smiled mockingly and showed me a newspaper.

" Now we know what you were doing over there," he said. " Here is your name. I see you wanted to hound Mexico against America."

I had an intuition that I was going to be extradited to the United States. My companions ridiculed me. Were there not, after conferences specially held at The Hague, in the midst of war, between British and German Foreign Office and War Office representatives, clearly defined rules established as regards prisoners of war ? Was there not—so expressed themselves some reserve officers, lawyers in civilian life—the altogether thorny problem of extradition ? No such thing could possibly occur in my case ; for not only would that be contrary to all law, to all existing treaties, but, besides, there remained always the weapon of reprisals in the hands of the German Government.

Many a year later I learned almost accidentally that the intention to surrender me to America had been there, for political reasons, for purposes of propaganda among the—even as late as early in 1917—still unwilling population of the United States. " Might goes before right ! " and the end sanctifies the means. A presentiment of misfortune came over me.

THE DARK INVADER

I began to be superstitious. I had been captured on Friday, August 13th, and I could not get rid of the obsession that the coming Friday, April 13th, would bring me bad luck. When this day arrived I went about in an ill humour, and as I was sitting in my room in the evening with a few friends my foreboding was fulfilled. Friday, the 13th, brought me bad luck again. In spite of all my protests to the Commandant and the representations of the other German officers, I was to be taken from the camp—and to my regret, not entirely because I knew what was waiting for me!

For I personally, without being in any way a spoiled child, was generously treated by the Commandant. This again was not so much due to the fact that I had been frequently in England before, and knew the best and worst about that country, but because a report had come to hand that my brother Ludwig, the Commandant of a camp for British Officers in Germany, had proved to be not only " Hun," which he couldn't help, but a gentleman besides.

Apropos, Hun : I can assure my readers that the news of the, shall I call it grotesque, execution of Nurse Cavell seemed most revolting to the vast majority of the inmates of Donington Hall. Many Front Officers openly expressed themselves that they would have flatly refused, had they been called upon, to order a firing squad to shoot a woman ; others, like myself, were grieved as well over the gross miscalculation of the British Spirit —oh ! *that* miscalculation !

.   .   .   .

BLIGHTY

Amid the uproar of the prisoners' camp, the *auf wiedersehen* celebrations of that night, the Hock and the Moselle, I managed to slip away to my room for a few quiet minutes. I could not keep myself from brooding.

"Where is this leading?" I asked myself. "Why had I merely stood by, when some others had tried to escape through the famous tunnel of Donington Hall? I might have been more successful than they, once beyond the barbed-wire fences!"

It's too late to consider that now; so let's go! The carbolic acid bath of 1915 seems not to have been sufficient: in 1917 there must be Purgatory thrown in as well.

PART IV

BACK IN AMERICA
" Grand Hotel ": Atlanta

IN the head-lights of a motor-car I saw armed English soldiers, and was driven away from " dear old Donington Hall," followed by the good wishes shouted out to me by my fellow-prisoners. The drive ended at Nottingham, where I was taken on board a train. I was surrounded by soldiers and detectives to protect me from the civil population, who looked menacing. When we reached Liverpool I received permission to telephone to Admiral Hall. When I was connected I said :

" I only want to tell you that this is a mean trick you are playing. I ask you to countermand the order at once. You must know that prisoners of war are not allowed to be taken through the battle zone. The U-boat blockade is a battle zone."

" You sail for America this morning," he replied. " I have nothing more to say to you at present."

He hung up the receiver, while I fired a few curses at his head.

My escort still had their bayonets fixed, and accompanied me at three paces interval to the left and right until we boarded the White Star Liner *Adriatic*.

The irony of this situation could not have been brought home to me more forcibly than by remembering what the *Berliner Lokal-Anzeiger* had said but a few months before :

" Rintelen is in no great danger ; he is interned as a prisoner of war in England, and the endeavours of the

American Government to obtain his extradition have
failed."

And now I was on my way to America!

I pulled myself together, and it became clear to me
that I could no longer escape my fate. We started off in
a queer way. The Captain invited the officers on board
to lunch, and I sat there in my German uniform among
dozens of Allied officers of numerous nations and all
branches of the Service. None of them was *au fait* with
all the various little differences in dress, and it did not
occur to anybody that I was a German.

We left harbour in the evening. I stood on deck with
the British officer who was accompanying me as my
escort and had orders to hand me over to the American
authorities. Like all the others, I had put on mufti, and
I was glad when the Englishman told me that no one
except the Captain and himself was aware that I was a
German officer. We had hardly left the harbour when
we turned back, because U-boats were supposed to be
in the vicinity. We left harbour and turned back a
number of times before we eventually got under way.
We were escorted by a dozen patrol-boats of the Royal
Navy, for we carried about a hundred British officers,
from admirals and generals down to second lieutenants,
who were being sent across as military instructors for the
American Army and Navy. We were preceded by a
large ship, the *Olympic*, with Mr. Balfour, the head of
the War Mission to the United States, and a whole
staff of civilian officials on board. I cannot describe
how for days I hoped that the two vessels would be

stopped by one of our U-boats. My hopes, however, were vain.

I fumed at a brutal precaution which my escort was compelled to take by the Admiralty. He locked me in my cabin every evening, and if the ship were torpedoed I should have been drowned like a rat. I had a scene with the officer, and we both got so agitated that it looked as if we should come to blows, but at last I succeeded in persuading him to leave my cabin door open at night.

There was only one woman on board, who had been permitted, as an exceptional case, to cross on the *Adriatic*. Her husband was on Mr. Balfour's staff on the *Olympic*. As the English officers were occupied mainly in playing cards and looking out for submarines, it was reserved for me to devote my time to her. She astonished me one day, as we were sitting at tea, by leaning towards me and whispering a secret in my ear :

" Do you know, they say there's a Hun on board ! "

" Good heavens," I replied, " that *would* be exciting. Let us go and look for him."

Strange to relate, we were unable to find him. At last we met my escort, the English officer, and she addressed him reproachfully :

" They say there's a Hun on board. Do you know anything about it ? "

I added hurriedly : " Yes, just imagine. We have been looking for him."

He stared at us, standing arm-in-arm, and then grinned as he said :

THE DARK INVADER

" All sorts of things happen on big ships."

Every one on board suffered from a U-boat psychosis, and I was also infected. It was not at all improbable that we should meet a German submarine, and I had an idea which I was unfortunately unable to put into practice. I sewed together a black, white and red flag out of ribbon and other materials, which I intended to tie round my waist if we should be held up by a U-boat. It was very unlikely that I should have time to make an elaborate speech to the officers who came on board, and somebody would be bound to stand behind me to prevent me from attracting their attention. If we all had to parade on deck I would open my coat, and it was certain that any German officer would inspect more closely a man wearing a black, red and white flag round his waist on an English auxiliary cruiser.

We saw neither U-boats nor German officers, however, and at last the American coast came into sight, and I, much to my resentment, was handcuffed and taken ashore in uniform under the cross-fire of a battery of cameras, which took my photograph for the New York evening papers.

I appeared before the District Attorney.

Detectives and police officials were waiting for me in a large room, but I refused to open my mouth until the handcuffs were taken off. I then protested against the way I had been treated, and demanded to be regarded as a prisoner of war, but I was told curtly that I was a civil prisoner. I therefore refused to say another word. As a result I was taken away and left to myself in a cell.

254

Next morning I was brought before the representative of the Attorney-General of the United States, who came straight to the point.

" You will remember," he said, " that you were in America in 1915. You must permit me to read out the charges against you. Do you remember having known Dr. Scheele and the Captains Wolpert, Bode, and Steinberg ? "

I held my tongue.

" Do you not recollect that you committed acts of sabotage against munition transports by means of incendiary bombs manufactured by this Dr. Scheele ? Don't you remember having damaged the rudders of munition transports by means of an apparatus constructed by a certain Mr. Fay ? "

" I remember nothing."

" That is a great pity. Perhaps, however, you will call to mind having founded a trade union called ' Labour's National Peace Council,' in order to corrupt our dockworkers by the organisation of strikes ? Of course, you never had an interview with General Huerta at the Manhattan Hotel ! You never heard of the firm of ' E. V. Gibbons,' or the ' Mexico North-Western Railway ' ! You were never on friendly terms with one of the most distinguished members of the New York Bar Association, Mr. Boniface, who put his comprehensive legal knowledge at your disposal ? "

I kept my mouth shut and said nothing. I was very uneasy, but I told myself it was by no means certain that they could prove everything they were trying to assert.

The Attorney appeared to read my thoughts. He gazed at me a while and then said :

" Come a little nearer, please. Let us have a quiet talk. You see, up to a short time ago we were convinced that there were some men here at work putting incendiary bombs on ships, calling men out on strike, negotiating with Mexican and Irish leaders, and carrying out all sorts of activities whose purpose was to help Germany, but which infringed the laws of this country. I must offer you my compliments. We know that all these happenings were directed or carried out by you. While you were still in America and violating our laws, we were unable, in spite of our most zealous efforts, to bring either you or any of your agents to book. It was only after some time we found your trail. Of course, we had been suspecting you for some time. You were watched, but we could never discover the slightest positive proof. The situation was changed suddenly when this book came into our hands. Take a look at it, please. As an intelligent man, you will not fail to notice that it is a cheque-book. Do me the favour to examine closely the different entries. It was very instructive to me to learn the names of the people to whom the owner of this book had paid out sums of money. I presume a perusal will help to refresh your memory. If you should happen not to recognise the handwriting, permit me to offer you the following information.

" This is a cheque-book that was formerly in the possession of Captain Papen, then German Military Attaché in Washington. He appears to have had a mania for preserving all his cheque-books, and he had a brilliant idea of taking them with him to Germany when he was recalled at the request of the United States Government as being no longer *persona grata*. You may be of the opinion that it was an unfriendly act on the part of the English to extract these cheque-books from his diplomatic luggage. But please turn over the pages."

I opened the book. It consisted only of counterfoils of the cheques which Captain Papen had made out. As I turned them over I suddenly had a dreadful shock. I saw clearly written the following entry : " To Dr. Scheele, $10,000." I remembered that item and knew for what purpose von Papen had made out the cheque. It had been a rather harmless affair, and I had had nothing to do with it personally.

I was certainly of the opinion that it was an unfriendly act on the part of the English to confiscate this book, as the Attorney had suggested, but my mind was dominated by the unshakable conviction that Captain Papen, in failing to destroy it, had perpetrated a blunder of such stupendous idiocy that he would never be able to atone for it as long as he lived.

" I see," said the Attorney, " that you have stopped at a certain counterfoil. I assume that you know a number of the people to whom these sums of money were paid. But at any rate you are looking at the entry which says that Captain Papen paid ten thousand dollars to Dr. Scheele. I will therefore tell you, briefly and to the point, that we have arrested this Dr. Scheele.

He was sensible enough to answer our questions. In other words, he has confessed. He has told us everything about your activities in this country, and it is really unnecessary for you to say anything at all. We know enough to secure a conviction so far as you are concerned. There is one other matter which will be of interest to you. Dr. Scheele's admissions enabled us to arrest all your friends. One said this and another said that, but I can assure you we know enough. Will you therefore talk, or do you prefer to keep silent ? "

I preferred to keep silent, and was sent back to prison. I passed the night visualising what would happen if I could suddenly have the vast pleasure of being alone in my cell with Captain Papen !

Friends engaged one of the most celebrated lawyers in America, Mr. George Gordon Battle, to undertake my defence. I cannot overstate my gratitude to this splendid man. In the middle of the Great War he was willing to risk much more than his wide popularity by undertaking the defence of a German officer on trial in an enemy country. He and his friend, the late Mr. Massey, proved the staunchest of allies and friends to me throughout those trying years and times. At our first interview he looked me up and down for a moment and said :

" Before I decide to undertake your defence, you must answer one question. Have you resolved to admit everything or do you intend, as a German officer, to say ' No ' to everything ? "

I told him that I intended to say nothing at all. He agreed to defend me, and immediately decided to send the

BACK IN AMERICA

following letter to the Attorney-General in Washington, Mr. Gregory :

" NEW YORK,
" *May the 1st*, 1917

" SIR,

" In the matter of Capt. Franz von Rintelen, for whom I am counsel, I respectfully beg to call your attention to the fact that he is now confined in the Tombs Prison, this City, while undergoing his trial upon an indictment for violation of the Sherman Anti-Trust Law. Capt. von Rintelen was a prisoner of war in England and was kept there with other German officers in comfortable and dignified quarters. He was sent to this country by the English Government without any extradition proceedings and to that extent he claims his status is continued as a prisoner of war. He is now confined in the Tombs under circumstances of great discomfort and indignity. The conditions of the prison are dirty and are most unbecoming. He is thrown in with the lowest class of criminals. He is an officer in the German Navy and it seems highly improper that he should be confined in such surroundings. He is subjected to constant filthy abuse from his fellow-prisoners in the Tombs. If he can be kept in the Military Prison at Governor's Island he will be equally secure, and I think if he is so confined our Government will occupy a more dignified position. I think such treatment should be accorded to a naval officer of Germany. John Z. Lowe, who is also a counsel for Capt. von Rintelen, went to Washington last night for the purpose of bringing this matter to your attention. I would come in person, except for the fact that I am actually engaged in the trial

259

of a case. I earnestly hope that you will instruct the Marshal of the Southern District of New York to have Capt. von Rintelen so confined in the Military Prison at Governor's Island.

"(Signed)   GEO. GORDON BATTLE "

I joined in the bombardment by writing post haste to His Excellency the British Ambassador, Sir Cecil Spring Rice, at Washington :

"YOUR EXCELLENCY,

"Permit me to lay before you the following.

"On the 13th of April I was brought over here from England, presumably at the request of the Department of Justice of the United States. Until then I was interned at Donington Hall, Derby, as an officer prisoner of war. Before sailing I was distinctly told that by the described procedure I would *not* lose my legal status as prisoner of war. Since my arrival in America, however, I am not accorded the treatment that, I think, I am entitled to as a naval officer of Germany, and that up to the present has been accorded vice-versa to officer prisoners of war by both Germany and England : I am being carried handcuffed through the streets of New York day after day : I am confined in the Tombs Prison under circumstances of great discomfort and indignity : the conditions of the prison are dirty and most unbecoming : I am thrown in with partly the lowest class of criminals, and repeatedly subjected to filthy abuse by some of them : and it seems, no matter what I am being tried for since my arrival, highly improper that an officer who has been in the active service of either navy in the course of the War, and subsequently become a prisoner of war, should be confined in such surroundings.

"Now, since my legal status as a German officer prisoner of war in English captivity seems not to be challenged by anybody, and as I am therefore under English authority, unless otherwise stated, I take liberty in asking your Excellency to see to those conditions being altered and brought up to a decent standard, on level with such conditions as are heretofore considered proper by both Germany and England.

"Expressing to you, sir, my sincere thanks for your intervention on my behalf,

"I have the honour to be, your Excellency,

"Respectfully yours,

"RINTELEN"

In vain! I was to become definitely a "common" prisoner!

.　　.　　.　　.　　.

My trial furnished the American newspapers, great and small, with abundant news for weeks. It began on May 5th, 1917. During my preliminary examination I had firmly insisted that I was innocent, and had not admitted any of the charges which were laid against me. The court in which my trial took place was a large rectangular room with wide windows and an arched roof. At one of the longer sides was a raised platform with a chair for the judge which dominated the whole room. He sat enthroned alone in a black robe, and to right and left of him were large portraits of George

THE DARK INVADER

Washington and Abraham Lincoln. On the right-hand side of the room was a large raised bench for the jury. In the centre, in front of the judge, stood a long table for the accommodation of the accused and their advocates, while the journalists sat at a smaller table on the left. One side was shut off by a barrier, behind which crowded the spectators.

The trial, in which I was the chief figure, was by no means on my account alone. The American police had done a great deal of work in the meantime. The case was *Government of the United States* v. *Captain Rintelen and Accomplices*. The charge was Violation of the Federal Laws under the following counts:

Endangering of transport at sea.

Transporting and storing of explosives within the territory of the United States without a police licence.

Violation of the Strike Laws by founding an illegal and fictitious trade union.

Endangering the security of the United States by contriving war plots with a foreign Power (Mexico).

Endangering the good relations between the United States and other Powers with which she was on friendly terms by contriving rebellions within the territory of these Powers (*Ireland—Great Britain*).

Altogether about thirty men were charged during the various stages of the trial, including Captain Wolpert, Herren Daeche, Fay, Binder, Uhde, Captain von Kleist, Dr. Scheele, the melancholy Mr. Boniface, and the

engineers Herren Schmidt, Becker, Praedel, and Paradiess
of the German steamer *Friedrich der Grosse*, who were
accused of endangering transport at sea. There were
also charges under this count against six German
captains and engineers of a German shipping-line, but
they had managed to get away in time.

Other accused persons were the executive of " Labour's
National Peace Council," the members of Congress
Buchanan and Fowler, who had had to resign over the
affair, and the former Attorney-General Monnett, who
were all charged with being concerned in the founding of
the trade union, and the notaries who had furnished their
signatures and their seals for the purpose of obtaining
the necessary documents. The plot with Mexico was
laid to my account alone, since Huerta was dead, but
the Irish intrigue was to be atoned for by Jeremiah
O'Leary as well. These more important prisoners were
flanked by a row of lesser sinners.

The trial lasted for weeks. I sat next to my lawyer
and listened, and hoped that it would eventually come
to an end. I maintained the attitude I had promised at
my first interview with Mr. Battle, and said nothing.
I let him do the talking, and he succeeded in turning
many doubtful points to my advantage.

On the other hand, however, I was in an impossible
position. I was charged with a large number of activities
of which I was innocent, particularly matters which had
been instigated by Captain Papen, but which I should
have to pay for. It would have been quite simple for
me to rebut them, for I only had to say who had been

responsible, but I could not do that—I could not, as a German officer, betray a comrade !

The trial drew towards its end and the accused were overwhelmed. There was not much of us left when it was over. When the Attorney for the prosecution rose to address the jury we were all very uneasy. I myself had special reasons for viewing the future pessimistically when he began to occupy himself with my person. He depicted the damage I had caused, and I still feel proud when I recall how he showed that I nearly succeeded in preventing the munition shipments over a long period through the organisation of a general strike. I still get excited when I remember how he expressed his gratitude to Captain Papen for delivering us all up to American justice by his confounded carelessness ! He then summed up my activities once more, and after he had taken a deep breath he demanded for me a sentence of four years' penal servitude. It was poor consolation when he proceeded to honour me with the following remarks : " I regret having to demand such a heavy penalty against this German officer. He has, as he believes, only done his duty. But in doing so he has violated the laws of the land, and the punishment I have demanded is therefore fitting. Let us, however, utter no harsh words. We have nothing but respect for him."

There was an interval of three days between the speech of the Attorney for the prosecution and the verdict, a period which I occupied by reading all the American newspapers I could get hold of. While one group of papers declared that it was unjust to demand a sentence of penal servitude against a German officer who was a prisoner of war, other journals attacked me bitterly. One headline ran : " What the Kaiser Wanted was Carried Out by Captain Rintelen with a Bloody Hand."

I hurled the " bloody hand " into a corner and picked up another paper : " Kaiser Demands Repatriation of Captain Rintelen."

I read in this paper that the German Government had threatened reprisals if I were sent to penal servitude. My hope that this would help was, however, shattered when I read that Mr. Lansing, the Secretary of State, had replied with pleasant irony that Germany should not indulge in any false ideas concerning the effect of her note on my behalf. There were more German nationals in the United States than there were American troops fighting in Europe. It might be possible to organise a competition to see who could imprison the greater number of people. This was the end. The American public had a good head for figures !

I was solemnly sentenced to four years' penal servitude. When I was asked if I had anything to say, I stood up. Feeling that Germany could not be defeated, I cried in exasperation :

" This will not help you to win the War."

The judge also jumped up and shouted :

" I regret nothing more than the fact that the law of the United States does not permit me to sentence you to death."

" I don't regret it at all," I replied.

THE DARK INVADER

He looked at me with a hard stare and gave a sort of grunt. I did not require anything else; the warder put on the handcuffs before leading me away.

That was in May 1917.

After all these distressful days I still remain deeply grateful to Attorney John C. Knox, who is now a judge, for all the consideration he showed me.

One more cloud appeared on the horizon, and that was when the British forces, under General Allenby, had rolled up the Turkish front in Palestine, in the autumn of 1918.

The pursuing cavalry came across a tent, the occupant of which had taken to his heels, leaving behind whatever documents the British had not taken away from him at Falmouth. Such perfect calm seemed to prevail down there that the tent's occupant, Captain Papen of course, found time and peace of mind for the filing of those "documents." A wire was sent to London, and the reply read, so rumour had it: "Forward papers. If Papen captured, do not intern; send him to lunatic asylum." The British and American Press roared!

Copies of those papers found their way soon afterwards to New York and Washington; and a new indictment against me was the sequence. Still, the American authorities had a sense of humour too, and amidst the derisory laughter over the ill-fated German officer's retreat in Palestine, the charge against the German officer in residence at Atlanta was dropped.

.   .   .   .   .

BACK IN AMERICA

Space allows only a few fleeting comments on what happened to me, ever since I " landed " in prison in America.

From jail to jail was I dragged—or, rather, as I styled it, as I was not brought *by right* from England to America, invited by one " hotel " after the other, until finally it was decided that the " Grand Hotel " was the most suitable place for me to stay at—the Federal Penitentiary at Atlanta, in the State of Georgia.

When I arrived in Atlanta, with the two detectives who had travelled with me by rail for forty hours, I decided at once that I did not like the town at all. We drove through it and finally came to a large building which stood in the midst of maize-fields. It had a façade like a palace, but it was a prison. For years I wore a blue linen jacket, blue linen trousers, shoes made of sail-cloth and a broad-brimmed hat. I lived in a cell together with international forgers, thieves, pickpockets and smugglers. My number was 8891, and at first some of the other prisoners promised themselves considerable profit from the hurling of stones at the head of the German captain who wore that number. They were people who were anxious to curry favour with the prison authorities ; but when the aristocracy of the place—that is to say, the respectable burglars, footpads and smugglers—discovered that I never betrayed a fellow-prisoner, the situation quickly changed to my advantage.

During all these years I was treated like any other prisoner. I took my " revenge " by standing guard when

267

the others broke into the warders' canteen to find something fit to eat. Many a celebrated criminal told me of his deeds, but I kept my mouth closed. I trembled when the convicts attacked a man who had betrayed a comrade and left him lying dead.

I had one surprise visitor in the person of Ronald Squire, who was sent over from Donington Hall to inquire into the welfare of its late guest. He reminded me of the day when I had complained that the local dentist was an incompetent plumber.

One morning I was given a new cell-mate; he was no longer a youngster, and so I offered to him the lower " cot." He introduced himself as a *Titanic* survivor; it was the famous Doc Owen, the card-sharper, who had succeeded in making his " get-away " from that ship, after having overheard two stokers: " The g.d. duck will sink in 'arf-an-hour." He quickly helped himself to a bottle of whisky, made one of the victims of his wits—who himself drowned—give him a cheque for what he was " owing " and got into a lifeboat, which was picked up by some vessel. This time, however, the " Doc " had been " caught with the goods " and had to serve " at hard " in Atlanta.

Then there were two intelligent young men, severely sentenced for having tried to sell forged French bank-notes in New York. They had been living in Paris during those anxious days of August 1914; and their next field of operations was London, where, during Zeppelin panics—they themselves having nothing to lose on this earth—they rifled bedrooms wholesale, whose occupants, male and especially female, had taken refuge in the hotel's cellars.

Besides Eugene Debs, the Socialist, a fine old fellow indeed and who was rather outspoken in his political views, there were plenty of anarchists and Bolshevists assembled in Atlanta : a " spiritual élite " altogether, and quite interesting to talk to !

One of them, however, a little Jew from Galicia, had material interests too. Having observed how two boiled eggs had been smuggled into the pockets of my stylish coat—" Number 8891 "—he felt a sudden pity for me lest I might get punished for irregular possession of the eggs. For when I found that they had " left " my pockets, his eyes smiled at me through the habitual horn-rimmed spectacles : " *Herr Kapitän, ich habe aufgegessen die Evidenz !* "

In the course of time I was put to work in the steam-laundry and the cotton factory ; then I worked at the cement press in the quarry and in the stone-mill, which is a hell where men toil in a thick cloud of stone-dust which penetrates into every pore ; and I have seen a couple of dozen negroes rise in a revolt which lasted until they were hit by the bullets of the warders and fell writhing to the ground.

I have learned to know American prisons. I have seen how the prisoners are treated, and, God knows, I can understand when now and then such revolts are reported. I can imagine that a convict prefers to meet his end under machine-gun fire than remain for fifteen years in a place which is a ghastly hell on earth.

THE DARK INVADER

Sometimes of an evening I would lie back in as comfortable a posture as I could achieve, and think over the events of the past few months.

There is an adage which states categorically that " the influence of cheerfulness upon success is well shown in time of war."

I certainly felt like laughing that one off. . . . I was the insider here and also the outsider. I had no business to be where I was, but I was most certainly there, and with every opportunity of thoroughly experiencing everything that any common prisoner might . . . with the added comfort of knowing myself, and knowing that my judges knew, that I was there *under false pretences*, in direct contravention of all civil or military law.

Though I said on a previous occasion in my narrative that it was the saddest moment in my life when I was captured by the British on Friday August 13th, 1915, I feel I must revise my opinion.

I do not know whether the British Admiralty and the British Foreign Office, who had agreed to my extradition to America, contrary to all law and to International agreements, did realise beforehand that the Americans might treat me as roughly as they actually did. . . .

There I was on board the *Adriatic*, running into the Port of New York, and, of course, had put on my naval uniform, as the mufti, which all on board had worn, had been more or less donned only on account of the ravaging of our U-boats.

In came two fierce-looking American detectives and without many further words handcuffed me. Only those

270

who have ever been handcuffed—and most of my readers never have been—can possibly imagine the horrible sensation it gives one. A bear on a chain is a thousand times freer than a man handcuffed to the wrist of a detective ; and, of course, those two fellows, though later they turned out to be quite decent chaps, thought it was a great stunt to drag me along the deck before the eyes of the other passengers. And who was there to meet us, when we came up the staircase, but my fair fellow-passenger, the only lady who was on board the *Adriatic*, whose husband was in the *Olympic* ahead of us as a member of Lord Balfour's War Mission to America. She leaned against the railing below, dumb-founded—Macbeth having to see Banquo's Ghost must have seemed child's play to her at that moment.

I, myself, shall never forget my journey from the Pier to the Federal Building in Park Row, and from there to the Tombs Prison.

What a beautiful name !

It was given this name in a former time when the prison consisted of actual dungeons, and now it was a sinister-looking fortress. After brief formalities—for up to this moment I was only a " suspect," and not yet a convicted prisoner—I was conducted to a cell, and with a rattling bang the iron-barred door slammed in its lock.

There was a small dirty cot, and simply abhorrent surroundings—appalling iron walls and an iron roof, all more or less dirty—a filthy wash-basin, and many other little things to prove that many a man had been here before, and they not such who laid the average stress on cleanliness.

In the course of time I measured this beautiful hole, and found it to be just five paces long and just two paces from cot to wall.

Fortunately, they had permitted me to carry one of my hand-bags with me, containing at least the barest of toilet necessities; and more fortunately still, while searching the bag they had mistaken a small bottle of brandy for eau-de-Cologne. Undescribable was the feeling of abhorrence at these surroundings, and undressing seemed impossible in this mass of filth, with vermin crawling about the bed-clothes and in the straw bag politely labelled " mattress." With the help of a sip of brandy—and I was very careful not to take too much at a time, as I did not know how long this bottle would have to be my " spiritual support "—and with a good hearty oath against the British Admiralty, and Sir Reginald Hall in particular, whom all the time I considered to be the villain in the piece—I fell asleep after the extraordinary experiences of this first day. But, alas! there was not much sleep to be had, as the well-fed passenger of the *Adriatic* seemed to be a particularly attractive morsel for the—I am sorry to say it right here —lice. Instead of throwing myself on the cot in all my clothes, I ought to have gone stark naked to this so-called bed, for from now on the lice made their headquarters in my naval uniform, my shirt and my underwear. When a few days later my splendid lawyer and adviser, Mr. George Gordon Battle, came to the prison for an interview, one of these charming little animals, quite red after it had soaked itself fully of " Hun " blood, actually crawled up my neck, straight across my face and looked surprisedly at Mr. Battle, who, because of the surroundings to which he was accustomed, could not imagine that such a thing really existed, and probably only recognised it as something he had heard of during the Natural History lesson when at school.

No wonder that after this first restless night I was simply foaming with rage because the British had delivered me into this mess, and that the Americans did not for a single moment pay any attention to the fact that, after all, they might place their own officers who might later become prisoners in German hands in a similar awkward position.

Not only had Mr. George Gordon Battle sent in his protest in detail in his letter to the U.S. Attorney-General, but there was one great friend of mine who was revolted over the whole business, and that was Admiral Albert P. Niblack, who had been American Naval Attaché at Berlin until shortly before the outbreak of the War, and had been repeatedly a guest at my house, and I at his. In fact, after having tried vainly to influence Joseph Daniels, the Secretary of the Navy, he went straight to Franklin D. Roosevelt, then Assistant Secretary of the Navy, and from what I know of my late friend Niblack he did not mince his words, and it is fair to suppose that Roosevelt was made to see the whole affair from all angles. But with no avail: Mr. Gregory, the Attorney-General, remained adamant. " Rintelen has admitted his offences, if not crimes, during America's neutrality period, and punishment will be meted out to him as if no state of war existed between the two countries. He will remain a common prisoner and not a prisoner of war."

Some " construction," after once America had declared war! But I was quick to realise that this whole thing was nothing but a piece of propaganda. Whenever during the neutrality period a horse had slipped in the streets of New York, rumour had it that this was arranged by German spies! But the American people would not believe all this, and thought it was merely newspaper stuff "made to order." Now here they had the arch-villain in their hands, and the papers—morning, noon and night—had headlines, increasing in size as the case went on, and gradually the public became convinced that any Germans who had stayed in America from 1914 to 1917 had occupied themselves with plots, nothing but plots.

Day after day went by, and I was still in the Tombs Prison, and had to go in the shower-bath with many human wrecks abhorrent to look at physically, among them men of all ages and formerly of all stations of life. Disgusting and degrading it was, and yet frightfully pitiful; but after a few days elapsed I decided to bite my lips and stick it out—as long as my country was winning this War, and as long as every morning brought us news of how much more Allied shipping had been sent to the bottom. For in the Tombs Prison one was allowed to read newspapers, as most of the inmates were only charged with crimes and not yet convicted. In turn, however, as there were no servants or even maids around, we had to scrub the floor ourselves, to mop up the corridors and, worst of all, to clean up that shower-bath now afloat with the filth of some hundreds of people. Cigarette after cigarette helped one to bear up in this atmosphere. In turn we had to go round the cells with " spray-guns " to fight the vermin.

How much extra strain it puts upon all these men by having to dress up decently in the morning when they are brought into criminal courts, so that they may make a good impression on judge and jury alike. Not one of these eminent gentlemen actually realises that these suspects undergoing trial have to put up a good appearance in order to live up to the word of the Law, namely, that as long as a man is not convicted he is not only innocent, but a respectable citizen !

But the Law in no country realises what it means to remain " respectable," after having gone through nights and days in such terrible circumstances, because in a good many cases men, who have in the meantime been sentenced, remained detained in the Tombs until all the formalities have gone through. And then come their paroxysms of depression, and rages of despair and revenge against what they naturally consider injustice, for it goes without saying that 90 per cent of all convicted men feel that they were unfairly treated and unjustly convicted.

Comes the question of their families, who are allowed to visit their dear ones once in a while. At times these give reciprocal consolation, but in so many other cases the visiting-room witnesses the most heartrending of scenes—lives are ruined, families are broken asunder, children have to be taken care of, money has to be found right and left for the sustenance of the family, and for finding a lawyer to appeal the case, while the accused man goes on hoping against hope. Some convicted men give in to fate and put up with the sentences they have received. In a great many cases the strain of fighting against experienced judges and stony public prosecutors proves all too much for the average man. Such men commence soliloquising—a habit which, by the way, I became a victim to for quite some time, and even to this present day I catch myself at times falling back into this bad habit. Men would get up in the middle of the night and either recount at the top of their voices the experiences which they have just gone through, or else prepare a fulminant address still to be delivered to the jury when under scrutiny and cross-examination in the dock. I have witnessed the most terrible scenes of that nature, with the orator throwing himself against the iron bars meanwhile.

There was one case I remember distinctly, when ten men, competitors in the Poultry Market had, out of sheer greed and jealousy against one other man, arranged an unbelievable plot and killed this unfortunate man, who had sold chickens two cents below market price! The plot was so fiendishly arranged, and the evidence had been so absolutely conclusive, that all of them had committed the murder or had aided in it, that after one of them had given " State's evidence " the whole gang was actually sentenced to the death which they had well deserved. Never shall I forget the screaming and howling, the rage and despair of these men, fathers of families, and some of them quite well-to-do, when they saw the electric chair before their eyes, which they had risked facing for a few cents on the market price of chickens ! They yelled and shouted, each accusing the other, and were locked up two together in different cells, all the while cursing and swearing and trying to batter down the walls with their heads, and rattling the doors in their despair. " Let me out, let me out," they shouted to the warders. Some shouted the names of their wives and their children, and all called down Death and Hell's punishment upon the one man who had given evidence against them. Poor wretch, by so doing he just earned imprisonment for life and so saved his skin, whilst actually all the men sentenced to death went, one after the other, to the electric chair a few months afterwards !

While bringing back to my memory this ghastly crime, the severe justice meted out to these men and the scenes which ensued, I can but once again record my definite and absolute conviction that the penalty of death, if carried out, is the only real and effective deterrent to deliberate murder ! While there is *life* there is hope ; and I have come across, in my past " career," so many men who gave thanks to Heaven each morning that they once more awoke alive—alive in the most miserable surroundings, and bereft of all human kindness ; but nevertheless—alive !

THE DARK INVADER

Men convicted of the most dastardly murders have narrated to me how they felt when they were granted a reprieve. Some of those wretched " lifers " were clinging from day to day to the faintest ray of hope that a day might come when they might be discharged, even though their families had dispersed, and though they had nothing to hope for outside these prison walls in a life for which they had become wholly unfitted through decades of incarceration, as they were now nothing but human rags.

There is one thing which I observed, namely, that after a given period a physical shrinkage sets in with convicts, so that about every five years they have to be given an entirely new outfit. My readers will not believe it, but after the four years that I " did time " I simply " drowned " in my beautiful dress clothes which had been made by a well-known tailoring firm in Bond Street! From top to bottom, hat, suit and shoes, all my measurements had to be readjusted to my new proportions. I was by no means " husky," as the Americans say, but much fuller than I am nowadays. Physically, Nature had gifted me with an india-rubber frame, and mentally I had the one great determination to win through and to survive it all, to keep fit, and, above all, never to admit to myself that I was actually in jail. In fact, I lived in a state of self-deception, and it was not only sarcasm, but the result of this state of mind, that when addressing the American authorities I referred to the Tombs as " the hotel to which you were graciously pleased to invite me," and when finally I

BACK IN AMERICA

landed in the great Federal Penitentiary in Atlanta the men in the Department of Justice in Washington seemed a little hurt when I called it the " Grand Hotel "—they did not realise that my underlying idea was that there *could* be no such thing as a Penitentiary for me. As a German officer I considered I had done nothing but my duty, which had consisted in a determination ever to prevent or delay shipments of munitions to Europe in order to save the lives of my fellow-countrymen.

For my readers may believe me that unless a man, or a woman for that matter, is innocent and has become a victim of a miscarriage of justice and is sustained by his or her clear conscience—though in a great many cases this is *not* a sufficient stimulant in the long run—the vast, vast majority of human beings, condemned to long sentences, are bound to become definitely harmful to civilisation.

Believe me, judges and juries alike—and, by the way, I may mention I was a foreman on a jury myself in Berlin, long before I ever thought I would become a convicted prisoner myself—think thrice before you mete out these long sentences! Of course, there are men who are born criminals and take things lightly ; but what is the use of huddling together men or women of all ages, when the juniors are nothing but raw High School pupils sitting in front of professors, of " *Membres de l'Acaêdmie.*" What a lack of wisdom it is to put together wretched creatures, such as our notorious criminals, into the same surroundings and abode along with people who have committed what the

French rightly call "*crimes de passion*," and, therefore, *are not* criminals in the true sense of the word, or—more abhorrent still according to my views—with young fellows who pull off some stunt or do mischief for the sake of their girls, perhaps stealing a ring to make her happy—or even with poor people who, out of sheer want, steal a loaf of bread out of a baker's shop.

I think in giving these four different types I have fairly sized up the population of prisons, and especially of prisons such as Atlanta or Dartmoor.

No one can imagine my feelings, or condemn even *my* temptation to have a "try," when one morning, during the time of my employment in the blacksmith's shop, one of those gentlemen members of the venerable Guild of Housebreakers, a man who had been in jail for thirty out of the fifty years of his life, and who had been sentenced at least ten times—pulled out of his pocket a heavy lock, threw it with a bang on the stone floor, and shouted to all the youngsters, some of whom had possibly only sold drugs in the streets of New York, or had carried "liquor" from one restaurant to another: "Now, boys, you try to open this lock; I have been working on this in my cell for the last two months, and I bet you five dollars none of you will be able to break that lock."

No, no, put all those who *are* "habituals" within prison walls, but send the rest of them, who have merely sinned against the Ten Commandments, to some wide space of open air, among forests and fields—not swamps, though !—and you will find that under the influence of nature, with all its beauty and glory, they will become again respectable human beings and valuable members of our civilisation.

Come, let us reason together, you judges and myself. What do all our penal codes say? They speak of so many years for such-and-such a crime, and you sentence them, sitting on your benches, and you accept the fact that your victims are getting their food and their drink, their clothes and occasionally some recreation. But has it ever occurred to you, living as you do as free men— and I realise what I mean by using the word " men " —that no law and no penal code lays down that a man should become an abstainer from the other sex? You know that we men are meant by nature to be active, and you must see what I am driving at. That is the crux of the whole question! That is the punishment which is meted out, and it is far beyond what any human being should ever mete out to his fellows; and I may respectfully remind you that there is one State in this world where they have sense enough to realise this greatest of all problems in our lives, and that is—Mexico ! Go and make inquiries for yourselves how beautifully they have solved that problem there. What happens in women's prisons I do not know, but passion does not die out because people are made to enter prison doors. The result of it all is that all those prisons are hot-beds of immorality, and nothing short of it—and our " *courts* " see to that !!

I hope and trust that my publishing an account of my

many years " at hard," and of my stay in five different
American prisons, along with my views on this essen-
tially human problem of prison life, may have at least
this one result—that *this* problem be tackled courageously
and solved, and, finally, that all the sheer humbug talked
on this subject will be condemned, as I have condemned
it, before and after imprisonment, as hypocrisy, and
nothing but hypocrisy!

.   .   .   .   .

I shall never forget how ptomaine poisoning once
broke out in the prison. In order to fill his own pockets
the governor had bought meat which had already been
rejected by a military commission. But this was nothing
to the conditions which prevailed in the winter of 1918.
The " White Death " made its way through the prison
gates and raged with merciless persistence. The " White
Death " was Spanish influenza, and the prison became a
cross between a madhouse and an inferno. Dozens of
convicts died, and still the infirmaries were full. The
dying lay on the ground, on the bare stones, where
hastily improvised mattresses had been thrown down,
and there they twisted and shrieked in their death-
agonies.

When the plague was at its height, a number of Germans were brought in who had helped me three years
ago, in 1915. Among them was Bünz, the former
Consul-General of New York, who was seriously ill.
He had been sentenced for furnishing German cruisers
with coal from American harbours. In his defence he

put forward the fact that millions of shells and innumerable tons of coal had been sent out of American harbours on British ships; but this did not help him, and he was condemned to penal servitude for violating American neutrality. I returned one day from my work in the quarries, and found him in my cell. I got a shock when I saw him, and we fell into each other's arms, for I could see straight away that he was very sick. One night I shouted in despair for the warders, for I realised that Bünz was dying. He was taken to the infirmary, and was carried out next day dead. To die at the age of seventy, in prison!

Captain von Kleist came to Atlanta about the same time as Bünz. I spoke to him, but he did not answer, and he went about as though dazed. I did not learn until later what had made him like this. I heard that he had had a complete mental breakdown. Some American detectives, who were examining him before his trial, played him a horrible trick. They put a narcotic into a glass of beer, and when he was in a state of semi-consciousness, they got him to sign a document stating that I had been at the head of all those activities which we had now to pay the penalty for. Kleist felt fearfully ashamed; but why should I not, as always, stretch out my hand to somebody asking forgiveness! I arranged for the fine old man to share my cell; and what little I could do for him—after all, one of the scores of victims of Papen's recklessness too—that was only too gladly done. Fate was with me and kept me in a supreme condition, both physically and mentally, throughout those terrible four years. If only I could have parted with some of my strength : too late—Captain Kleist finally died in my arms from general debility ! And before many more months had elapsed one of our most active and patriotic agents, a writer, Stephan Binder, from Forchheim, in Baden, succumbed to influenza.

Immediately afterwards the German-American bookseller, Feldmann of New York, died in a dreadful way. He had been sentenced for supplying prohibited strike literature. He also fell a victim to influenza, at a time when the infection was at its worst, and conditions in the infirmary beggared description. He lay in bed with a high temperature ; and one night, when he was delirious, he got up, threw off all his clothes, and went out quite naked, in the depth of winter, to the yard, where he sat down. Next day he was found frozen to death. He was buried at the same time as a German sailor who had died of ptomaine poisoning.

Those who did not survive are all lying by the prison wall of Atlanta. A simple cross indicates the name and the prison number which each of them bore while under sentence.

That sailor had, to the very last, refused to disclose even to me his identity ! He is, in the truest sense of the word, an Unknown Warrior. " *Hoch kling' das Lied vom braven Mann !* " Highly be praised those brave of the brave ! For the worst that could befall man, that befell them, who either died or survived—for their country ! Heroes they were and are ! but forgotten are their names and their deeds ; and this book is written in praise of their fame, in contempt of those " diplomats " and otherwise whom " immunity " has saved from what they deserved a hundred times more than those poor fellows !

. . . . .

When I looked at these crosses I was seized with sullen energy. They should not bury my body there. I had to escape a prison death.

I was determined to get out of this " hole " alive ! The sick list seemed to be the only alternative, and from now on I was condemned to " light diet," the menu of which consisted of porridge and toast—morning, noon and night. As there were still 300 days " time " ahead of me, the prison became a " spa "—900 meals of porridge sustained me until the day I was once more to be a free man. Assuredly *Hunger ist der beste Koch* !

I took exercise in my cell and wherever possible.

Diplomatic immunity is a very fine phrase !—and I could have done with some of it—for I had to protest very strongly on my own behalf against what " diplomats " felt they could afford to say under cover of that immunity !

Twice did a telegram—in 1919 and in 1920, the " whitewash period " in Berlin—make the following Grand Tour, from No. 8891, all that was left of Rintelen —to . . . the Warden of the Penitentiary, to the Department of Justice in Washington, to the Secretary of State, to the Swiss Legation in Washington, then representing German interests in America, thence to

Berne, to the Swiss Government, from them to the Auswärtige Amt in Berlin, to be handed to the President of the Reichstag.

Twice had I to protest, in the most outspoken fashion, against what I called " the brave attacks upon a defence-less prisoner." Bernstorff and Papen alike had told the Reichstag Committee the meanest of tales about me and my mission. How angered I was, " doing time " in Atlanta—with two more years before me!—by these wanton distortions of facts—for so they seemed to me.

But still no answer came from Berlin; they knew how to forestall that, and the shame of these cowardly attacks still rests upon those two.

And after a grey eternity the gates of Atlanta were opened. I stood outside surrounded by reporters, whom I managed to evade, and eventually reached New York, where I took a boat for home.

This was early in 1921.

The most bitter disillusionment awaited me. Nobody expected me. Nobody was able to understand the psychology of a man who had passed the transition period from war to peace in prison. When I spoke about the War, in which alone I still retained interest, I discovered that everyone else had almost forgotten it, and was living not for the past, but for the future. For me war and fight were still realities, and my world was in the past, and would still be, were it not for my beloved daughter !

When I had recovered from my disillusionment, there

BACK IN AMERICA

came the recognition that man is not made immortal by what he destroys but by what he constructs.

May the bombs we once employed never be brought forth again !

.   .   .   .   .

POSTSCRIPT FROM ADMIRAL BEHNCKE

" BERLIN,
" February 16th, 1921

" My dear Captain,

" It has given me the greatest pleasure to hear, at last, of your safe return to this country. The Navy has always felt very closely the hard fate which overtook you while attached to the Army. To-day, remembering our work together on the Admiralty War Staff, I send you my warmest congratulations on your return ; and I do so in the name of all your brother-officers and of the whole Navy. I hope that you will soon recover from the consequences of the harsh treatment which you received at the enemy's hands and that you will always recollect with satisfaction the part which you played with such admirable devotion and patriotism.

" While it is not within my province to thank you for the service which you rendered to your country abroad, I do not hesitate, on behalf of the Navy, to express to you my thanks for all you did. It is my hope that, when your case has been given the necessary consideration, you will receive recognition in some visible form. I am already in communication with the former Ministry of War on the subject

287

THE DARK INVADER

of your affairs, and will draw its attention to that part of your report from which it is clear that the release accorded to you by the American Government is in no way to be regarded as a special favour, and therefore must certainly not be overestimated.

" *With every good wish,*
" *I remain, my dear Captain,*
" *Yours very sincerely,*
" *(Signed)* BEHNCKE,
"*Admiral and Chief of the Admiralty.*"